Education and
change in a village community

Roger Thabault

Education and change in a village community

Mazières-en-Gâtine 1848–1914

translated by
Peter Tregear

SCHOCKEN BOOKS · NEW YORK

Published in U.S.A. in 1971
by Schocken Books Inc.
67 Park Avenue, New York, N.Y. 10016
Translated from the French
Mon Village
1848–1914
L'Ascension d'un Peuple
Published by Librairie Delagrave & Cie 1945
© this translation Routledge & Kegan Paul Ltd 1971
Library of Congress Catalog Card No. 71-110251

Printed in Great Britain

Contents

1579604

CONTENTS

Foreword

by J. A. Lauwerys

Commandeur des Palmes Académiques
Professeur Associé à la Sorbonne
Director, Atlantic Institute of Education

In 1957, I had the good fortune of being invited to travel round some of the less developed parts of Morocco, to study the ways in which, under the guidance of France, schools and teachers were contributing to social and economic advance. On my return to Rabat, in Roger Thabault's gracious and beautiful residence, after a generous meal, I asked him to explain what had led him to write that gem of a book, *Mon Village*, remarkable alike from a literary and a sociological point of view. Why should the Director of Education of Morocco be so lovingly concerned with the educational history of his own small village during the nineteenth century? What had Mazières-en-Gâtine to do with Marrakesh or Fez?

So Thabault told me, with a wealth of fascinating detail, about his visit to Morocco in 1938. He described the isolated villages, the miserable huts, the poor diet of the peasants, their superstitions, the closed nature of their culture and society, their primitive ways of tilling the soil and of raising cattle. And he had been struck by the resemblance between this state of affairs and the situation of his own homeland a hundred and fifty years earlier. He went on to explain how he had come to the notion that if only he could understand more fully what forces had transformed a French village and what contributions public education had made to progress, he would have a theory that would guide him in his own professional efforts. He went on to explain that the chief forces making for change were certainly political, social and technical. But all these were ineffective unless popular education and enlightenment sustained them. The school gave form, purpose and direction: it trained the people by developing their skill and put in their hands an ideological compass.

All this can be expressed somewhat differently – and generalized. The first step in the modernization of a rural society anywhere in the world is the transformation of a subsistence into a market economy. Wielders of hoes, raising corn or potatoes or bananas, getting eggs and milk from their domestic animals, exchanging and consuming their own products within their little circle have to be brought into contact with cities and markets. They must sell their products and get money in order to buy the tools, machines, seeds and fertilizers which will make it possible for them to increase vastly their output, thereby enabling them to begin to enjoy the products of modern industry and technology: more varied food, medical care, cultural facilities, and so on.

The first need is the improvement of communications: isolation must be broken down. Roads, railways, bridges, telegraphs, postal services, buses and trucks: all these are needed. So are schools: they too, and particularly they, are part of the communications network which is the nervous system of every modern society.

It is the dynamic aspect of this process of opening up a closed society that Thabault seizes so wonderfully in his remarkable case study. No one has excelled him in his imaginative use of apparently trivial detail. He draws meanings of universal significance from ancient school registers and from dull statistical records of transport on the local lines of national railways. And thus, stroke by stroke, he offers us a rich picture of the development of a French village during the nineteenth century. It is a canvas as carefully planned and composed as a Breughel. Consider how he describes his old headmaster, M. Auguste Bouet – an affectionate portrait of one of those *instituteurs* whose contribution to the culture of France and her people cannot be overestimated. Here was one of those men to whom a whole region was deeply indebted, and who was admired and respected by all his fellow citizens. A loyal son of his village and a radiating focus of optimism, faith, morality and, yes, culture.

The importance of teachers of this sort may have diminished in highly industrialized, largely anonymous, societies. But what about Africa and the Middle East, Latin America and Asia? How can such leaders be found, recruited and trained? What ideals should now be put before them? Until the elementary schools of those countries can do what the schools of France did a century ago, the progress they seek will elude them. True, those French schools were not really rural: they were orientated towards the cities. But they were, at least, deeply rooted in local needs and local aspirations. And the teachers were passionately devoted to the well-being of the children they taught and to the improvement of the communities to which they belonged.

Here then are some of the themes handled in *Mon Village* and a few of the ideas it evokes. André Siegfried – Roger Thabault's teacher and friend – has described the chief qualities of the book. He comments on the imaginative percipience of his pupil. He writes . . . 'You go so far not only into the research itself but into the deeper meaning of details . . . that our curiosity is satisfied and we are given the feeling of truly understanding . . . But this infinite detail is interesting and fruitful only when it is part of a whole: the individual case must lead us to know the species . . .' Siegfried goes on to compare Thabault's method with that often adopted by American sociologists and particularly with that of the Lynds: 'Reading your book, I thought continually about Middletown, saying to myself that, without doubt, you did not have in your hands the heavy and costly tools which were at the disposal of Mr Lynd. But as a member by right of birth of your small community, intimately concerned with its life since your childhood, plunging directly into the memories of the preceding generation, you had the advantage of a power of penetration and of an inner understanding possibly greater than that of the American enquirers, despite their immense means and their splendid intelligence. If they went deep you, I think, have gone deeper still.'

Here then is a book which, at first sight, seems to be chiefly a brilliant contribution to our knowledge of the history of France and of French education. No one can fail to be attracted by the charm of Thabault's writing, by his imaginative grasp, by the clarity and precision of his writing. Soon, one begins to see more. Here is a collection of lovingly drawn miniature studies where every detail really is an intrinsic part of a concrete whole, a microcosm which mirrors the social macrocosm. One learns without quite realizing how the teaching is going on that education can be the instrument of genuine political, social, economic and spiritual advance.

Peter Tregear has succeeded admirably in his translation: correct to the letter and to the spirit of the original, pleasant to read, and with many a felicitous phrase. His was no easy task. Thabault's style is deceptively clear and limpid; French prose of the purest and most balanced kind, beautifully integrating form and content. But how hard to put into English! I hope he feels pleasure at the thought that he has made available to many who are concerned with the theory of education, and particularly with comparative education, a most remarkable and original book, full of valuable lessons and insights.

J. A. LAUWERYS

Preface

by the Translator

Some twelve years ago M. Roger Thabault came to London and delivered a lecture at the University of London Institute of Education in which he gave an account of the research which had led up to the writing of his book *Mon Village: l'ascension d'un Peuple*. The description that he gave of the rôle of the school in the social and economic changes which took place during the nineteenth century in an 'undeveloped' region of France was closely paralleled in the minds of many who had had long experience of work in education in what is now known as 'the Developing World'. For many years the idea of the school being 'the major agent of social change' had been current but was now being questioned as to its true validity. Today in all parts of the developing world the rôle of education in socio-economic change is being more and more closely examined. Many communities remain in the state of subsistence agriculture in a closed economy resembling that described by M. Thabault in Mazières some 120 years ago. What is the relevance of the school to people in that situation? This was the question that M. Thabault set out to examine when considering the opening of a school on the edge of the Saharan desert. It is a question which exercises the minds of many educationists and administrators in Africa, Asia and Latin America today.

The minimal impact of the Farm School and the problems involved in the development of the Co-operative Dairy are but two instances of situations experienced even today in many parts of the world. It would be unwise to attempt to draw too close parallels between nineteenth-century France and

twentieth-century Africa: for example, the world of space satel-
lites and jet travel is not comparable with that of the Mazières
peasant of 1840. And yet there remains a large proportion of the
world's population to whom the Concorde and Telstar are completely irrelevant in their daily experience. Most of these communities, however, have schools in which children learn a
curriculum apparently inappropriate to their needs. A dicho-
tomy between school and community exists which is in many
ways comparable to that of Mazières before the advent of the
railway linked the commune with the wider exchange economy
of France.

The detailed and affectionate portrait drawn by M. Thabault
of his native commune shows the progress of the school from
an institution of little relevance to the majority of the inhabitants to one which became indispensable for their social and
economic development.

It was in relation to the rôle of the school in social change in
the developing world that the book first attracted my attention
and more than ten generations of students at the Institute
of Education from many parts of the world have, from their
own experience, seen this relevance. It is not only in this
connection, however, that the book deserves a wide public.
Students of Comparative Education will find in it an analysis
of the consequences of policies and controversies over education
in France over a century of time, examined in detail in a microcosm of society. We follow the doctrine of Enlightenment
through Reason, the conflict between Tradition and Reform,
between Church and State and the influence of men who saw
their people as they wanted them to be, not always as they
were. Perhaps, above all, we see the influence of a band of
devoted men and women, teaching in humble schools, imbued
with a sense of mission because they believed wholeheartedly
in the value of what they had been given as their task. The
instituteur today no longer plays the rôle of M. Bouet. We are
fortunate to have such a meticulous description of what men
like him could and did perform in other days when the world
seemed more secure.

P. S. T.

Glossary

Arrondissement	administrative district under a *Sous-préfet*, i.e. next in importance to a *département*. There are about 300 *arrondissements* in France.
Bocage	agricultural land characterized by scattered woodland and many high, thick hedges.
Boisselée	an old measure both of capacity (bushel) and of area – a field sown by a bushel of seed.
Borderie	a small farm leased on a share-cropping basis.
Bordier	a farmer operating a *borderie*.
Canton	administrative unit in importance between *commune* and *arrondissement*.
Chouans	Royalist insurgents during the First Republic in the Vendée province: a term extended sometimes to refer any of pronounced royalist or pro-aristocracy tendencies.
Collège	a secondary school established and maintained by a *commune* with State aid.
Commune	the smallest administrative unit in France. Each *commune* has a Mayor and municipal council. There are over 38,000 *communes* in France.
Département	the chief administrative division in France under a Prefect (*Préfet*) and advised by a council elected on universal suffrage on the basis of one member from each *canton*.

Ecole normale	training college for elementary school teachers.
Landes	sandy, infertile tracts of land.
Métairie	farm similar to a *borderie*.
Métayer	share-cropper.
Métayage	share-cropping.
Pourrin	cow dung in the field (cow pat).
Pourrinier	farm labourer who collects *pourrin* and makes manure.

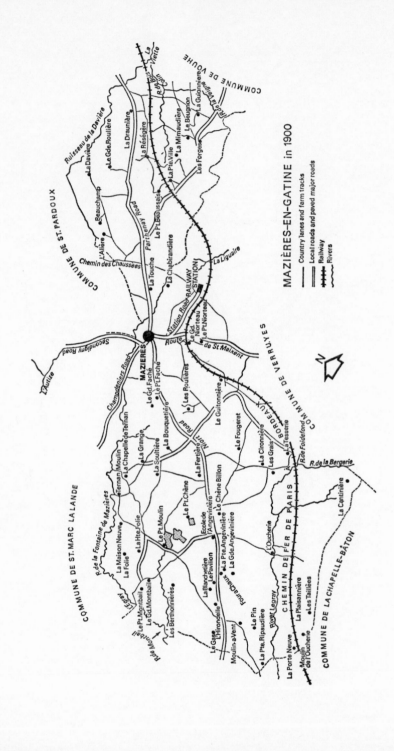

MAZIÈRES-EN-GATINE in 1900

———— Country lanes and farm tracks
═══ Local roads and paved major roads
+++ Railway
～～ Rivers

COMMUNE DE VOUHÉ

COMMUNE DE ST.PARDOUX

COMMUNE DE ST.MARC LA LANDE

COMMUNE DE VERRUYES

COMMUNE DE LA CHAPELLE-BÂTON

COMMUNE DE L'OUCHERIE

CHEMIN DE FER DE PARIS A BORDEAUX

La Vrie
R. de Bois
R. de Bois Vrie
R. de la Vrie
Ruisseau de la Davière
La Davière
Le Gde.Roulière
La Draunière
La Résérère
La Pte.Ville
Le Mimaudière
Le Beugnon
La Guionnière
Les Forgeas
Beauchamp
L'Alière
La Touche
Le Pt.Beaussais
La Chabirandière
La Liguaire
Chemin des Chaussées
Parthenay Road
RAILWAY STATION
Le Grd.Niorteau
Le Pt.Niorteau
Station Road
Route de St Maixent
de St Maixent
Secondary Road
Champdeniers Road
MAZIÈRES
Le Grd.Faché
Le Pt.Faché
Les Roulières
La Guitonnière
L'Autize
Ternan/Moulin
La Chapelle de Ternan
La Grange
La Soultière
La Bouquetière
Niort Road
La Fertière
Le Chêne Billon
Le Fougeret
La Cironnière
Les Grais
La Tesserie
R.de la Bergerie
La Cantinière
Le Pt.Chêne
Ecole de l'Angevinière
La Pte.Angevinière
La Gde.Angevinière
L'Oucherie
R. de Foidefond
R. de la Fontaine de Mazières
La Maison Neuve
La Folie
La Hte.Folie
Le Pt.Moulin
La Blanchetière
Le Pavillon
Fou la Chaux
Le Gd.Montbail
Le Pt.Montbail
Les Berthonnières
R. de Montbail
L'Hirondelle
Moulin-à-Vent
Le Pin
La Pte.Ripaudière
River Legray
La Plaisannière
Les Taillées
La Porte Neuve
Moulin de l'Oucherie

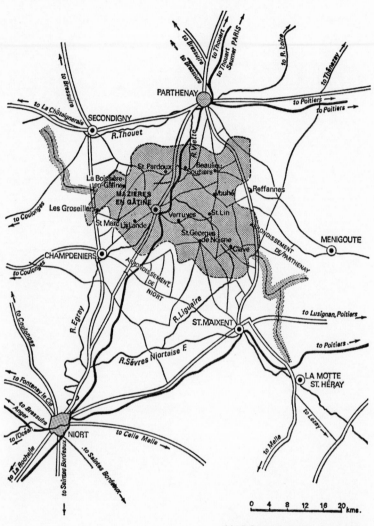

MAP OF MAZIERES CANTON

part one

From 1789 to 1850
The school in a
subsistence economy

one

Introduction

In the spring of 1938 I was called upon, with my friend M. Lucien Paye, head of the department of Moslem education in Morocco, to visit the schools in the extreme south of the country. Our journey took us after Oudjda to Berguent, Tendrara, Figuig, Erfoud and Ksar-es-Souk.

As far as Berguent I saw nothing in the landscape which was unfamiliar. But the High Plateau aroused my interest with its vast empty space, its monotony and barrenness. Scattered clumps of alfa stretched out of sight on every side. Nothing caught the eye: no change of slope, no tree, no human dwelling. The wide track alone, as it sped straight to the south, acted as guide to travellers new to the desert. At rare intervals the practised eye could discern, far in the distance against the clear sky, the tiny silhouettes of herds of sheep or gazelles.

After one has travelled for sixty miles through this cheerless immensity, some distant hills take on the guise of mountains. At the foot of these heights squat the few pisé huts which comprise Tendrara. A hundred people eke out a meagre livelihood by trading with the nomads: a couple of hundred yards of track between these huts and one is back in the monotonous desert of the alfa plateau.

Application had been made for a school at Tendrara. I was struck by the strange contrast between the image of the level of civilization and concentration of population which our kind of school conjures up and the empty immensity separating the people of this settlement from the rest of the world not only in

3

the matter of physical remoteness but also in their way of life in direct contact with nature in the raw.

For the next ninety miles M. Paye and I kept coming back to the concept of a school. We saw it as a response to the needs of a particular economic stage of a society's development; but neither of us could go any further than this rather obvious and vague statement.

A few days later we discovered that the Moslem schools of Boudenib and Erfoud were attended almost entirely by the Jews in the settlement. 'The Moslems in the oases,' said the teachers, 'don't want to come to school; the Jews, on the other hand, are eager to enrol.'

I was then struck by the very simple thought that our school had become above all a school for initiation to the symbols (reading, writing, arithmetic) required for communication at a distance, for keeping records. It is part and parcel of an economy of frequent and varied exchange. The Moslem farmers of the oases living in a closed economy, in a country where cash itself was rare and barter the order of the day, felt no need to acquire the use of these symbols. On the other hand, a few Moslems and particularly the Jews of the settlement of Boudenib and Erfoud – the artisans and traders, middlemen by necessity or choice – were vividly conscious of the value to them of a knowledge of symbols which would allow them to communicate with the outside world and to preserve records of their transactions. To the former, attendance at school seemed to be an incomprehensible and detestable invention of the French: to the latter, an unlooked-for golden opportunity. This was only one side of the question, although perhaps one of the most important.

I was then led to consider whether the school is indeed, as Durkheim teaches, essentially the means by which one generation transmits to the next the moral values it wishes to preserve or impose: or whether it is at the same time an economic organism indispensable to a society of a diversified exchange economy. It was perhaps to this second reason that the school owed the greater part of its success among those who attended it.

I tried to verify my theory by examining the development of schools in Morocco. By and large it is true that their success was related to the development of trade in a changing economy with a resultant increase in employment. But the problems raised in

4

such a study are surprisingly complex and numerous. In particular, it demands a re-orientation of ideas, a surrender of religious and moral prejudices which add further complications making it extremely hard for a foreigner, even if he is alive to the problems and sympathetically understanding, to attempt a precise evaluation. I myself would never have been able to speak other than as an outsider.

It seemed to me that a more certain method would be to study how the problem of the primary school arose and was solved in France, in relation to the economic and social changes which took place in the second half of the nineteenth century.

Clearly it arose in different ways in different regions. I could have compared regions from this point of view: or I could have studied one larger region, such as Western France. Indeed I did embark on writing something which might have been a modest supplement to André Siegfried's famous thesis: 'Political description of Western France'. But a work of this kind, if it were not to be superficial, would have required a number of local studies, and there are very few of real value.

Moreover, in order to understand why a peasant is willing to do without the labour of his children and send them to school; why, at about 1890, a peasant farmer's son was no longer willing to stay at home but sought paid employment, one must have very precise knowledge of the environment, and be able to relive in oneself all the doubts and reasons which led to the making of the decision.

This is why I have deliberately confined my subject to the commune of my birth and I have attempted to gain in precision what I may have lost in breadth.

I have restricted the study to the nineteenth century and particularly to the second half of the century, since it was in 1850 that the construction of roads began to assist change in the economy. Another reason is that the operation of the education law of 1850 (the *Loi Falloux*) allowed me to trace, from that date onwards, important statistics on school enrolment. I end the study in 1914 because by that time the case for the school had clearly been won.

I have tried to show how the exchange economy, which step by step replaced the closed economy in which the people of my country existed in 1850, convinced first the town dwellers and later the peasants of the value of symbols: how the habit of

5

travel, the rise in the standard of living, and social change all broadened their horizon, made possible a change in outlook, aroused a more lively interest in the school and led them more or less consciously, more or less completely through a maze of paths to share in the grand ideal of a visible and splendid faith in mankind and man's Reason so clearly to be seen in the great movement towards mass education since 1882.

two

The commune of Mazières-en-Gâtine Introduction: geography and history

La Gâtine

The traveller on the railway from Bordeaux to Paris via Saintes and Thonars may notice, some dozen miles after Niort, a change in the landscape. The monotonous, bare plain, dissected by dry-stone walls, is replaced by an undulating and wooded countryside where fields are separated by high, thick hedges: this is La Gâtine. At this same moment the train slows down as it climbs a steep gradient to reach, we are told, the highest point on the line.

If he is alert and has been briefed beforehand he may notice, just after a wide bend where the engine begins to pick up speed, a level crossing on a rough secondary road and, away to the left, disclosing itself above a fold in the ground and beyond the hedges and trees, the sharp outline of a church tower. Five hundred yards further on, slow trains stop at a little station. The church tower is Mazières-en-Gâtine: the station is Mazières-Verruyes.

If you wish to get to know the countryside, it is better to go by road. About eight miles from Niort, from the top of the little hill of Echiré and before dropping down into the valley of the river Sèvre, you will see, rising abruptly some ten miles away across the valley, a ridge covered with trees and running from north-west to south-east, which has all the appearance of a vast forest barrier on the horizon. This ridge is the southern edge of the ancient lands which are the prolongation into the region of the Armorican Massif before it disappears beneath the limestone of Poitou.

Echiré Hill is some 300 feet high and the road, after crossing the Sèvre, climbs to 450 feet until it enters Gâtine at the village of Champeaux. It reaches the parish of Mazières barely half a mile on, at the village of L'Hirondelle. It is now at a height of some 550 feet above sea level and for another six or seven miles it proceeds to cut the commune in half along its entire length.

Until it reaches the township, the road crosses some extremely broken ground composed of impermeable schists. No houses border it: only with difficulty can one pick out through the trees a few isolated farms at the end of earth tracks.

The township of Mazières is built entirely on the schist except on the northern edge where a few houses have recently been built on jurassic formations. Then after a steeper slope which marks the end of the secondary formations, the road comes out on to a sort of raised plateau (700 feet above sea-level) of alluvial deposits. Presently patches of secondary formations are met with and, at the intersection of permeable and impermeable rocks, larger villages may have been established.

Thus half the area of the commune is at the southern end of a band of ancient rock, running from north-west to south-east and half in a small structural basin made up chiefly of alluvial deposits with a few narrow outcrops of jurassic rock.

The commune: population distribution

The population as a whole is extremely scattered. Of the 1,032 inhabitants at the last census, only 349 were resident in the township: the remainder were dispersed among 48 villages or isolated farms.

Moreover, this distribution is not uniform. The schist lands, stretching south-west from the town, contain 12 isolated farms, nine hamlets of two or three homesteads and a few relatively important villages (Montbail, Ternan, Faché, making a total of 30 households or villages, 97 houses, 379 inhabitants).

The north-eastern part of the commune, smaller in area, comprises only two farmsteads, four hamlets of two or three households and large villages: le Beugnon, la Mimaudière, les Forges, la Guionnière, Beauchamp, la Lière: in total 17 households or villages, 73 houses, 299 inhabitants.

Thus there is a tendency for the population to be more sparse in the south-western sector than in the north-eastern.

Age of the settlement

As stated above, the township of Mazières is built at the point of contact between the jurassic and schist formations. It is probable that the presence of a spring which never ran dry even in the hottest season led to the first settlement. Several other, equally abundant, springs are found nearby, but from the former runs an earth road with a few remaining elements of rough paving. The thick hedges, the enormous banks, and the age of the trees which border it are evidence of its age. Moreover, in less than a mile, it joins a road formerly called the *chemin des chaussées* which was the ancient Roman road leaving Rom between Poitiers and Saintes to reach the port of Maillard at Nantes.

The very name Mazières reflects a long history. M. Dauzat,[1] in his work on place names, states in his chapter on name forms in the Frankish era: 'One may quote the Latin word crystallized in the toponym *maceria* as the prototype of Mazères. In the south Mazières, further north Maizères, Mezières (with the derivatives Mazenet, Maizenet, etc.) indicating homesteads and villages reconstructed from "ruined walls": the relics of plundered towns: the symbol of a bygone civilization.' A related origin is given by Longnon in his dictionary of place names: 'Place names in Normandy in which the word "toft" (today tôt) is found suggest a meaning similar to the French place names of Mezières, Maizières, Mazères and their derivatives, Mazeroy, Maizeret, Mazeret – which are often applied to localities built in the middle ages near ancient ruins.'

There would thus appear to be every reason to believe that this area has been inhabited for very many years.

The names of villages also are significant and interesting.

First, Ternant, which Longnon connects with the Gaulish *nantos* (valley), and the fact that the village of Ternant is situated in a small deep valley near an abundant spring, the source of a stream. The name Niorteau in Petit Niorteau and Grand Niorteau would also seem to have a Gaulish origin from Norioritos (new ford) given to a farm and village near the town of Mazières close to the source of a stream. It is amusing and perhaps worth noting that the village and farm of Niorteau adjoin the railway level crossing. They have given their name to this 'new ford'.

9

The term 'Petite Ville' recalls the Latin sense of the word 'villa'.

Other names have Roman origins: Fâchet probably derives from an early word Fagetines from Fagus (beech). La Mimaudière, la Ressegere, la Guittonnière, la Cantinière, la Chabirandière, la Texerie, etc., were certainly formed from family names by the addition of the suffix -ière or -erie.

The name of the farm La Fertière goes back to the Latin *firmitas, -atis* which was used in the early middle ages in the sense of 'fortress'. 'The origin of these names – fermeté, ferté,' states Longnon, 'goes back certainly to before the middle of the thirteenth century for it was then that the noun "ferté" ceased to be in common use.' There is no trace of any fortress in La Fertière but the village is situated at the top of a very steep slope and near the château of Petit-Chêne which was for long the residence of the lords of the manor. The name of the village of Angevinière doubtless recalls the establishment of the Angevins at the time when the Count of Parthenay was the ally of the Count of Anjou against the Count of Poitiers. It coincides perhaps with an expedition of the Count of Anjou which penetrated early in the twelfth century as far as Champdeniers.

Other names, such as Maison-Neuve, are self-explanatory or are connected with the vegetable kingdom: Le Petit Chêne, Le Chêne Billon, La Touche (Tuscha, Fosca, inlay wood).

Brief Survey of Mediaeval and Modern History

All these village names are evidence of the relatively ancient origins of the area's settlement. This is not to say that it was a rich country. The very name 'Gâtine', which is derived from the idea of 'tainting', is an indication of the poverty of the land which in early days was suitable for hardly anything more than a little cattle herding. A few village names are significant in this respect: les Gâts,[2] le Fougeret, les Naides.[3] The population was in all probability sparse and poor.

A fine oak wood near the farm of Pressigny, the exceptional importance of this farm of over 200 acres, the remains of a chapel in the village of Ternant, the thick walls of the farm of Oucherie are the only evidence remaining that noblemen once resided in an area now inhabited only by peasant farmers.

Little is to be found about Mazières-en-Gâtine in works of

local history. The following is the information given by the learned Belisaire Ledain in his toponymic dictionary of the department of Deux-Sèvres (Poitiers 1902):

> Mazières-en-Gâtine, Parthenay district. Maceriac 1041–1044 (cart. Saint-Maixent, 121); Matheriac 1093 (id. 213); Macheries 1108–1115 (id. 288); Mazerres 12th cent. (cart. Saint Maixent II); Maseriac 1625 (f.xvi); Mazères 1269 (collection Belisaire Ledain); Materiac 1300 (gr. Ganthier); Saint-Barnabé-de-Mazières (. . . 1648 to 1782).

Mazières was part of the manor of Bailliage Baton, linked to the barony of Parthenay and in the jurisdiction of the bailiwick of Parthenay. It was subject to the archbishopric of Saint-Maixent, to the seneschal's court of Poitiers and to the electoral district of Niort, after having been part of that of Parthenay in the sixteenth century. The church living was in the gift of the abbot of Saint Maixent. There were 90 households in 1716 and 106 in 1750.

The district blue book drawn up in 1716 gives a few precise details:[4]

> Mazières is a poor parish consisting of 90 households including 24 properties situated five leagues to the north of Niort in a land of mixed heath, cultivable fields, woods and with much excellent well-watered pasture land. The only crops grown are rye and oats. A good number of cattle are raised for sale.
>
> Its revenue is derived from rye, oats, timber and the proceeds of cattle sales.

> *Tax assessment*
>
> | | |
> |---|---|
> | Poll tax | 3,300 livres |
> | Forage | 180 |
> | Capitation | 420 |
> | Tithe | 479 |
> | | 4,379 livres |

This parish is in the diocese of Poitiers. It is the property of the Sieur de Breuillac by right of law vested in Pressigny.[5] His house is unpretentious but well wooded. It is called *Petit Chesgne*.

The population has decreased by 25 households since 1686.

This noticeable drop in population is probably explained by the years of extreme hardship experienced in the French countryside at the beginning of the eighteenth century, particularly during the terrible winter of 1709.

Statistics for 1744 show:

Mazières, five leagues north of Niort, Poitiers diocese
Number of households

1744	1716	Increase
100	90	10

Tax

	1744	1716
Poll tax	3,400 l.	3,300 l.
Forage	588	180
? Tools Equipment	819	—
Capitation	1,378	420
Tithe	855 l. 10s	479
	7,040 l. 10s	4,379

Increase 2,661 livres 10 sous

This parish is entirely within the boundaries of Gâtine but, since it is on the edge of the Plain, it has an easier market for its timber. It contains 24 tenant farms and three mills. There is good well watered pasturage for all kinds of livestock.

It is no more heavily taxed than others but the assessments are never equally distributed which has led to complaints from every quarter in turn.

The Pressigny family are lords of the manor. Their estate has always been the best timbered of the region: all the mature trees have been sold but some fine young timber remains.

Twenty-four farms; three mills. There could not have been much agriculture. The chief source of livelihood must have remained timber and livestock as it was in 1716.

The district records for Niort compiled in 1789 for the meeting
of the States General having disappeared, it is not possible to
know what were the grievances of the inhabitants of Mazières
at that time. But more precise information can be gathered
from a neighbouring parish – Verruyes in the Saint-Maixent
electoral district, the townships being barely two miles apart:
conditions in the two parishes were sure to have been very
similar.

Complaints Register, Verruyes.

Lord of the Manor, 1750:   Mme. de Breuillac of Petit-Chêne
Lord of the Manor, 1789:   Charles-Jean Viault, Squire, lord
                                of de Breuillac of Petit-Chêne
                                Verruyes.
Population   1790:   1,450

Court Hearing

Date : 1st March
Presiding Magistrate: Jean Metayer, syndic deputising for
                              the judge.
Population: 250 households

His Majesty being desirous of lightening the burden
of his subjects by requesting them, as is stated here
above, to make known their grievances, our parish will
provide instances which will cause any man to shudder,
torn with pity for mankind.

It is a wondrous way in which Providence has shed
and still sheds its bountiful rays on the aforesaid parish
to furnish means of relief sufficient to meet the dues
and taxes levied upon this parish of but some 250
homesteads with small resource in corn since not
enough is gathered for the sowing of an unprofitable
soil nor for the nourishment of the unfortunates who
inhabit it albeit they spend part of their time clearing
fields which are filled with reeds, with thistle and with
heather so that their beasts may graze there more
favourably, for this is the only resource of this parish
which is not one of the greatest and which is in a wet
situation filled with numbers of springs which are the
occasion of much mist. It is perchance this which has
been the cause of mortality among divers species of
cattle for several years; undoubted testimony of this is

shown by numberless petitions which have been
addressed by the unfortunates of this parish to
M. l'Intendant.

There are to be found in this parish a multitude of
poor miserable beggars who swarm under the roofs with
straw for their beds with numerous children who lack
strength to seek bread for their sustenance.

And for the other part, ploughmen, herdsmen,
hedgers and ditchers, exhausted by toil and themselves
in need of succour, hasten to aid their indigent brothers
as far as lies within their power.

Our pastors are unable to carry out their charitable
function either within the parish which is their first
concern or in the neighbouring parishes as well as to the
strangers who pass through, leading by the hand bands
of unfortunate little ones . . .

It is of the greatest moment for this miserable parish
to make known how it strives and exhausts itself in
efforts to pay the taxes and subsidies levied upon it.
Seventy or eighty years past it paid but 2,000 livres in
principal tax; but today it finds itself burdened with
a sum of 6,000 livres in principal taxes not counting
considerable other charges in tithes and forced labour.

Again this parish is burdened with a multitude of
manorial rents and other dues amounting to considerable
sums.

There followed seventeen signatures.

This is a dark picture. It was probably painted in darker
colours than reality in justification of the protest in the last
few lines. All that follows after the first lines referring to the
payment of taxes, to the exceptional mortality rate of the
cattle, to the petitions previously addressed to M. l'Intendant
is evidence in this direction.

Nevertheless the picture of these poor miserable beggars
lying on straw under the roofs; of those children lacking strength
to find bread for themselves; the allusions to a barren land
covered with reeds, thistles and heather and barely cultivable
– all seems to be based on actual experience. It can be reckoned
as true that in 1789 the country was very poor and yet, at the
same time, thickly populated.[6]

three

From 1789 to 1850
The commune in
mid-nineteenth century

Chief Events: Historical Summary

Various documents – uncatalogued and unclassified – preserved
in the town hall of Mazières allow one to follow with more
precision the history of the commune during the Revolution.

It was situated between Niort, a republican centre, and
Parthenay which was disputed between the forces of the Vendée
and those of the Republic. Consequently it does not appear to
have been directly affected by the struggles of the Vendée.
However, two documents bear evidence of the insecurity of the
times. On the 2 Frimaire in the Year III of the French Republic,
the *curé* Cavanoc, a constitutional priest, and by virtue of that
position acting as registrar for Mazières, was assassinated in his
house and the account of his death reported at the time speaks
of the pillaging of the township.[1]

The following year, on the 16 Vendémiaire, Year IV of the
French Republic, the health officer Pierre Morel, who lived at
Mazières, was murdered a few miles from his house between
Allonne and La Boissière. The Mayor was unable to make a
first-hand report of the death 'in view of the fact that the
country is in a state of insurrection and overrun'.[2]

The conscription of men under the Revolution for the
Republican armies cannot have been very burdensome. In any
case, that of the Empire was not. In 1808 there were 79 conscripts for the canton of Mazières: 18 were declared fit for
service; five were sent for base duties; three were postponed,
and 52 were discharged. In 1813, of eleven conscripts in the
commune, two were exempted, one as the older brother of an
orphan family, the other as the brother of a conscript killed on

active service; one was declared fit for service, another one for marching after having attempted to hoodwink the tribunal by pretending to be lame; two were deferred; five were discharged as unfit and as such eligible for pensions varying between 100 and 1200 francs a year.

A report from the Prefect of Deux-Sèvres gives some idea of the atmosphere in which these decisions were made:

> The conscript classes are far from good. . . . It appears that the quality is deteriorating. The forced labour to which the peasants subject their children from the age of fourteen or fifteen harms their physical development. Moreover, in this Department, and particularly in Gâtine, the body is not fully developed before the age of twenty-five and nothing is more difficult than to find conscripts five feet five inches in height. The best come from the cantons of La Mothe-Sainte-Heraye, Thouars, and Airvault; the most stunted from Ménigoute, Mazières and Parthenay. This region, like the whole of Gâtine, produces ulcerated legs, deaf people and epileptics in prodigious numbers. The gorse which covers the land pricks the legs of the young men who wear for work, wide canvas trousers and no stockings. The dampness of the soil impedes the healing of sores and the sufferers purposely infect them so that the conscript may be rejected. These precautions are taken three years in advance. . . . The disasters of the Vendée war may have given rise to epilepsy. In respect of this condition, as for deafness, the recruiting tribunal is faced with many traps. Surgeons come up with sheaves of certificates; there is no conscript who does not present himself without one, although one takes little notice of them and hardly ever reads them (I myself even tear them up in their presence). Every year these abuses are repeated with a more serious effect than might be thought, adding a heavy monetary burden to the human factor of conscription. These certificates are sold for amounts varying from three to as much as 200 francs and respectable persons of standing in society come to bear witness in support of these claims, nearly always in order to effect an unjustified exemption. The tribunal

must take strict action: those who have self-inflicted
burns and sores must be sent to the pioneer battalion.
By this means it is possible each year to deal with one
disease but, the following year, the doctors will find
a way of producing a different case for exemption.
The great problem is that, since most of the registers
of births, deaths and marriages for the Bressuire and
Parthenay districts have been destroyed, parents swear
statements declaring their children to be older than
their true age. One can only deal with a lie when the
deceit is quite obvious and natural evidence is in clear
conflict with legal evidence. I am sure we are often
deceived; I have just sent back for the 1812 call-up a
child brought before the tribunal as being twenty
years old.

As time went on and the State became both weaker and more
demanding, attempts at deception became more ingenious and
more frequent. They were encouraged and assisted by the
people as a whole, even by those whose task it was to combat
them.

The following letter written to the Mayor of Mazières by the
Deputy Prefect at Parthenay on 18th March, 1814, is of
particular significance:

> Parthenay 18 March 1814
> The Deputy Prefect
> to His Worship the Mayor, Mazières.
>
> Sir,
> The present necessity of repelling a bold foe requires
> us to furnish a further contingent of men. The quota
> for your commune is three. You should select them
> yourself from among those least needed at home. They
> should report to Niort on Thursday next, 24th of this
> month equipped with fowling piece or rifle, sabre, pistol
> and all other arms they can obtain. Under no pretext
> can your commune be exempted from providing its
> quota and the responsibility which rests on your
> shoulders in this respect is not an empty word. You
> should forward to me the list of the men requisitioned.
> I have the honour to greet you.

In such manner is evidenced the spirit of anarchic individualism among the peasants.

The Chouan rising

No event worthy of note after 1816 seems to have affected the routine of the people until 1832. The 1830 revolution appears to have taken place without notice; in any case no document exists to show that it had any effect whatever in the commune.

But the Chouan rising in 1832 was the cause of many incidents – some bloody – and aroused such feeling that it was still discussed round the fires twenty years later. The following was written in 1934 by M. Bouet in the *Echo de la Vallée* under the heading 'The Chouan Rising in Mazières-en-Gâtine, 1832–3'.[3]

> The Duchess of Berry had raised in Gâtine a body of partisans who took the name of 'chouans' after those of the great Revolution. They were commanded by a Corsican and, for two or three years, terrorised the countryside.
>
> At Mazières itself on 18th January 1832 they raided the safe of the collector of taxes, named Taffoireau, giving him a receipt for 3,092 francs 50 signed 'Chouans, soldiers of Henri V'.
>
> They murdered a man called Billant whose descendants still live in Mazières.
>
> At Verruyes they committed another murder, the victim named Obi. . . .
>
> In the commune of Vouhe, at the village of La Mounère, there was a veritable battle one day. . . .

Order was restored when the Duchess of Berry was arrested and discredited in circumstances which are well known.

Such are the chief events in local history until 1850, a date which is of importance to our study since it was at that moment in time that roads were constructed and the economy began to change.

Social and economic conditions

The cadastral survey of 1832 gives the commune of Mazières-en-Gâtine an area of 1,857 hectares 29 ares 58 centares, distributed as follows:

Arable land	1426 ha.	23 a.	90 ca.
Pasture	270 ,,	81 ,,	12 ,,
Rough grazing	21 ,,	37 ,,	90 ,,
Woodland	91 ,,	00 ,,	80 ,,
Gardens	31 ,,	96 ,,	31 ,,
Residential land	15 ,,	39 ,,	55 ,,

In 1791 ninety-one landowners were inscribed on the tax roll. On a total income calculated at 12,149 livres 11 sous, M. Henri Viault, owner of the château of Petit Chêne, was assessed on his sole account at an amount of 3,674 livres 15 sous. This Henri Viault was the Comte of Breuillac, a descendant of the names we quoted in the electoral list drawn up at Niort in 1716 (see page 11). He belonged to an old family of the region. One of his ancestors, René Viault, squire, lord of the manor of Breuillac, entered into possession of the fief of Pressigny, with jurisdiction over the parishes of Mazières and Verruyes, in 1672 and, three years earlier, of the fief of Angevinière in the parish of Mazières. In 1789 the Comte de Breuillac was a very considerable landowner indeed, not only in Mazières parish but also in the neighbouring parishes, particularly in Verruyes and Chapelle Bâton. He also had property in Vendée through his wife, Jeanne-Marie-Pétronille de la Taste. In Mazières parish alone he owned the following estates: Petit Chêne, his residence, Petit Moulin, Angevinière, Chêne-Billon, Bretommières, Bouquetière, Soultière, Moulin-de-Ternant, Oucherie, La Grange, Fâchet, as well as several pieces of land belonging to Pressigny (in Verruyes parish): in all, a total of more than 600 hectares out of 1,800.

The income of the other major landowners living outside the parish, sometimes at some distance (Poitiers, Fontenay, Airvault) was assessed at 4,850 francs 5 sous. This means that more than two-thirds of the commune was owned either by the lord of the manor or by proprietors who lived outside its boundaries.

These 'absentee' landowners, each of whom had a taxable income of more than 100 livres, were members of religious communities (the Commanderie of Saint-Marc-la-Lande, the Maison-Dieu of Parthenay) or government officials (a lieutenant of the Forestry Service living at La Foye-Monjault, a magistrate living at Poitiers) or *rentiers*, some of noble rank like Mme. de Chainelay living at Fontenay-le-Comte, owning property at Le Beugnon. Worthy of note among them are: a farmer named Bordier who lived at La Bouchetière, and owned property in the township with a taxable income of 518 livres, and a fuller named Clisson, living at La Varnière, assessed at 173 livres 10 sous.

The other relatively important land owners – those whose taxable income was more than 100 livres and who were domiciled in the parish – came to a total of ten. Among them were the Mayor, René Galin, whose profession is not given, a farrier living at Beugnon, an innkeeper in the town, a certain Louis Vivier, cabinet maker in the town, and six farmers in villages to the north of the parish, the southern part being mainly owned by the Breuillac family.

In 1836 the taxable income amounted to 11,310 livres. The number of landowners had grown from 91 to 138. The sale of some national property belonging to the de Breuillac family,[4] or to the Commanderie of Saint-Marc-la-Lande or to the monks of the Maison-Dieu at Parthenay helped to produce this result.[5] The increase is most noticeable among the number of owners living in the commune. It rose from 47 in 1791 to 89 in 1836. But it was largely a question of very small properties limited to a house and a garden or a few fields. Of these 89 owners, 70 had a taxable income of less than 50 livres (as against 31 in 1791). The number of owners with a taxable income between 50 and 100 livres had risen from six to nine, of whom eight were small farmers. The number with a taxable income of over 100 livres had not changed at ten. It should be noted that of these ten, seven were small farmers, but only two (of whom one had bought the Fâchet farm, sold as national property) had a taxable income of more than 200 livres. It is also worth recording that three notables of the town (a notary, a doctor and a landowner) did not work their land themselves.

Most of the important landowners still lived outside the commune. Prominent among them is the Comte de la Laurencie who owned more than 500 hectares and nine working estates.

He lived at his country seat of Petit-Chêne for only a few months of the year.

The great wealth in real estate, dating from the *ancien régime*, to which attention has been drawn, had thus maintained itself. Not without some difficulty, however. M. de Breuillac seems to have taken part during the Revolution in the Vendée movement and, for this, his property had been confiscated. Two farms even – La Grange and Grand-Fâchet – had been sold on 16 Brumaire, Year VIII, for 13,770 livres. But the amnesty of 7 Nivôse, Year VIII, having established a distinction between the émigrés and the Vendéens, he was able to profit therefrom and regain provisional possession of his estates through an order of the prefect of Deux-Sèvres dated 25 Nivôse, Year IX. On 12 Nivôse, Year X, all the sequestration orders were lifted. Compensation to the amount of 32,868 livres was paid to the nieces of the Comtess de Breuillac on 25 April 1826 as compensation for the sale of the farms of La Grange and Grand-Fâchet and of some land in the commune of Saint-Georges.[6]

Changes in the numbers of landowners at different income levels may be summarized as follows:

	Owners resident in the commune Level of taxable income			Owners resident outside the commune Level of taxable income		
	−50 l.	+50 l.	+100 l.	−50 l.	+50 l.	+100 l.
1791	31	6	10	19	7	18
1836	70	9	10	22	7	16
1852	68	21	7	20	19	23

Thus, from the standpoint of real estate in 1852 in Mazières commune, together with clear and important survivals of large estates dating from the *ancien régime*, there was a clear tendency for an increase in the number of small owners whose assets consisted of no more than a house, a garden and one or two fields and also a marked increase in the number of middle-sized owners. The number of proprietors living outside the commune tended to decrease. On the other hand, an important fact is worthy of note in the growth of a class of leading figures in a rural society (a notary, a doctor, a few rentiers) dependent mainly on their income.

Method of cultivation: tenant farming or share cropping (*métayage*)

Since there were in 1840 some 30 estates of more than 25 hectares, of which only 7 were worked by their owners, the remainder (averaging between four and ten hectares and including most of the *borderies*) were being worked by tenant-farmers or *métayer* share-croppers. It is difficult to make a clear distinction between the two.

The term *métairie* cannot be used with any exactitude. In a deed handing over property to the community dated 6 Vendémiaire, Year VII, of the Republic, the Comtesse de Breuillac complains that her tenants had paid no rent for five years, by reason of the Vendée wars. She mentions in particular that the *métairie* of Les Bretommières (in the commune of Mazières) had a rental of 400 livres. It would appear that the word *métairie* has the meaning of a farm of medium size but with no implication of the idea of *métayage* (share-cropping).

The same meaning occurs in an account of land sown to crops at Les Boisselées drawn up by the Mayor of Mazières in 1817. He makes a distinction between the *métairies* and the *borderies*, but the *métairies* are always of larger area than the *borderies*.

The farm of Les Bretommières is classed as a *métairie*: it comprised fields requiring sixteen bushels of seed. Within living memory in the region the term *borderie* is used to describe small farms: it does not necessarily imply any idea of share-cropping, as it would appear to do historically and etymologically.

An inscription on the wall of the most important house in the Lower Town at Mazières tells that it was built in 1774 by Maître François Gaillard, bailiff and tenant farmer of M. de Breuillac. It seems probable that this village legal luminary was responsible for collecting the rents due to the Comte de Breuillac for the Pressigny estates. But the deed of renunciation executed by Mme. de Breuillac mentioned above indicates that she leased land around Petit-Chêne directly on cash tenancies. From the time of the Revolution, therefore, a certain number of estates appear to have been worked on tenancy agreements and not on the basis of share-cropping or *métayage*.

In any case, from the middle of the nineteenth century onwards, the system of tenant farming was more widespread than
that of *métayage*. Of ten leases recorded in 1840 and 1841 in the
study made by Maître Bobin (successor to Maître Pastureau of
Mazières) only one was a *métayage* agreement.

This point is confirmed for the area in an address given by
General Allard, member of the Chamber of Deputies, at an
agricultural show at Parthenay in 1852:

> Abundant harvests will soon be visible instead of the
> wasteland of moor and heath which are such a sad
> spectacle today and may lead people to think you lack
> intelligence. Above all, do not believe, because of a
> mistaken distrust of your landlords, that any
> improvements that you may make will have as their
> sole effect an increase in the rents they may charge for
> their farms.[7]

This is not to say that between 1840 and 1850 there was no
share cropper (*métayer*) in Mazières commune. On the contrary,
I was able by questioning villagers to discover several – one on
a farm of considerable size (70 hectares at Niorteau) which
changed to a rental basis only in 1867. But such were the
exception.

The tenants were, moreover, extremely subservient towards
their landlords. They called him 'Master' – a title which was
still in use at the end of the century. They were proud and happy
if their landlords would come and share a meal in their house,
even if they were a large party, on hunt days. They would
willingly present them with gifts of fowls and eggs in addition
to the 'supplements' which were added to all leases and of
which we shall have more to say. As a general rule, especially
in the larger farms, the generations of the same family succeeded
each other: the eldest son, if married, followed his father or, in
exceptional cases, two brothers would share a large property.
The younger sons who could find no place of their own would
sometimes stay with their elder brothers and assist in bringing
up the family. Similarly the estates changed hands but rarely.
The heirs of the Comtesse de Breuillac remained, right up to
1885, in possession of the lands they had inherited. One farm
(La Davidière) was still owned in 1940 by the same family
who had possessed it in 1791. Close personal relations existed

between landlord and tenant particularly since within living memory the commune has never experienced, for example, a 'Registrar General' as registrar of property. Maître François Gaillard has had no successor since the Revolution.

So the region would appear to have been the scene of relatively marked economic change by the middle of the nineteenth century, bringing a little prosperity to a certain number of farmers who had become wealthy enough to own their own stock and implements.

Besides the owner-farmers, some of whom could be considered as almost wealthy, besides the relatively comfortable tenant farmers and besides the small *bordiers* who eked out a meagre living, there were also a few craftsmen (of whom we shall have occasion to speak later) and a number of very poor daily paid workers – twenty families being classed as indigent. Some, in order to make a living, acted as foster parents for children registered as foundlings.

Poverty

The need for unskilled labour, the prevalent custom of gleaning and public charity, enabled them to live during the summer. But the winters, when warmth was needed – and the supply of dried wood was soon exhausted – were terrible. To provide aid for the poor, workhouses were opened. In 1848 there were no fewer than six in the commune paid for from a national fund of six million francs. By this means the roads were maintained after a fashion. But it was still not enough to overcome this abject poverty.

In 1852 the Mayor of Mazières was asked by the sub-prefect of Parthenay in a letter dated 14 June to provide a list of beggars in the commune. He found 63 names which included only seven old or chronically sick persons. Among them were several widows, two of whom each had three children and also two families, one with five and the other with three children. It was the usual custom – which oral tradition confirms – for the children of large and needy or very poor families to beg for their bread. This they did by visiting the tenant farmers on regular days. Others went into domestic service at a very early age: one maidservant aged eight is recorded at Le Beugnon in the register of 1846.

In 1853, after an extremely poor harvest, the price of bread rose swiftly. A meeting of the town council on 26 June fixed the price of top grade bread at o fr. 30 the kilogram, of second grade at o fr. 25 and third grade at o fr. 225. Subsequent price levels were:

	1st grade	2nd grade	3rd grade
29 September	o fr. 37	o fr. 325	o fr. 30
3 October	o fr. 40	o fr. 35	o fr. 325
30 October	o fr. 42	o fr. 37	o fr. 35
5 November	o fr. 47	o fr. 47	o fr. 35

The frequency of these changes demonstrates how the local authority strove to resist price increases and its impotence to prevent them. The number of necessitous cases registered on 4 December 1853 reached 87 and a public subscription was opened to counter begging. In October 1855 the mayor of Mazières answered a questionnaire on begging as follows:

Estimated number of indigent persons in your commune living exclusively upon public or private charity during the bad season:

Men 12
Women 27
Children below 12 years of age 49

How many inhabitants are there who, although not asking for alms and not indigent, lack sufficient resources for existence during the winter and will require assistance:

Men 29
Women 12
Children under 12 years of age 10

Total necessitous cases 139

Of this total how many will require assistance in the form of food? 102
How many will need assistance in the form of work . . 57

Thus in 1855, out of a total population of approximately 970, 159, i.e. one-sixth, depended on charity when the harvest was bad.

The State of Agriculture

This can be explained, at least in part, by the economic state of the region. The only economic resources were, in effect, agricultural: and agriculture was in a poor state.

In a remarkable memorandum addressed to the Ministry of the Interior by the prefect Dupin in Year IX of the French Republic, the country is described as follows:

> The environs of Parthenay present no pattern of symmetry.... The country is a jumble of deep valleys, mountains, ponds and forests: the scene is one of varied and picturesque landscapes. The soil is dry, stony and sandy, swampy in the lowest parts and generally unfertile. It produces little rye but pasture and forage are excellent. The growing of crops is at an early stage; the thin soil needs to be manured every year which demands considerable expense and the low level of wealth in the country is an obstacle to improvement. Moreover, few of the landlords undertake true farming; they resign themselves to the narrow way of life of the peasant (pp. 29–30).

There follow these precise details on the methods of cultivation:

> A farm is divided into thirds in three parcels – one in meadows, one in rough pasture, the third under the plough. These last fields, which are the best land, however, are productive only as the result of endless hard work and need to rest fallow for five, six, even eight years – sometimes longer. To prepare a field for the type of grain to which it is suited will require ten ploughings.... All this is done with oxen only and generally four or six oxen are needed for one plough.... Land lying fallow produces, like the heathland, broom, gorse and abundant forage fodder, providing excellent grazing for cattle. When the grass is exhausted the broom is fired; the ash fertilizes the soil; the grass recovers.

Doubtless the same procedure could be seen twenty-five years later. On the 14 March 1826 the sub-prefect of Parthenay requested the mayor of Mazières to complete two returns relating to the crops and the number of livestock in the commune. The mayor, the Vicomte de la Laurencie, held a meeting at Petit-Chêne of all the farmers and husbandmen. In the light of the information then given he drew up the following tables (viz., minutes of administrative actions in the commune of Mazières 1826):

Crops and livestock: average for the years 1821–5

(amounts in double decalitres)

wheat	nil	pulses	nil
rye & maslim	3,078,821 mililt.	potatoes	1,800,336
maize	nil	oats	1,302,407
buckwheat	56,442	spring corn	nil
barley	30,133	chestnuts	40,050

Notes

(1) From these estimates, which state as accurately as possible what the farmers of this commune have harvested during the last five years (on average), may be deducted that part which, each year, they retain as seed for their lands to ensure the next season's crop. The average for this part is one-eighth of the above amounts, at least.

(2) The population of the commune consisting of more than 600 consumers, it is correct to say that the one-eighth having been deducted, the commune is far from producing sufficient rye and potatoes to feed its inhabitants; there is, in consequence, a regular and considerable importation of grain.

Table showing the number of each kind of stock

horses	5	bulls	41
mares	62	oxen	108
foals			
(under 3 years)	14	cows	245
mules	7	heifers	71
mules			
(under 3 years)	14	sheep: merino	nil
asses	nil	cross bred	nil
		local	597
		goats	82

Notes

(1) Nothing varies more than the number of young livestock. Each market day shows increases and decreases.

(2) Many farmers harness cows to their carts or ploughs together with oxen. The number of cows used for ploughing or submitted to the yoke in this commune may even be put at over one hundred.

Vicomte de la Laurencie.

Near to the houses were to be found some rather better places, usually relatively small fields on which much care was lavished and fertilizer spread (i.e. farmyard manure – the only fertilizer known at that time in the region) and around which cultivation decreased as distance increased. As their distance from the centre of the farm increased and as they became less and less cultivated, so the fields increased in size. Doubtless the more fertile but more distant fields were sometimes put under the plough but, in view of the impossibility of manuring them after one harvest, they lay fallow for four, six or eight years.

Jacques Bujault, a farmer from Chaloux near Melle, was indignant at this state of affairs:[8]

In the Bocage, however large a farm may be, it possesses but one plough. Broom, gorse, couch grass, bracken, thistle and thorn cover any uncultivated land.

Some poor beasts starve with hunger for nine months of the year, live well during three. This is the agriculture of the Arabs of Mascara, a little better than that of the Iroquois or the Tartars who roam the high steppes with their herds – but it bears a close resemblance to it.

Oxen, cows and calves all sleep out of doors during four to six months. If it were not for the wolves (who render great service in this respect) they would never be put inside the byre. Under this system you can make heaps of manure – as big as your fist. And without manure, there is no crop.

The Vendéens and the men of Gâtine plant a little rye for themselves and their workers. This grain is exported in one year in ten and then at a low price.

The better land, if well treated, would produce wheat.

They grow none and get it from the plain. A cunning lot, these folk.

The very names of the fields in Gâtine are of significance. In the northern sector 'A' of the commune: The Naiads, Gorse Fields, Sand Pit. In the town sector 'B': Lost Bread, Thorny Field. In sector 'C': Lost Land, Big Pasture, The Burrows. In sector 'D': Great Thistle, Gavachons, Champs de Gas. The gorse and broom (especially the latter) sometimes grew ten feet high. Some old men declare that oxen would lose themselves in it and never be recovered.

*

By 1850 there had been some progress.

The report on the state of agriculture in the Parthenay district presented to the Committee of the *Exposition Universelle* of 1855 remarked, concerning the soils of the Bocage:

The impoverished soil, exhausted by broom, bracken, thistle, couch-grass and a hundred other parasitic plants used to yield every nine or ten years a meagre crop of rye, barely sufficient to feed the farmer and his family.

The remedies indicated were:

1. breaking in new land;
2. the use of lime;
3. the cultivation of plants for grazing.

We will confine ourselves (wrote the reporter) to stating that the market gardening industry in the neighbourhood of Parthenay has developed to an almost unbelievable extent but, nevertheless, is unable to meet the ever-increasing demand for seedlings of beetroot, cabbage, parsnips, turnips, etc. All this notwithstanding the increasing number of growers planting the crops suitable to their lands.

4. wheat to replace barley.

Eighteen years ago the growing of wheat was to all intents unknown in the whole Bocage area. Recently its cultivation has begun. I was able to record, in the Vasles and Mazières communes, a yield of 40 hectolitres per hectare or of 30 to one per seed – and this with no expense of capital. It will take the place of rye.

The report emphasized the need for the creation of sown pastures and said: 'They have doubled in a few years.'

There, indeed, lay the salvation, as M. Jacques Bujault wrote in his almanac for 1830: 'No fodder without pasture; no cattle without fodder ... is that not true? But no manure without cattle and no grain without manure. Thus, pasture, fodder, cattle and manure lead to grain. All these form a unity; if one is lacking, goodbye to the harvest.

Do you want corn? Then create pasture.'[9]

For the Mazières canton this development began in 1850. Besides the allusion made in the report just quoted, the following letter from the Mayor of Mazières to the sub-prefect of Parthenay is further evidence:

> In reply to your letter of first instant, I have the honour to forward to you the following information which I have hastened to gather as regards my canton.
>
> For 1850 the following areas have been sown: 180 hectares of wheat, 750 hectares of rye, 750 hectares of oats, 350 hectares of buckwheat, 550 hectares of potatoes, 15 hectares of beans. Maize is not grown for grain but only *brizeaux*. No summer or winter barley is grown: our soil is unsuitable:
>
> The harvest has been good and the yield above that of an average year. The yield of crop for seed has been in the ratio of 8 for wheat, 14 for rye, 17 for oats, 18 for pulses. The buckwheat has not yet been harvested. The rains have harmed it and it is not ripening so that the yield will not be as good as had been hoped for. Potatoes go from bad to worse. They yield at least 10 for one but the farmers will be obliged to cease growing them. This has already happened on several farms where they have been replaced by swedes. The amount of old grain may be estimated at approximately 200 hectolitres of wheat and 800 hectolitres of rye: oats and other grain are never kept for long – they are nearly always sold or consumed before the following harvest.

One hundred and eighty hectares of wheat, 750 hectares of rye, 750 hectares of oats, 350 hectares of buckwheat, 350 hectares of potatoes, 15 hectares of beans come to a total for the canton (eight communes of about 15,000 hectares) of 2,595 hectares of farmland, of which approximately 300 probably were in Mazières. The progress reported was still barely noticeable.

The dwellings

It is not surprising that these poor peasants, scattered among these fields covered in gorse, heather, bracken and broom lived in houses equally poor and comfortless.

There seems to have been no plan in the arrangement of buildings. Only one farm near Mazières (La Menardière), by the ordering of its buildings round an interior courtyard, recalls the great farms of Beauce – and this was an accidental whim of its owner, the health officer Fraigneau. In most of the isolated farms the general pattern was one of open courtyards with an irregular layout of farm-house and out-buildings according to the lie of the land. It is difficult to discern in most of the villages any attempt to align the buildings around a common courtyard.

The use to which the outbuildings of 1850 were put confirms what has been said earlier concerning the agricultural resources of the country. It was a country of stock, not arable, farming. The typical building was a fairly narrow barn flanked by two byres and surmounted by a hayloft with apertures to the animals' food-racks. Granaries were rare, and, where they existed, very small.

The houses themselves were low, with tiled roofs. Entrance was through a solid door, the height of a man and surmounted by three rows of narrow tiles. Only the more important houses had a window at the side of this door.[10] A lower, roughly made wooden wicket gate, hooked to the outside wall, allowed the door to be kept open to admit air and light while barring the entry of the hens and domestic animals.

Many houses had only one room and on the floor of beaten earth there would be a large table flanked by two backless benches, one or two wooden chests and, against the wall, one or two beds. They were dark and unhealthy dwellings 'where diseases of the chest are dangerous', particularly in a damp climate.

Thus wrote Dr. Pouzet, mayor of Mazières, in 1853. Nevertheless, he hardly showed much zeal in enforcing in his commune the law of 13 April 1850 regarding unhealthy houses. This minor point is worth closer consideration: it gives a vivid picture of the difficulties the central government may have in applying laws which are in advance of change in society's culture.

That the houses were unhealthy is impossible to doubt when those which remain unaltered are studied. In the eyes of a man who, in 1850, was capable of seeing them as they were because he was not in the habit of seeing them every day, they were barely habitable. The mayor of Saint-Pardoux, a neighbouring commune of Mazières, on 22 October 1853 asked Dr. Pouzet to come and help him 'to clean these new Augean stables, if I may so express myself'. It was, in his opinion, a matter of 'philanthropic work'. This mayor signed himself: 'Mayor C. C. Imbert, retired'. He was not, or was no longer, familiar with the region. Dr. Pouzet, who seems to have been a good mayor, who knew and loved those under his charge but who kept them in their place and would not have dreamt comparing them to himself, had also nominated a committee appointed to inspect unhealthy houses in the commune. But a reminder from the sub-prefect of Parthenay was needed before he replied on 4 April 1854 as follows: 'The committee has met and visited the houses of the commune. It found everywhere houses in a reasonable condition: none seem to come under the legal classification of unhealthy dwelling. The committee, therefore, confined itself to advising that some houses be whitewashed and that some owners provide a little light. This advice has been followed and all is now in a proper state.' In so doing he no doubt had the approval of his people: the owners who were put to but little expense, the tenants whose rents had not changed.

The township—a village: its topography

The centre of the commune, the township, differed very little at that time in the way of life of its inhabitants from the larger surrounding villages. It had, moreover, a relatively small population. About 1840 it held between 180 and 190 inhabitants[11] in some forty houses while the whole commune had 842 inhabitants and 914 in 1846.

The centre was still near the spring, close to which an open air wash-house and a drinking trough had been set up. Highway No. 2 from Niort to Parthenay passed in front of this spring;

this was where the main district road No. 22 from Mazières to Thénezay started (the road which joined the ancient Roman road a kilometre further on). The houses were not built beside the spring (the ground was too wet for building) but opposite it. There the land seems to have been entirely covered by houses, stables or gardens. One of these houses dating from the eighteenth century (1776 to be exact)[12] was particularly large. The gendarmes were billeted there. The village inn which is still today called the Auberge de la Fontaine was at the end of this conglomeration of houses. Such as it was, it formed a focal point of sufficient importance to have led to the building – along a narrow earth road which, starting between the gendarmerie and the inn, lost itself in the fields – of several dwelling houses now transformed into stables. (One of them, so strong is tradition, has been rebuilt and is still lived in.)

All this was situated in a valley about a hundred yards wide at this point, enclosed between two slopes, one fairly high and steep towards Parthenay, the other lower and more gentle towards Niort. No dwelling was built on the Parthenay slope.

In contrast, the church had been built (probably in the twelfth century) at the top of the second slope. It marked the junction of the Road No. 2 – from Parthenay to Niort and Road No. 23 leading down towards Champdeniers. A certain number of houses were collected together at this privileged spot, but they, too, were in no kind of alignment along the roads. Nothing is more indicative of the little importance given to roads at that time than the way in which the building of houses had so little regard for them. First, they gathered together at will in interior courtyards round a well; for example, in this collection of thirty odd houses there were no fewer than three courtyards denying at least ten dwellings any direct access to the road. Quite clearly the type plan of the surrounding villages, gathering their houses around interior courts, had stamped itself on the construction of the township. It goes without saying that even those houses which were built by the roadside observed no rule of alignment. The survey and line trace for Route No. 2 in the traverse for Mazières town, drawn up in 1844, shows that at one spot the Mazières road was barely three yards wide.

The houses referred to above, moreover, still exist and it is still possible to trace in their frontages the line to which they had to keep. The Niort–Parthenay road was at times eight yards wide, at others twenty and at others again – notably opposite the presbytery garden and the cemetery – hardly five.

These houses were built of undressed stone covered with a greyish plaster and roofed with tiles. Most had a second storey; some were of one floor only. But all, apart from three or four where the town notables lived, were less than modest. For example, No. 85 at the beginning of this century consisted of one large room with a floor of beaten earth entered directly from the front door and which served as workshop, shop and bedroom at one and the same time. This room was lighted by a large glassed door and one window. It was warmed by an enormous fireplace. Three steps gave access to the kitchen. This was a narrow, dark, low-ceilinged room from which a steep wooden staircase led to two bedrooms on the first floor. Thus, the town of Mazières was made up of two islets of houses separated by meadows; the one built near the spring and drinking trough, the other near the church at the crossroads. Needless to say, the cemetery was close to the church and between the two islets of houses.

The town's inhabitants

Around 1850 this little collection of dwellings housed a few notable figures. First and foremost there were three landowners living on the rent of their estates. The mayor of the commune was typical of these gentry. The fortune on which he lived dated from before the Revolution. One of his female ancestors is recorded in the communal register as tenant of La Ménardière (a large farm of some 70 hectares near Mazières town but in the commune of Saint-Marc-la-Lande). He owned considerable land in the communes of Mazières and Saint-Marc-la-Lande. In 1841 he built himself a large house in a large garden at the lower end of the town and lived there with a manservant and two maids.

Before him another landed gentleman also living in Mazières town had been mayor. At the beginning of the century the mayor had been the Comte de la Laurencie, son-in-law and heir of the Comtesse de Breuillac. But when he died, the Comte de Tusseau, his heir, had left the office of mayor to be discharged by the notables of the town. The exactitude of numerous registers and the minutes of meetings show, moreover, that these notables were well-educated and conscientious people.[13]

Next comes the doctor, in reality a health officer but whose daughter was shortly to marry a true doctor: the former appears on the register as 'medical man' (*médecin*), the latter, very correctly, as 'doctor' (*docteur-médecin*). This 'doctor', Dr. Pouzet, was to become mayor of the commune for more than twenty years from 1841 to 1871 and an excellent mayor, too, whose activities we shall have cause to study in detail. Health Officer Fraigneau lived in a comparatively modest house near the church, but in 1848 he had it considerably extended at the time of his daughter's wedding. He was, indeed, a wealthy man owning five farms (of about 300 hectares) one of which – Fâchet – was in the commune, acquired at the time of the sale of national property. The others were in the commune of Saint-Marc-la-Lande. The solicitor, the beadle, the registrar were notables in a second category. The priest, the venerable Abbé Dru (so described in official records dealing with church affairs), was much respected and loved. There were only a few civil servants: one tax collector, four gendarmes and a police sergeant. There was, in addition, a teacher. The gendarmes and the teacher can only be regarded as comfortably off in comparison with the artisans and shopkeepers of the town. In the census of 1841 the only artisans recorded were:

1 wheelwright	1 woodcutter
1 mason with 3 workmen	1 smith with 4 workers
1 tiler	1 baker with 2 workers
1 clog-maker with 1 workman	2 joiners (1 with 3 workers)

There were also mentioned:

1 carter	1 costumier (who would have worked at home)
1 gelder	
1 miller	1 dressmaker with 5 workers (who worked from house to house)
1 laundress with 2 workers	

The records of 1846 reveal certain interesting changes. The gelder had been replaced by a veterinary surgeon, the brother of Dr. Pouzet. A new civil servant, whose importance will become apparent, had appeared: the road mender.

The number of artisans had increased with the addition of another clog-maker and a weaver. On the other hand, the carter had vanished. A new inn had been established. The wood-cutter had assumed the title of pit-sawyer. In particular a tobacconist and two store keepers had set up business. These store keepers – one man and one woman – were not content to wait for customers in the shop: they peddled their goods in great baskets from door to door on foot through the farms and villages. One of them was styled 'resin merchant'.

By the side of these notabilities, civil servants, artisans and small shop keepers, lived families of peasant farmers. It was, therefore, a very small township – more a large village of peasant farmers.

This, indeed, is how the Mayor of Mazières-en-Gâtine wrote of it a few years later on 4 December 1860 in answer to a letter from the Sub-Prefect of Parthenay requesting a report on the implementation of the law of 22 June 1854 and the order of 30 April 1853 concerning workers' record-books:

> In reply to your letters of 27 October last, I have the honour to inform you that, in the canton of Mazières, where the population is engaged almost exclusively in agriculture, the laws of 22 February 1851 on apprenticeship contracts and of 22 June 1854 on workers' record books are to all intents unknown. We have no more than a few blacksmiths and clog-makers and they, more often than not, are out in the fields rather than in their workshops. These professions are most commonly hereditary: son succeeds father and the law is of little purpose.
>
> As for the workers' books, since 1855 I have received only one request. As long as the law is not applicable to farm servants, I consider that these regulations will seldom be of relevance in the canton of Mazières.
>
> I have heard of no difficulties arising between employers and workers.

Weekly markets were held regularly under an order issued by the Ministry of Agriculture and Trade dated 22 August 1837. They continued until 1849.[14]

At this time the larger villages of the commune all had their taverns (there was one at L'Hirondelle, another at L'Angevinière, another at Le Beugnon) and their artisans. There was a carter at Le Beugnon, a joiner at La Forge, a pit-sawyer at La Mimaudière, a stone mason at La Texerie, another at La

Ressegère, another with an assistant at Ternant, two hoopers and a dressmaker at L'Oucherie. Weavers were to be found in almost every village: one at Le Beugnon, one at La Texerie, one at La Blanchetière.

These craftsmen were at the same time farmers: that is to say, they had a big garden, one or two fields, two or three goats. They were, in the words of the mayor of Mazières, 'more often in the fields than in the workshop'.

Consequently, at that time, the town was no more than a village slightly larger than the others. Most of its inhabitants were small farmers and journeymen craftsmen: the villages, for their part, also had their craftsmen. No important social factor differentiated the town from the villages except for the presence in the town of a few civil servants and notabilities.

How the people lived

The very small number of craftsmen in the town, and the kinds of craft they plied, reflect the way of life of the people of the commune.

They strove to exist as far as possible on their own resources, their own industry, without having to buy anything essential to their needs and, since communications were extremely difficult, they lived in a very closely restricted world, without even being able to imagine anything different.

A semi-closed economy: houses and furniture

It is remarkable that there were in the commune only three stone masons in 1841 and five (two master masons and three workmen) in 1846. This could be taken to mean that little building activity took place at the time. I do not believe this was so. The register of taxes on buildings from 1838 to 1842, it is true, does not show any new assessment. This indicates that no new building had been erected between 1835 and 1839, since houses were taxed three years after their construction. But in 1843 nine new assessments at 2 francs each appear: this was certainly a revision of earlier assessments. In 1844 we find three more assessments: one at 2 francs, one at 6 francs and another, very considerable, at 24 francs – the house of M. Jorigny, the Mayor.

In 1845 three new buildings (two in the township) for the lesser notabilities were taxed: in 1846 there was one only, in 1847 and 1848 none, in 1849 five, 1850 two, 1851 two, 1852 one, 1853 nine – one at 24 francs, another at 16 francs and a third at 9 francs. Between 1860 and 1870 and particularly by 1890 the rhythm of building activity had increased. But already in 1851 there were twelve masons in the commune. There were probably two causes for this sharp increase in the number of masons in relation to the houses built: first, the growing size of the buildings undertaken and, secondly, the increasing part played by trained craftsmen in the work. More often than not the peasants were accustomed to build for themselves the simple shelters they felt they needed. Even in larger construction work, the quarrying of the stone, the transport of material, the material itself – all the manual labour would usually be provided by them. The local masons before 1850 were not small entrepreneurs capable of drawing up estimates and who would be paid on completion of a work. They were more often simply daily paid workmen (at the rate of about 1 fr. 50 a day) who were engaged for as short a time as possible. Little by little their share in building activity increased. The custom of entering into 'contracts' became established.

This was true for the masons. It was still more true and in a more precise and easily visible way where carpenters and joiners are concerned.

Everyone who owned trees made sure they provided their own timber when they wished to build a house or ordered furniture. The trees were felled and sawn on the spot by pit-sawyers according to the measurements given by joiners: planks were more easily transported than trees. The pit-sawyers earned for this long, hard work a maximum of one franc a day – and they provided their own food. This was little enough reward. But they retained the off-cuts and did a good business with them. Thus, for their labour they received two payments – one in cash, one in kind. The joiners were always paid in cash. The steep wooden staircases with their solid but rough and unevenly spaced treads, the massive but ill-squared joists showing the kind of work required of them, are evidence of the extent to which economy in construction was pushed.

Here and there a few pieces of beautiful old furniture (particularly wardrobes and sideboards) show what could be produced by these country craftsmen when one did not haggle over the time taken. But usually furniture was reduced to the minimum. There were comparatively few wardrobes but plenty of chests. Sideboards were rarely seen for few houses possessed much in the way of crockery. Beds, on the contrary, were veritable monuments: an uncurtained bed would be regarded as unfinished. These beds were made for the most part of a palliasse of maize straw (a little maize was grown in the area), a feather bed, rough home-woven sheets and a coverlet stuffed, not with wool but with feathers and down.[15]

Clothing

The peasants managed to clothe themselves from their own resources, without cost to themselves. Winter and summer alike they wore rough canvas smocks and trousers made entirely in the area.

The cultivation of hemp has already been mentioned. It was harvested at the end of August and put to soak in the ponds for about a month. At Michaelmas it was taken from the water and spread to dry in the fields. Towards the second week of October it was hackled, then dried again and once more hackled when the tow maker travelled from farm to farm combing it. Women spun the yarn sitting round the evening fire. They then washed the yarn, arranged the skeins on a *châtelet* and then wound them into balls. The yarn was taken to the weavers – who were relatively numerous (three in Mazières in 1851 – all in villages: La Texerie, La Blanchetière, Le Beugnon). The weavers were often paid in kind: that is, they would take as their reward an agreed amount of hemp (around ten per cent). They would buy cotton thread and the cloth they made was then their property. Every weaver was at the same time a cloth merchant. He would sell his cloth in the township or larger towns. The peasant farmers, for their part, had their cloth free, the weaver having been paid for his work in kind. The women dyed the cloth with *bois violet* bought at the grocer's. The many travelling needlewomen, paid at the rate of fifty centimes a day plus food, soon cut out and sewed simple trousers (with no flies) and smocks which fastened at the neck by a cord: and, if required, shirts or sheets. Headgear consisted of rabbit skin bonnets or cotton caps. Footwear – when people did not go barefoot – was heavy clogs stuffed with straw in winter.

Certainly, the small farmer – particularly those relatively well-off – possessed some woollen clothing usually made in stiff black cloth, but these garments would be rare. A 'best' smock, one of those colourful, almost varnished, smocks described by de Maupassant among Norman peasants, would last almost a lifetime. It was the same for hats – those great hats with high round crowns with upturned brim bought in Parthenay or Saint Maixent – and for shoes which cost 10 to 12 francs a pair and were very carefully treated.

Food

Purchases of food were kept as low as possible. There was no butcher in the commune. This is easily explained by the fact that hardly any meat was eaten other than pork killed in every household and salted down. There was indeed a baker – a baker who bought flour,[16] who made and sold bread rather than merely bake the dough brought to him. But his customers were few: nearly all those who grew grain made their own bread.

The millers (of whom there were two) collected the grain from the houses, i.e. rye and buckwheat and, after 1845, wheat from richer households. They were paid in kind by retaining two decalitres of every ten provided. They returned the flour (bran, grits and mixed meal) to their customers. The peasants sifted their own meal. Fine flour was used for making best quality bread: second-grade bread was made from coarser flour, and it was often the case that third-grade bread was made from a mixture of meal and potato reduced to flour on one of those old graters two feet long by one foot wide still to be found in the area and which were once a household article.

A few took their flour to the baker. To bake 50 kgs. of flour cost 5 francs and they received in return 65 kgs. of bread. Those who made bread at home baked every ten to twelve days or every three weeks. A small lump of dough, carefully kept, served as yeast (for there were few who bought yeast from the baker). Once the dough had dried it was put to rise under an eiderdown. Bread was eaten with potatoes, cabbage, bacon and milk products. Their drink was apple cider or cider made from wild sloe berries or simply water: wine was seldom drunk even in the richer houses for it had to be brought from Mirebalais and was expensive.

Little was bought from the grocer. Oil was made from nuts gathered in the district and cracked by the winter evening fire. Every house had its small barrel of vinegar into which was poured the lees of cider or wine. The only regular purchases from the grocer were salt, pepper and resin candles. Matches were unknown: the fire was kept glowing beneath the ashes. It is not surprising that in these conditions there were so few grocers in the township.

Farm implements

The same care to use home resources, at any cost, can be seen in the ploughs of the time. 'The ploughs,' writes Leclerc-Thouin in his paper on agriculture in Anjou in 1843, 'barely scratch the soil. However, this instrument has several advantages which perpetuate its use: a single man and a feeble animal can use it; except for the share, it costs only 9 or 10 francs. Being wooden it can be made almost entirely on the farm; the speed of the work with the possibility of extending his ploughing without fatigue means that quite reasonable results can be achieved.'[17]

It is important to remember the fact that the ploughs were nearly always made on the farm. This was certainly not a minor reason for their continuing to be used. Harrows, too, were made of wood. Forks were the stems of young trees or forked branches, polished and sharpened; rakes were wooden. Every peasant was, moreover, something of a carpenter and possessed a few tools. Only ploughshares, spades and picks were made of iron. Harvesting was done with a sickle by cutting the grain at mid-height, à la beuille as it was called. Grain was threshed by flail, sometimes with long poles for oats and buckwheat. After threshing it was winnowed with great winnowing shovels by throwing it into the wind, the heavier good grain falling short of the husk and dust. Flails, shovels, poles were all made on the farm.

Briefly, then, in every area the peasant economy reduced to a minimum any trade and particularly any purchases in money. Money was indeed extremely rare: an agricultural employee was paid 150 francs for a year's work and was fed by his employer. The doctor charged one franc for a visit. An ox fetched 350 francs, a cow 100 francs and a calf 60. A large cart could be bought for 150 francs, a trap for 100 and a barrow for 10.

Communications

It would, moreover, have been impossible or at least very difficult for there to have been much trade in view of the state of the roads.

It is possible to gain a fairly exact idea of the state of the roads at that time by looking at those which today serve only fields: with an impervious subsoil which retains the lightest rain and high, thick hedges screening them from the sun, they are nearly always muddy, even in summer, and often impassable. It is possible to venture on them only in a heavy ox-cart; a pedestrian would plunge up to the ankles in mud if he ventured on them. It must be added that, as far as the village service roads were concerned around 1850, it was difficult to prevent broom and bracken from encroaching. Also the mere moving of fences by the Vicomte de Tusseau was enough for a whole section of the road to be accepted as a field belonging to him.[18]

Prefect Dupin noted in Year IX:[19] 'The branch roads, although rather better than the trunk roads, are generally in a very bad state. Those of Gâtine in the valleys are passable only at the end of the summer; and on the higher levels are encumbered with massive rocks which can only be shifted with explosives. There are many deep holes filled with damp earth and covered with a layer of dry soil which gives way beneath a horse's hoofs: to pull your horse out will require a team of oxen.'

Since the expenditure budgets for Mazières commune contain no, or at very best very meagre, provision for the improvement of roads, it may be assumed that in 1850 they were in the same condition as in 1800.

Prefect Dupin in his memorandum requested considerable funds for the repair and upkeep of the chief roads in his department. Only one of these roads passed through Mazières-en-Gâtine: Highway 2 from Niort to Parthenay.

As for the rest, the stretches which remain – between the township and railway station (the old road from Mazières to La Fournière) and between the lower town and the causeway (the old major branch road from Mazières to Thézenay) – show that they were narrow and unpaved – or very ill-paved. It would seem that the main concern had been to carry out terracing and paving on the steeper slopes and that work on the level sections had been kept to the minimum. Even the main road – Highway No. 2 – between Niort and Parthenay was sometimes impassable, as can be seen from this story told by M. Bouet, the schoolmaster at Mazières, in a paper on agriculture in the commune prepared for the Exhibition of 1900:

> There was no passenger transport. The first carriage to appear in Mazières, a small tilbury, was bought by Dr Pouzet in 1849. Doctors and veterinary surgeons had to make their rounds on horseback. They generally used small horses trained to go at a special gait – a 'high-stepping' amble.
>
> This anecdote which I can vouch for as true will give an idea of the difficulties experienced if one wanted to go out of the village:
>
> In 1838 a young man from Mazières, M. Fraigneau, was lodging in Niort. One holiday his family and friends, five or six people altogether, had the idea of visiting him and spending a day or two in the town. A carriage was borrowed from the neighbouring Château du Petit-Chêne; two strong horses were harnessed to it – and the journey began. They managed to go about five kilometres but, on reaching the boundaries of the commune and near a spot called the Mélusine Ditch, the vehicle became bogged. It was impossible to proceed. Oxen had to be obtained to pull the carriage out and the travellers returned to Mazières, covered in mud but not surprised at the mishap for such incidents must have been common at the time.
>
> To go from her Château du Petit-Chêne, three kilometres south of Mazières, the Vicomtesse de Tusseau was always carried by sedan chair to attend mass.

These statements are confirmed by Jacques Bujault in his almanac, by many articles in contemporary newspapers and particularly in one in the *Echo des Deux-Sèvres* of 23 September 1851 where the writer complains that the roads in Gâtine had been rendered completely impassable by the early autumn rains, and that this had prevented the transport of manure from the cavalry stables at Saint-Maixent, despite the peasants' need for it.

Towards 1900 nearly all the boundary fences of the fields were still provided with stiles which were used less and less but which, fifty years earlier, had allowed the locals to walk from one place to another: most of the time, if they had tried the roads, they would have been bogged.

Society's attitudes

Superstition: passion: religion

Try to imagine what might have been the state of mind, the attitudes of the people of this poor trackless land.

In 1850 it was not long since the roads had become safe. Besides the fact that in 1853 (by order of the Prefect of Deux-Sèvres dated 22 March 1853) drives against wolves were still organized, the memories of the 1832 Chouan uprising were still fresh and were to be found in numerous memoirs. By the fireside the story of Robert le Chouan was told, of how he was nearly killed by two soldiers at La Monnère-de-Vouhé during a fight which resulted in two deaths; of the attempt on the life of tax collector Taffoireau made in Mazières itself in 1833 between 4 o'clock and 5 o'clock in the evening; of the murder of gamekeeper Billaud at Verruyes on the following 22 February.

The roads went across vast fields of gorse and heather and the peasants still believed in ghosts, in *galipotes* and *loups-garous*.[20]

Travellers crossing the fields at night expected to be confronted at every stile by a *galipote* and at the least noise they would imagine themselves pursued by *loups-garous*. I spoke about this to an old man of eighty. He declared that when he was a young man returning at night from the neighbouring town he had been overtaken by white-robed horsemen travelling without a sound. When he told his parents of his adventure and terror they were not in the least surprised and even gave him the name of the horses, which they called *chevaux mallets*.[21]

'The Bocage peasant,' wrote Jacques Bujault,[22] 'is a wolf in the thicket: he sees nothing, hears nothing, knows nothing. He is ignorant, credulous, obstinate, dull and full of fear. He is what isolation has made him. He talks to his oxen, sings to them; tells tales of sorcerers and *loups-garous*.'

This judgment is too severe.

The world of ideas in which the Gâtine peasants of 1850 lived was as rich as the world of the peasants of today. Without any doubt, in many households there was displayed a wealth of energy and intelligence, of cunning, if you like, needed just to live. Beneath an apparent uniformity social relations were as complex as they are today. To have seen at the turn of the last century old farmers' wives, uneducated perhaps but intelligent, full of experience and good sense who had been able to put by a little money is enough to understand the extent of their independence on the one hand and also, beneath the warmth of their manners, their contempt for all who were not like them, their respect with no hint of servility for the notabilities they had contact with.

Entertainments were rare. The inn was an attraction for the men (and even women if J. Bujault is a reliable informant) and drunkenness was rife. Village gatherings attracted the young folk who would dance on the grass. It would be unusual if the young vigorous males, stimulated by wine or rivalry in love, did not come to blows. Even pitched battles often took place between young men of neighbouring communes where the memory of ancient enmities still rankled. On winter evenings people would gather together round a single candle or a single fireside where the men would twist wisps of straw or crack nuts while the women spun. Stories would be told, not only stories of wizards and *loups-garous* in which credulity and imagination had a free rein, but malicious local tales of gossip against one or another in which moral judgment was involved. A raconteur well-known locally for his skill in playing on words, using patois assonance to sharpen points with great liveliness, would be invited from house to house. In this way a form of popular art developed of which no trace remains except in the patois tales collected by students of local history.

Religion held a special place in the minds of men. In every family grace was said before meals: family prayers were held morning and evening and every effort was made not to miss Sunday mass. Doubtless their religion was shot through with pagan customs: a piece of consecrated wood would be placed in the byre to protect the cattle; and in the fields for the protection of the crops. Holy water was carefully preserved in each house for anointing in case of illness.

Doubtless, too, the smart alecks poked fun at the priests. Old songs current in the region speak of their chambermaids and very probably the well-known song[23] which pictures a magpie (*ageasson*) making its way into church and giving the responses to the priest saw first light in the region or, at least, was popular there. It may well be, again, that children during prayers pulled faces, teased each other and parodied the text of the prayers. But religious faith was deep and sincere; it is clear that the peasants held to it all the more because it was imbued with customs which formed part of their daily life and because in the mass and saints' days it provided them with their only occasion for entertainment. Only through their religion did they gain a consciousness of their dignity as human beings.

The mental world in which they were evolving was, therefore, by no means void or uniform. It was, on the contrary, very complex: but it was a *closed* world.

A closed world

Practically no one travelled.

The townsfolk, artisans and traders, having 'thirty-six trades and not one of them good', hardly stirred from their homes. The peasants would sometimes go to market at Champdeniers or Parthenay, the richer on horseback, the poor on foot.[24] A Sunday visit to the township, that poor place which we have seen to be hardly more than a village rather bigger than the rest, was reckoned as a considerable 'expedition' justified by the necessity of going to church.

The thoughts of one and all strayed barely beyond the bounds of the commune or its neighbourhood. The town meeting at Beaulieu, 8 km. from Mazières, was held on the same day at Mazières. There was nothing wrong or strange in this. The Mazières folk had less contact with Reffanes, 14 km. away, than they had with Paris.[25]

It is hard nowadays to understand the particularism of that time. There is no family today which does not have relations or friends living in regions more or less far apart. The exchange of news, visits paid and children coming and going are enough to widen horizons. There was nothing like this in 1850. The first statistics giving the birth-place of the inhabitants date from 1872. Then in Mazières there were only five people who had not been born in the *département*: one doctor and one baker's assistant living in the town, the owner of the Château of Petit-Chêne (M. de Tusseau) and his steward, one other owner of a *maison bourgeoise* at La Cantinière. Two notabilities and sixteen civil servants or gendarmes, artisans or journeymen in the town had been born in communes bordering on Mazières: but in the country all had been born either within the commune itself or in the neighbouring communes. All the evidence leads one to believe that conditions were the same in 1850 and even that there were at that time fewer 'foreigners' than in 1872.

Only those notabilities who had been educated in church boarding schools, at the Niort lycée or the Collège at Parthenay, had widened their circle of contacts. It was for them that a foot messenger carried mail once a week from Parthenay to Mazières – a distance of 15 km. The mail was, moreover, too light to justify the employment of a postman on horseback. Such was the reply given by the Inspector of Posts and Telegraphs to the Mayor of Mazières' requests for the service to be undertaken on horseback rather than on foot.[26]

People were all the more attached to their own little locality because they knew no other. The considerable number of indigent persons living in abject poverty has already been mentioned. Despite this, there appears to have been little emigration or even movement of seasonal labour as was the case in other regions. And I have been able to identify in the register of army volunteers for the canton only six names: two in 1849, one in 1850, one in 1853, another in 1856 and a final one in 1860 – these last three only belonging to Mazières canton, all three seventeen years old. It is noticeable that these were sons of a police sergeant, a farmer resident in the township and the innkeeper: none came from a village or a farm.

Indifference to Wider Events

All this makes it clear that events in the outside world must have passed unperceived by a population which was wrapped up in its own affairs.

There is nothing in the records to show any spontaneous

expression of opinion of any depth at the time of the 1848 Revolution. All the documents that I have been able to consult merely indicate that the orders of the central government were correctly carried out.

On 19 March 1848 an address, based on a model drawn up in the Prefecture, was sent to the members of the provisional government by the municipal council and the inhabitants of Mazières commune. It was signed at the town hall by all those who could write (twenty in all). A tree of liberty was planted on 16 April 1848 as described in the following account:

'The Council, considering that the tree of liberty should, as far as is possible, be planted at the most commanding and most frequented place in the commune, orders that it shall be planted in the public square of the town near the Cross, on Sunday next after the celebration of the Mass.'

On Sunday, 19 November 1848, at one o'clock in the afternoon after the mass, the constitution was promulgated. The ceremony had been announced before the church service to the sound of the drum. This account is to be found in the municipal archives:

'After mass Citizen Drue sang a solemn Te Deum: then the Mayor, wearing his official scarf, read aloud the constitution. After this reading cries of "Vive la République" were heard. The citizen-mayor distributed to the poor of the commune one hundred kilogrammes of bread together with the twenty francs granted by the Prefect in accordance with his letter of the 15th of this month.'

This ceremony was held in the presence of the municipal council, the police sergeant and four gendarmes, the beadle, the schoolmaster and the tax collector. In the background there must have been peasants and artisans clad in smock with cap on head, women and children. But it is doubtful whether they understood a word of what had been read to them. Besides the fact that they would understand only the local patois, anything happening beyond the limits of their own experience would be unintelligible to them. The attempts of the men of the 1848 Revolution to associate the rural population with their republican zeal does not seem to have met with any success with most of the peasants of Mazières-en-Gâtine. They had no chance of success in view of the state of intellectual isolation prevailing among the people and their incapacity to take any interest in anything which was not of their immediate neighbourhood.

The only notable and truly local effect was a change of mayor. The resolution of 3 September 1848 notes that 'Citizen Pouzet is nominated Mayor by the Municipal Council by virtue of the decree of 3 July 1848'. M. Jorigné (the former mayor) was nominated as deputy: but he resigned. He was replaced as deputy mayor by M. Guichard. M. Jorigné has been mentioned earlier: he was a landowner-*rentier*. Dr. Pouzet was wealthy only through his marriage; he combined merit with wealth. M. Guichard was a well-off owner-farmer living in a large village in the north of the commune. The changes were, indeed, not very noticeable.

The *coup d'état* of 2 December 1851 itself passed unnoticed. This comes quite clearly from a note by Dr. Pouzet in reply to this letter from the Sub-Prefect of Parthenay:

> Monsieur le Maire,
>   Having received a request from the Minister and the Prefect for a daily report on the political situation in this district I seek your assistance in providing me with the necessary information.
>   I would, therefore, be most grateful if you would report to me all noteworthy facts within your canton on which you have knowledge.

Dr. Pouzet's usual and most valuable practice used to be to write the draft of his replies on the letters he received. This is how he now answered:

> In your letter of 6th inst. you ask for information on the political situation in the canton.
>   The canton of Mazières, as you know, Sir, is little concerned with politics. Therefore the recent events have been received by the majority of the population with indifference. A few people have expressed great surprise and a fear of civil war. Public order, however, has not been disturbed in any way: no shouts, no rumours, everyone going about their daily business. The tax collector received 1500 francs at Beaulieu on Friday last and 600 francs at Mazières on Sunday last!

If I hear of anything out of the ordinary I will inform you at once . . .

Allow me, Sir, to make a protest to you concerning the inquisitorial behaviour of the military authorities towards the Mayors who have been placed under the surveillance of the police sergeant and are even required to report the number of decrees and telegrams that they have made public and posted up in their communes.

Conclusions

Thus, at Mazières between 1830 and 1850, there lived a rural population relatively dense but scattered, in a country covered with bracken, broom and heather, farmed in a very slack and desultory fashion. It was, in large measure, very poor, living in a semi-closed economy which exaggerated rather than abolished social distinctions and, in the absence of contact with the outside world or a passable road system, in a state of intellectual isolation undisturbed by news from distant parts, such as Paris, which might be picked up in the market-place and peddled through the region. The only events of national importance to attract attention were those which had obvious local repercussions. The Chouan rising of 1832 had a long-term effect because several incidents happened in the neighbourhood or within the commune itself. The 1851 *coup d'état* aroused no excitement among the poor who formed the great majority of the population. This habit of living from day to day, of struggling against nature close at hand in order to live or to live a little better, their inability to form abstract ideas or to conceive the possible consequences of far-off events and the extreme difficulty that most peasants and artisans had in imagining any country other than their own, resulted in the people being deeply rooted in their own little area and in great social stability even if it was in poverty. This stability was reinforced by religion both by satisfying the spirit and imagination of some and by the habits and customs it imposed on all.

We will not ask whether or not these people were happy. To answer this question would require an ability to recreate in ourselves with exactitude the mentality of those whose way of life we have described. One cannot judge their happiness with merely an idea of man and what is due to him, a concept which those people did not have and could not have.

Everything that Flaubert wrote of the Norman peasants he studied in 1840 seems to apply very closely to the Gâtine peasants of that time. One cannot call unhappy the serving-girl in *Madame Bovary* who, in her clumsiness and folly, symbolized 'half a century of servitude in the presence of bourgeoisie in full bloom' at the agricultural show. She was not conscious of her servitude and probably found a humble, but genuine, joy in washing clothes successfully and receiving, now and then, a word of praise from her masters. Similarly, the maid whose life Flaubert has described with such pure and penetrating simplicity in one of his finest tales – *Un Cœur Simple* – experienced a happiness of her own in her daily habits, her piety and her parrot. It is not unlikely that the poor folk of Mazières, in 1850, also were lacking in imagination and found it impossible to dream dreams. But they, too, possessed in their fashion a humble happiness mingled with insensitivity, resignation and a multitude of little joys.

Lastly, if the State did nothing for them, it demanded little from them in its turn.

four

The school

Its birth

Today, 10 June 1832, the undersigned members of the
Municipal Council of the commune of Mazières, at an
extraordinary meeting called in response to the circular
letter from the Prefect dated 17 May last, under the
chairmanship of the Deputy Mayor of the commune, in
the absence of the Mayor, have discussed the allocation
of funds for the primary school teacher.

Considering that the commune has never had a
recognized primary school teacher, having no house for
one nor any vote which could be used for that purpose

and nevertheless recognizing the urgency of having a
primary school teacher

is unanimously of the opinion that the commune of
Mazières be authorized to levy a supplementary tax to
the extent of sixty francs for the salary of the primary
school teacher, while requesting the Government, having
regard to the insufficiency of this amount, to undertake
to make up the difference, the Municipal Council having
answered, after due study, the questions raised in the
second table addressed to them by the Prefect.

Such is the birth certificate of the public school at Mazières-
en-Gâtine.

Before 1832

This is not to say that before that date the people of the region
had never received schooling.

Prefect Dupin[1] in Year IX wrote: 'The public schools are in a very unsatisfactory state . . . Primary schools are few in number and badly organized Lacking educated persons willing to undertake the honorable task of teaching I have been obliged to entrust it to men who, at best, are able to form their letters passably well. The following are the numbers of teachers and pupils during winter: in summer the schools are quite empty.'

District	No. of teachers	No. of pupils
Parthenay	24	600

In the following year[2] he continued on this theme and regretted that the number of primary schools in Year X were fewer and less well run than before the Revolution:

In the towns and the countryside the poor remain without schools; and the better-off citizens believe they have done enough for their children's education when they have sent them either to a boarding school or to the Central School where they gain some superficial knowledge. There they spend three or four years, a very short time for learning. At the age of seventeen the young man returns to the bosom of his family and devotes his time to the pleasures of society awaiting the opportunity to make an advantageous marriage when his only business in life will be to look after his estate.

Before the Revolution every town in the *département* (Châtillon excepted) had its secondary school (*collège*). . . . The poor, in some towns, were able to find free schooling . . . and there were also some fee-paying private schools which taught reading, writing and the elements of arithmetic.

Of all the *collèges* which existed in 1789 not one remains. The turmoil of the Revolution and then the war have destroyed everything. There are no longer any entirely free schools; only the primary schools offer the poor any chance of obtaining education for their children. One hundred and four of these are established; in winter about three thousand pupils attend. This number is reduced by three-quarters during the season of work in the fields.

Under the Empire, then, there were very few schools. Most

probably there were no more during the reigns of Louis XVIII and Charles X. Nevertheless, when a public school was about to be opened in Mazières a certain number of the people did know how to sign their names.

In 1835, the very year the school opened, among 119 people, ranging from 25 to 78 years of age, who were summoned to witness the registration of births, deaths and marriages, 22 could write their names.

The general custom at that time was to teach reading before giving the least instruction in writing. It may be assumed that people could read more or less fluently and it is reasonably certain that they could count as well. In my childhood I knew many completely illiterate old men who were perfectly able to count.

Doubtless many of the signatures were extremely crude, which shows that their authors were little used to writing. Probably, too, the witnesses were deliberately chosen from among those who knew how to write. Be this as it may, in 1835, before any school had been opened, nearly 18 per cent of the male population was not completely illiterate.

It would be surprising if the more wealthy landowners of the commune whose names appear in the registers had received no schooling at all. At Parthenay and Niort there were public secondary schools and at Niort a private boarding school.

It is not surprising, either, that the village constable and the sacristan could sign their names: they had probably been appointed for that very reason.

But how and where had the peasants, the weaver, the flour-merchant, the artisan whose signatures appear on the registers, acquired the rudiments of education that they possessed?

One can only guess at the answer. It may be that here, as in other communes, the priest considered that his duty of teaching did not end at the church door but should extend into the school. Perhaps he had subscribed to the upkeep of one of those charity schools which, according to Prefect Dupin's memorandum, were to be found in a relatively large number of parishes before the Revolution. Perhaps, too, the carpenter-sacristan Louis Vivier, whose name appears frequently on the registers, taught a few children the elements of reading, writing and arithmetic in his spare time during the winter.

The very words of the resolution of 10 June 1832 – 'In view

of the fact that the commune has never had a recognized teacher' – presupposes that there had been in the township or larger villages one or more 'unrecognized teachers'.

The results must have been quite unsatisfactory since the urgency of having a public school had been recognized and that, to obtain it, the commune agreed to extra public expense in the same resolution.

The influence of Guizot

The resolution was passed at an extraordinary meeting called to consider a circular from the Prefect, dated 17 May 1832.

The Prefect had issued the circular only in obedience to orders from Guizot who was preparing his famous Law, promulgated in 1833, for the organization of primary education in France.

It is very doubtful that the Municipal Council would have taken the initiative of asking for a public teacher and of paying for him. The sum offered of 60 francs was minimal in the light of the normal salary of 200 francs. And Mazières commune was the only one of the whole canton which 'warmly welcomed the school'. Three others were 'agreeable'; five were 'indifferent'; one 'disagreed'.[3] Another asked that its pupils should join those of a neighbouring commune. Verruyes commune, indeed, offered to repair the priest's woodshed to act as school room, once the priest had agreed to give it up temporarily.

The few notabilities of Mazières who signed the resolution of 10 June 1832 and who, in the Mayor's absence, were administering the commune, were thus the exception.

It is unlikely that their views were, in general, very different from those of the councillors of other communes. Their eagerness to start a school – while keeping its cost to themselves to the minimum – can only be explained by special motives. Perhaps M. de la Laurencie, or one or two important people, were interested in the mental development of the peasants; perhaps the priest at Mazières saw in the opening of a public school – which would naturally be under his control – another means of spreading the faith and also a means of recruiting a most useful helper who would bring children to the church to sing at services. Perhaps, again, the Council thought it would be useful to have men who could read and write.[4]

Lastly, perhaps a few leaders of this poor little township,

which chance had made the chief place of the canton, had children of their own of school age. In any case, as will shortly be seen, the Council speedily lost all interest in the school once it had been established.

The reasons which led Guizot to take the initiative in organizing public primary education throughout France are better known. His memoirs are explicit in the matter.

The 1832 Ministry of which he was a member had limited itself to completing plans of which the outline had been drawn by all previous governments. 'It cannot be said,' he wrote, 'that from 1814 to 1830 primary education was free from political influence but it did not perish from this dangerous contact; either from a sense of equity or from prudence, the very powers who worried over its claims thought it best to treat it with kindness and support its development.'[5] The government of Louis Philippe was forced politically to organize a system of popular education.

Guizot saw clearly, moreover, that the evolution of ideas rendered such an organization necessary:

> Family feeling and duty is of great influence today: the
> political and legal bonds of the family have weakened;
> the natural and moral bonds have strengthened . . . a
> new idea has joined forces with these sentiments and
> given them greater effect – the idea that personal merit
> is today the greatest force and prime condition for
> success in life and that without it nothing can be done.
> It is to this feeling of ambitious foresight in families
> that the Ministry of Education owes its popularity. Now
> a matter of great public interest has taken its place
> beside this powerful domestic interest. Necessary as it
> is for the family, the Ministry of Education, it is no less
> necessary for the State . . . The great problem of modern
> society is the government of men's minds.

Guizot counted on the development of reason as a means of controlling minds. His letter of 16 July 1833 accompanying the text of the Law of 1833 announced to all teachers:

> Make no mistake, even if a primary school
> teacher's career lacks glamour, even if the daily round
> of duty is performed within the bounds of a commune,

his work is of moment to the whole of society and his profession shares in the importance of public affairs. It is not for the commune alone nor for the purely local interest that the law desires that all Frenchmen should acquire, if it is at all possible, that knowledge which is indispensable for social life and without which intelligence languishes and may decay; it is also on behalf of the State and public interest, it is because liberty becomes firmly established only among a people sufficiently enlightened to hear the voice of reason. Universal primary education from henceforth will be a guarantee of order and stability in society. Since everything, in the principles of our government, is true and rational, to develop intelligence and to propagate enlightenment will be to ensure the continued reign of constitutional monarchy.[6]

Thus it was above all to buttress a stable social order that Guizot developed primary education, because it seemed impossible to him that a man could be intelligent and educated and not share his views, and not recognize that the principles of constitutional monarchy were completely true and rational.[7]

In 1860 in his memoirs he declared that 'the Church formerly was the sole governor of minds' and he added: 'This is no longer so; intelligence and knowledge have become secularized and in so doing have claimed more freedom for themselves. But precisely because they are now more secular, more powerful and more free than before, intelligence and knowledge cannot remain out of the hands of the government of the society.'

But he insisted on the absolute necessity of associating Church and State in all that pertained to primary education. Only higher education could be permitted to enjoy a degree of freedom: the primary school must be profoundly religious:

While the co-operation of State and Church is essential for the wide establishment of popular education on a solid basis, it is also necessary if that education is to have true social value that it should be deeply religious. By that I do not mean only that religious instruction should have its place and religious customs observed in school. A people is not brought up in religion by such petty and mechanical means. Popular education must be given and received in the midst of a truly religious atmosphere permeated from all sides by religious attitudes and habits. Religion is not a study or exercise to which one can assign its time and place; it is a faith and a law which must make itself constantly felt everywhere: only in this way can it exert all its beneficent influence on the soul and life itself.

This means that the religious influence must always be present in the primary school. If the priest mistrusts or shuns the teacher; if the teacher looks on himself as the independent rival and not the trusty aid of the priest, then the moral value of the school is lost and it is near to becoming a danger.[8]

He found some difficulty in carrying through his ideas to success:

The dominant fact that I met with in the Chamber of Deputies as in the country as a whole was precisely a feeling of mistrust of, almost of hostility towards, the Church and the State. What was feared most in schools was the influence of the priest and the central government. The strongest desire was to ensure in advance and through the law protection for the action of local government and the independence of teachers vis-à-vis the priests. (p. 70)

The question of compulsory education arose. 'The first question was to know whether, in universal primary education, the law should make it compulsory on all parents with the sanction of penalties in cases of negligence, as is the practice in Prussia and most of the States of Germany.'

Guizot said 'No'. 'I deliberately left out compulsion in my proposed law for primary education.'

Next came the question of independent primary schools. On this there was no room for doubt.

A third question was more debatable: in public schools should primary education be completely free and provided by the State for all children? 'The State must offer primary education to every family and give it without fees to those unable to pay: in so acting it will do more for the moral life of the people than it can for their material well being' (p. 61).

The curriculum of the elementary school was to include – in

addition to religion – reading, writing, the elements of the French language and arithmetic, the systems of weights and measures: that is to say 'the understanding of the simplest notions in universal use . . . Precisely because it is necessary for all, elementary education must be very simple and undifferentiated' (p. 65). If this kind of education was to be fruitful, competent teachers were essential: therefore, training colleges were opened. Teachers had to be supervised and posts of inspectors of schools were created in every *département*.

The teacher received a fixed annual salary of 200 francs, paid by the commune, plus the product of school fees. He was to be provided with a suitable house to serve him both as lodging and a place to receive his pupils. Finally he must possess the certificate of elementary education (*Brevet élémentaire*). A local committee including, besides the mayor, the priest and several leading members of the community was charged with supervising and aiding him. The committee was nominated by the District (*arrondissement*) Committee on which sat the Sub-Prefect, the Public Prosecutor, the mayor of the chief town, representatives of the religious denominations and two teachers. But it was appointed by the Minister.

A point to be noted clearly at the outset is this: at Mazières it was a matter of teaching little peasant children who lived in poverty amid fields of broom and gorse. The education designed for them by the statesman who wished to open their eyes to an intellectual view of life, was not compulsory and was free only in necessitous cases. They were to acquire those basic ideas which were indispensable for society and to become sufficiently enlightened 'to hear the voice of reason in all circumstances'. This indeed was a guarantee for social peace, 'the principles of constitutional monarchy being of their essence true and rational'. In addition, the school was to strengthen religious faith in the child, for this was its truly educative function: the teacher must be the faithful auxiliary of the priest.

It was difficult at that time to conceive of any other kind of education for this closed community, lacking roads or trade where the great problem was the struggle against the deadening of the mind, to render the people capable of playing their part in the life of the country as a whole. It should be understood that what was offered was a very general body of knowledge in universal use; that which was to be developed in the child was solely those wider attributes and qualities appropriate to all mankind. The idea of creating a system of technical primary education either on a regional or national basis, if it had been considered, had been quickly put aside. Guizot offered a coherent and complete system, already centralized in the State, which paid no heed to provincial differences, superimposed itself over any local initiatives and tended to take their place.[9]

Guizot's proposals implemented in Mazières

How were the central government's intentions interpreted in Mazières? What opportunities for education did they offer to the people we know so much about? What kind of welcome did they receive?

The school was opened in a building rented by the commune which was considered satisfactory by the primary schools inspector for the department of Deux-Sèvres. The statistical table 'The State of the Communes concerning School Buildings' compiled on 15 August 1836 by this official shows, indeed, these premises as 'sufficiently large' and suitable accommodation for fifty boys and twenty girls. A certain amount of repairs were, however, needed and 2,400 francs would be required for purchase and repairs. The supply of school furniture was sufficient but it did not belong to the commune. The only things lacking were a crucifix and a bust of the king. The municipal council was well disposed and would do its best to find the necessary funds.

The teacher was M. Michel. From school returns for the year 1835–6 we learn that he enrolled fifty boys and ten girls during the winter. In the summer only twenty boys were left. The textbooks used were *Simon de Nantua*, Fénelon's *Télémaque* and the Catechism. School fees brought in 400 francs and so he had a total of 600 francs a year to live on. His character, ability, enthusiasm and his standing in the community all appeared to be good. Nevertheless, by 1838, M. Michel was no longer teaching at the commune school. He conducted a private school in Mazières with a roll of sixteen pupils in summer and eight in winter. The inspector reported on him: 'This teacher was formerly the commune teacher: he has lost the confidence of the people.'

This severe judgment must have been correct, since the

District Committee at its meeting on 2 May 1840 recommended that he be charged in court with misconduct and immorality and he be subject, if found guilty, to the sanctions of Article 7 of the Primary Education Act of 28 June 1833.

By that date the commune teacher was a certain Thébeau, who was a property owner in the village of La Touche near Mazières as well as being a teacher. He held the elementary Diploma, but it is clear from the documents published by M. Dauthuile, Academy Inspector, in his work on primary education in Deux-Sèvres district from its origin to the present day,[10] that the elementary Diploma was the equivalent, in academic standard, only of our elementary Certificate.

M. Jacques Texier, who was a teacher at an independent school at Teillé until 1875, tells how he passed his Brevet examination at Niort in 1850: 'The tests,' he says, 'were limited to a short dictation, two simple problems, a grammatical analysis of no difficulty, a few questions on grammar, religious history and arithmetic.' This is what we should require, except for religious history, for our elementary Certificate today.

M. Dauthuile adds: 'A study that we undertook of the reports of the examining boards of Niort and Parthenay revealed no marks nor any question papers but merely vague notes on the capability and moral character of the candidates' (p. 223).

Teacher Thébeau appears to have used teaching methods which would be strange to us today. According to an old man whose father attended the school for two years without learning to read, the teacher did not make use of the spelling book. He would read out a sentence from the reading book and have the children repeat it.[11] This method, however, does not make him a precursor of the Sentence Method in honour today: it is the same procedure as that used by the *Fquih* in the Koranic schools. The children were not required to make any effort to understand the words or to attempt to associate the shapes with sounds and meaning. They merely repeated what had been said to them and gradually discovered, thanks to those clever on-the-spot 'tricks of the trade' known to all teachers who care for their pupils, by the place on the page or the approximate shape of what they were given to read, the sounds they were required to emit to avoid being beaten.

The few children who did learn to read would read religious books or various school readers. Old men whom I knew as a child remember particularly vividly *Simon de Nantua*[12] and the *Story of the Four Sons of Aymon.*[13]

The teaching of arithmetic, an easier and more immediately useful skill, bore more fruit. Many illiterate old men could count perfectly well.

Furthermore, the teacher was required to teach reading before writing, as he himself had learnt, instead of teaching both together as is done nowadays.

M. Thébeau was a teacher of adequate competence who came to neglect his pupils. The Parthenay district inspector in his annual reports to the Prefecture reported on him in these terms:

In 1838 the report is favourable: 'This teacher has come to the commune in happy circumstances; his appearance is somewhat neglected, he is not punctual in starting school; I have recommended to him that he should be diligent and do his best to merit the confidence of the parents. Apart from this he is a good teacher.'

Attendance at the school was 20 boys, 15 girls in winter; ten boys, ten girls in summer.

In 1840, the report was summary: 'Capable, moral, not sufficiently zealous.' In winter 42 boys and 20 girls were enrolled; in summer, 12 boys and six girls. School fees brought in about 355 francs a year for the teacher's benefit.

In 1842 the inspector had changed: the new one, kinder perhaps than his predecessor, considered M. Thébeau to be capable and zealous and that he had a 'good school'. In winter attendance was 52 boys, 20 girls; in summer eight boys, five girls.

M. Thébeau must have been very like the people of the commune in his habits and his way of thought and action. He was to end his days as a farmer at La Touche.

There is every reason to believe that he followed closely the recommendations of the Mayor and the priest and that – as was required by the school regulation of the Parthenay district, dated 1835 – every lesson opened and closed with prayer. He certainly would have led his pupils to mass on Sundays and Saints' days. And he must have taught them in class religious history and the Old and New Testaments. It was probably because he conformed to these strict requirements that the municipal council allowed him to carry on his work with a slackness that the inspector could not always condone and which seems to have increased over the years.

In 1851 M. Thébeau had occasion to seek the support of the Sub-Prefect of Parthenay for his request for an increment in salary from the commune. This official wrote on 10 July:

> School fee revenue during the past year (1850) reached only a total of 263 francs 50. This small amount is the result of the long illness of the teacher's wife who has unfortunately since died and of the fact that he has felt it necessary to neglect his class slightly in order to care for her. It is on these grounds that M. Thébeau bases his request.
>
> I fully recognize the seriousness of the misfortune which has befallen this teacher, but, as soon as he saw that his presence was needed at his wife's side, he should have arranged for his school to have been continued by a person acceptable to the administration.

Thus, for some time, M. Thébeau had abandoned charge of his class to nurse his wife and this circumstance would most certainly have been noticed by the local council if the teacher had not shown himself a man of excellent character.

The pupils can be divided into two categories: those who paid the school fee of 1 fr. 50 a month and the needy, for whom the commune paid. According to a letter from the Mayor of Mazières to the Mayor of Saint-Pardoux dated 20 July 1854 these were fifteen in number. This letter throws a curious light on Dr Pouzet's ideas on the necessary length of school life:

'In reply to your letter of 18th inst., I have the honour to inform you that, since I have been Mayor of Mazières, the communal school has accepted, without fee, fifteen pupils enrolled each year by groups of five. Thus, the pupils admitted three years ago will leave next month and will be replaced by five new entrants. In this way our list always contains fifteen names. I intend to propose the same for 1855.'

In 1851 and 1852 there were 120 children between the ages of seven and thirteen years. In fact the monthly school enrolment was as follows:

	1851	1852
January	20	45
February	28	44

	1851	*1852*
March	26	44
April	23	36
May	20	17
June	14	19
July	6	19
August	7	17
September	7	17
October	10	17
November	22	22
December	37	48[14]

Thus it is clear the majority of the children did not go to school. That is the first point. It is necessary now to look more closely into the attendance of those who were enrolled.

In 1851 there were 20 pupils (all boys) on 1 January: two attended school for one month; two for three months; 13 stayed until 1 March and three remained for five months.

Ten new pupils were enrolled in February: two of them came for one month, seven for two months and one stayed for four months.

In 1852 of the 45 pupils enrolled in January three left on 1 February, nine on 1 March, seven on 1 April, 19 on 1 May, two on 1 July, one on 1 August, one on 1 September. Only three pupils remained the whole year at school and these were the ones who had attended the whole of the previous year.

Thus practically all the pupils attended school for a few months only, chiefly in winter and on average for three or four months, although it is true that they would go on attending until they were 15 up to 18 years old.

This was long enough to learn the elements of reading, arithmetic and to be able to write their names. While in 1833 only 22 out of the 119 inhabitants of the commune who were summoned to sign their names knew how to write, there had been 35 out of 94 in 1813 and 37 out of 69 in 1853. But the amount of knowledge that most of them had acquired did not make them very different from the completely illiterate.

It should be noted – and this is important – that of the three pupils who regularly attended school, two came from the township – the sons of the smith and the inn-keeper. The third was the son of an independent farmer at La Coutancière. Similarly all those who in 1852 were at school for more than four months were the children of poor craftsmen in the township.

Thus by the years 1850–2 the school placed at the service of the people of Mazières by virtue of the law of 1833 had achieved only a relatively small success.

Reasons for this lack of success

The reasons for this are fairly easily found. They derive in the first place from the personality of the teacher. It would have needed an apostle to attract to and hold at school children who must have preferred wandering about in the fields to working shut up in an uncomfortable room and who, moreover, were put to work at a very early age by their parents. And Teacher Thébeau, although very probably a good-hearted, rather gentle man, had nothing of the apostle about him.

Lack of success derives, also, from the indifference of the local authorities towards education. This is clearly seen in their lack of action when the teacher stayed away from his school.[15] This attitude is echoed in the following letter from the Mayor of Mazières to the Sub-Prefect at Parthenay on 18 February 1851:

> The majority of the municipal council is unwilling to accept the resolution contained in Circular No. 12 from the Ministry of Education in the sense that they will not vote any salary increment to the teacher above his 200 francs plus the product of school fees. Being unable to reconcile the two views it has been agreed to refer the matter to you before recording the resolution in the minutes.
>
> School fees amounted to 263 francs and the sum which would have to be added to the budget, already in deficit, is rather too much.

This was a precaution which the mayor, as a prudent man, took *vis-à-vis* the central government. Here, in fact, is the resolution carried on 16 February 1851 as recorded in the council minutes: 'The Municipal Council records here that it is expressly agreed to place nothing to the charge of the commune and, even if the budget were not in deficit, it would not consent, under any pretext, to add any sum whatever as an increase to this salary.

If forced to do so, the Council would prefer to have an independent teacher.'

In point of fact the teacher did get his increment but it was under pressure from the government. The local Education Committee did not concern itself as much as it should have with the teacher's attention to his duties: and the Municipal Council refused to improve the teacher's material lot, as it was required to do by law.

Finally, I discovered in a letter written in September 1848 by M. Pouzet to M. de Grandenay (*conseilleur général*), informing him of the commune's needs, proof of the little importance he attached to the school and particularly to its buildings. After speaking of the need to maintain the road-work depôts and the value of classifying at least one road as departmental, he emphasized the question of repairs to the presbytery: 'Our presbytery is in the worst possible state: it has been occupied for more than forty years by the Venerable Abbé Pressac who has had practically nothing done to it and it is now in great need of repair. . . .'

'Another very great need would be the establishment at Mazières of a registry office.' And he ends by saying: 'These, my dear Sir, are the most pressing requirements. As regards a school house, we will bring this up later, since repairs to the presbytery will completely absorb all our few resources.'

I must again point out that Dr Pouzet was a remarkably good administrator who loved the people among whom he lived, devoting himself to their service. But he loved them as they were. It was not possible for him to imagine that they should or could change or evolve as a whole.

And finally the school's lack of success stems from the people's indifference. This is not to say that the mass were completely indifferent to education: they could not be for already the red tape of the administration had begun to enmesh individuals, illiterate and literate alike. One had to sign leases or make one's mark at the bottom of important contracts that one could not read. Forms had to be filled for conscription and for marriage: and there were the court cases. When loans of money were made, the written word was a precious piece of evidence. Thus it was useful not only to know how to count – which everyone could do more or less well – but also to read and to write.

Also education was respected for its own sake. I have already mentioned how proud the old men were in knowing how to read, write and figure. But there is more than that. In many peasant houses you will still find, religiously preserved in some corner, exercise books in which some learned ancestor kept his accounts and wrote notes. The care with which these books have been kept shows the respect given to knowledge. I have looked at many and they are all alike. They contain accounts, fragmentary and haphazard, drafts of letters, receipts, models of contracts and agreements and recipes, all written higgledy-piggledy with no thought of making a methodical collection of useful information. Many even give the impression of having been written by their authors more as a means of maintaining their pride in writing than with a thought of practical use. Take, for example, the book of the owner of a large farm in a neighbouring commune to Mazières – Saint-Marc-la-Lande. This book was started in 1836 when the author must have just left school. It was kept up until 1860. It contains estimates, probably relating to the farm he was working:

The grey mare is valued at	450 fr.
The black mare ,, ,, ,, ...	350 fr.
The pony ,, ,, ,, ...	100 fr.

It also contains many rough workings of sums (he must have used the book to work out all his bargains); recipes for tisanes, models of contracts or family and business letters but also the correct way to address petitions:

'When one speaks or presents a petition either to a great dignitary of the State, or to a Minister or to a Prefect or to any other person belonging to the constitutional authorities of the first degree, one must use the title appropriate to him; for example, to a Prince of France or a Princess the title of Royal Highness, to the high dignitaries of the Realm, that of Most Serene Highness,' etc. Then there is an unexpected copy of a letter, truly moving in its piety and resignation, from a priest of the neighbourhood – the Curé Bastard – who had had to flee to Spain during the Revolution.

So, in this book, one can discern not only the practical use of education to a peasant in 1850 but also the scope of his imagination and the matters which affected him most deeply. It is remarkable that, in this document which was so honoured that it had been preserved for more than a century, one finds side by side with matters which are purely utilitarian, other matters which are there purely because they are worthy of veneration.

There existed, therefore, a widespread respect for knowledge which derived not only nor even especially from its utility but because it is in itself worthy of honour and because it permits a man to raise himself up and maintain himself through thought and memory to a higher mental level.

And yet, as we have seen, the peasants did not send their children to school.

The first argument that comes to mind to explain this abstention is the length of the journeys to be undertaken and the bad state of the roads. This may have played a certain part but it was not an important part. To go four kilometres on foot over difficult ground seems to us today a considerable undertaking. This was not the case in those days: remember that teacher who used to walk ten kilometres every day to save two sous.

In actual fact those peasants who wanted to send their children to school did so. In 1852 a boy from La Coutancière attended school for the whole year. Now La Coutancière is nearly four kilometres from the town, which was reached only over particularly bad roads. Moreover, the roads to Mazières were stone-surfaced between 1848 and 1855 and completed in 1855, but school attendance hardly changed from 1851 to 1855, the year in which M. Thébeau was replaced by another teacher, M. Bertout, or even during the two years that the latter remained there. Here are the figures:

1851	69 pupils (in August)	
1852	87 ,,	,,
1853	83 ,,	,,
1854	87 ,,	,,
1855	67 ,,	,,
1856	80 ,,	,,
1857	92 ,,	,,
1858	83 ,,	,,

Thus, it is not because they lived far from the school that the peasants in 1850 did not send their children there.

School fees might have been a burden: 1 fr. 50 per month in 1850 constituted no negligible sum. But here again this is not a fundamental reason: indigent children, whose fees were remitted, did not attend school regularly.

Furthermore, if school fees had been considered burdensome by those involved, one would have found traces in the archives of demands either for their abolition or for an increase in the number of pupils receiving free schooling. Quite to the contrary, the Mayor of Mazières, writing to the Sub-Prefect at Parthenay on 20 February 1850, stated categorically that there was no knowledge in the commune or even in the canton of a petition circulating in the neighbourhood – probably in the lowlands – which called for free schooling.

In fact, the widespread respect for knowledge among the people, however real it may have been, was not sufficiently strong in 1850 to shake the peasants out of their normal way of life and lead them to give up their children's labour and subject them, at the cost of continual nagging, to the discipline necessary for regular attendance.

The illiterate were too many to feel shame at their lack of knowledge, and the state of isolation in which the commune lived forbade the development of any deep intellectual curiosity. Moreover, the semi-closed economy and the narrow horizons of the world in which they lived did not require a constant use of the symbols taught at school.

They needed to know how to count. Most of them could do so, thanks either to the school or the help of their parents or friends and many achieved great facility in mental calculations of the simple matters they most often had to deal with. There was, moreover, more than one ingenious device to supplement the use of written symbols. For example, the *coches*,[16] which were still used in bakers' shops twenty years ago, were current custom in 1850 among millers, etc. For the rest, they had no letters to write or read – or very seldom. They had no accounts to keep, for their money expenditure was kept to a minimum. Important official statements which should be known by all were announced by the town crier. People existed without much consciousness of their ignorance of symbols and it must be recognized that what was taught at school did not fit the needs of the peasants – as far as they could see. In the commune only the local patois was spoken: at school the teacher taught children to read in French, that is to say, in a learned language which one needed to use only on very rare occasions. People measured length in *toises*, *ligues* and *pouces*; firewood was charged by the *corde*; area was measured in *boisselées*: and things were valued only in *pistoles* and *écus*. At school the metric system was taught, even if only the bright pupils really learnt it.

The main reason for the poor attendance at school, therefore, is found much less in external causes such as the length and difficulty of the journeys to reach it, or in school fees, but rather in deeper causes relating to the state of mind of the people and the kind of life they lived. No one compelled them to send their children regularly to school. They had respect for learning but rather as a luxury of little use to a peasant. Neither from the point of view of personal dignity nor for daily practical use could they see the necessity of learning to read or write. So they would not undertake the effort to send their children regularly to school.

But roads were being built from 1848 onward: they were completed in 1855. At the same time the system of agriculture was changing and the country becoming more wealthy. It was entering a cycle where economic exchange became both necessary and possible. The way of life and state of mind changed as communications became easier and trade expanded. We shall see how parallel with this development, the enrolment at school increased and the peasants themselves became more demanding for the education of their children.

part two

From 1850 to 1882
The school: a consequence of economic and social change

one

Economic and social evolution

Road construction

Work on Highway 2 from Niort to Parthenay was begun in 1844, very probably in implementation of the *Loi Montalivet* of 21 May 1836. The *Loi Guizot* for the organization of primary education in France had come into force after 1833. There was probably little connexion between the two laws in the minds of the legislators of Louis-Philippe's government; yet, nevertheless, their enactment within a few years of each other is of some importance, for it was partly owing to the second that the first was able to have an impact on the life of the people.

Thus, in 1844, the *Loi Montalivet* was in the position of coming to the aid of the *Loi Guizot* which Government had tried to administer ten years earlier. The local authorities were more interested in the state of the roads than in the progress of the school.

Many Council resolutions had requested improvement in the roads. In point of fact the question of road works was often linked with that of the workhouses required for the relief of the destitute. For example, the resolution of 8 October 1848 requests 'a subsidy to provide work for the destitute and draws attention to the great value of rendering viable, as early as possible, the highways which traverse the commune of Mazières'. That year no fewer than ten work depôts were opened for that purpose, of which two were on Route 2. It has already been mentioned that, in his letter of September 1848 to the *conseilleur général* at Grandmay, the mayor of Mazières emphasized the urgency of this undertaking. He pressed that Route 2 should be classified as a departmental road. 'This change,' he said, 'would be of great benefit to us, for it would transfer to other roads funds used annually on Route 2, which would then be constructed and maintained entirely at the expense of the department.' He added: 'Route 23: to request for 1849 an allocation of 300 metres on the boundary of Mazières: this road leading to Champdeniers is much used but it is in a very bad state at this point during winter.'

'Route 24 goes at present from Saint Maixent to Mazières; we have requested and the Sub-Prefect will recommend that it be extended to Secondigny. This extension will pass close to Château-Bourdin, La Boissière and Allonne: it would open up a very wooded area which has no communications. It would thus be of considerable benefit to these parts and once funds for the road have been voted, we could add to them part of the precepts from the communes of La Boissière and Allonne.'

But because technical resources were limited the work took a long time. It was undertaken through contractors (the name of one contractor – Courtial – often appears in letters and documents) aided by loans. Great difficulties were encountered: the widening of roads and the rectification of the line necessitated negotiations with land-owners and sometimes compulsory purchase.

For example, for some time it was not possible to work on Route 2 out of Mazières at the spot called *la butte de la Touche* because of the obstinate opposition of a land-owner who claimed that a change in the line would cut one of his pastures in two. This led the Mayor of Mazières to write some forceful letters.

On 20 December 1850 he wrote to the chief roads surveyor: 'I cannot understand how the ill-will of a single proprietor can jeopardize the prosperity of the whole region.' On 10 January 1851 again: 'I had the honour to write to you on 22 December last concerning the bad condition of Route 2 at the spot called *la butte de la Touche*. I do not know if, since that time, you have looked into the question of halting as soon as possible this truly pitiful state of affairs. Up to now I have been able to prevent complaints from reaching the *Prefecture*, but this is no longer possible and before long they will arrive there en masse ... Until now your name has been honoured and blessed; but before long, beware: things have changed and murmurings of discontent have begun.'

The chief surveyor replied in a long letter on 18 January,

written in firm but subtly tactful terms which speak well for the administrator of the time: the delay was not his fault; he was, on the contrary, doing his best with the means at his disposal.

Moreover, road-making material was lacking. The shaly rock found in the area had a poor reputation and had to be brought in from elsewhere. When supplies were short, excavations would be made in one place for the stone obtained to be used in another.

On this subject the district roads inspector requested the mayor of Mazières, in a letter dated 23 October 1853, to bring a case against Courtial and the contractor of Route 2 for failing to fill in excavations they had made on Road 24 to provide material for their contract.

In November 1854 the same inspector was forced to make a similar complaint to the Mayor himself:

> Monsieur Le Maire,
> You have caused to be dug on the edge and even on the surface itself of Highway 2 from Niort to Parthenay excavations for material required for road works in the commune.
> I must emphasize to you, M. le Maire, the danger that this state of affairs causes to traffic, the trouble it may cause the police and the false position in which I am placed if it continues.
> Therefore, in order that this quarrying may be of the temporary nature that it should be, I must ask you to issue instructions that excavation no longer be undertaken on the surface of the roads or from the ditches and that, where this has been done, the excavations are filled in as soon as possible.
> In so doing, M. le Maire, you will oblige your most humble and obedient servant.

Dr Pouzet immediately complied with this request and, in a letter of 18 January 1855, the inspector provides some curious details of the kind of difficulty a traveller could experience at the time:

> I have to thank you for the promptness that you have so kindly shown in filling in the excavations made for commune work on the surface and borders of Highway 2.

I was unaware that M. le Préfet had authorized the work, but he certainly would not have included in his authorization permission to undertake excavations such as those indicated by M. le Procureur Imperial at Niort as constituting a danger to traffic.

If, by any chance, the weather should halt your waggons before the holes are filled in and the earth consolidated, it would seem useful to indicate the boundaries of the safe road by a few posts. Our road gangs will be available, on your request, to help you in this.

Few details could be more indicative of the technical difficulty faced in rapid road building in a land where manual labour alone was in plentiful supply.

Nevertheless in 1852 construction had begun on the secondary road from Mazières to Secondigny which Dr Pouzet had asked for in his letter to the *conseilleur général* at Grandmay in September 1848.

The Sub-Prefect in a letter dated 28 September 1852 stated that the total cost for the construction of the road would amount to a sum of 30,028 fr. 18,[1] of which 460 fr. was for work to be undertaken within the commune. He added: 'But you will understand, M. le Maire, that in accordance with Article 6 of the Law of 21 May 1836 communes must contribute to the cost in proportion to the benefit they enjoy from the road. Now it appears from the report submitted to me by the Roads Surveyor that, because of the advantage that the aforesaid road will bring to your commune, it must bear responsibility for the construction of 829 m. 96 cm. estimated at a cost of 4,289 fr. 74.'

A letter from the district Roads Surveyor to the Mayor of Mazières indicates that work was in progress in December 1855.

In 1855 the network of roads which still serves the area today was in a state which permitted relatively easy communication, having regard to the means of transport available at that time. This was an essential element in economic change in the region. Road construction answered the urgent and constant desire of people of the commune but it clearly could only have been undertaken under the impetus of the central government.

The Farm School at Petit-Chêne

A further stimulus came from without: a farm school had been opened in 1849 inside the commune itself.[2] It seems clear, however, that the choice of Mazières-en-Gâtine as the site for a farm school formed no part of any considered plan drawn up by the authorities concerned as part of an over-all grand design but came about by accident. Funds had been provided to the *département* for the establishment of a farm school.

M. de Tusseau, who, as we know, owned many farms in Mazières, had one near his personal residence which he operated either on his own account or through *métayers*. It was one of the worst estates in the commune, more covered than most by woods, heather, bracken and broom, very wet, and dotted with ponds and marshes. He offered it to the government as the site of a farm school. It was a gesture both generous and clever, for the property which had for long brought no return would now be improved at little cost to him. The government accepted the offer and thus it was that, in 1849, 17 pupils and a bursar were installed at Petit-Chêne.

M. de Tusseau was principal: as such he drew a salary of 2,400 francs. He had the right to appoint and discharge the farm manager, the bookkeeper and the gardener. He corresponded with the Ministry of Agriculture through the Prefect.[3]

The first bursar seems to have been a former teacher. He at once gained the confidence of the local authority. By 1850 Dr Pouzet wanted him to be appointed to the administration of the Relief Committee, while the Sub-Prefect wanted this office to be filled by a proprietor of the commune.

The pupils were recruited throughout the neighbouring region, both from the lowlands and the *gâtine*,[4] from among the sons of prosperous farmers between 16 and 18 years of age and with a satisfactory standard of primary education.

Thus the farm school was situated by chance at Mazières-en-Gâtine. There was no particular intention in the minds of its founders that it should, by its example and through a special method of teaching, transform the farming of the Gâtine country. It was the farm school for the whole *département* of Deux-Sèvres.

This is evident, not only from the text of the order establishing it but from the courses taught there.[5]

The 1850 course deals with the land and the different varieties of soil, then with *agricultural geography*. The introduction to the chapter reads:

> Agriculture's rôle is the distribution of the plants cultivated by man in France; the position of places must be the first study undertaken by a farmer because it is this which regulates cultivation.
>
> We will follow a division by provinces; as a general rule plants are distributed in France on the same lines as elsewhere from the *ecuator* [*sic*] to the *paules* [*sic*] . . . Forests and woodland are met with in greater quantity as one moves southward; the plants (*végétaux*) which resist the cold best are birch, beech and particularly pine. As regards the plants that we shall cultivate we shall classify them in the following order:
>
> 1. Barley
> 2. Rye
> 3. Oats
> 4. Wheat.

This is manifestly a course which its author made no attempt to adapt to the region in which it was taught. In point of fact he seems to have concerned himself about it only twice. When speaking of liming he gives the example of two neighbouring *départements* – Sarthe and Mayenne – where the annual rental of farms had doubled and trebled: 'from a rent of twenty francs they now are leased at fifty and even sixty francs' (p. 25 of the first-year course). Then, when speaking of artificial pastures, he quotes the slogan of Jacques Bujault, well known to the people of the area: 'A farm without cattle is like a bell without a clapper.' He adds: 'Unfortunately, the fodder crops possible in our *bocage* country are very few. Lucerne, for example, is rarely found,[6] sainfoin is impossible to grow; only clover succeeds well. Therefore we recommend its cultivation to you, if one day you farm in this area' (p. 55, second-year course). This remark does not, however, prevent the author from discussing the cultivation of lucerne and sainfoin, but it is the only passage in the whole of this course of dictated lessons in which can be felt any concern for conditions peculiar to the area where he was teaching. It must be remembered, too, that the pupils at the Petit-Chêne farm school were unable to farm in the Gâtine or *bocage* country.

Be that as it may, this course provides nevertheless valuable insight into the approach which could be made to the solution of the major problems confronting farmers in this land of heath and broom, where the opening of roads had permitted an entry into the cycle of trade and exchange, viz. the problems of land clearance, of equipment, of the use of fertilizers, of lime and of making artificial pastures.

The problem of clearing was approached very carefully. Farmers were advised to reckon the cash return to be expected before embarking on any large expenditure. 'Taking the value of wooded land at 400 francs the hectare, if the return from clearing is 200 francs, one then obtains from this operation land worth 600 francs the hectare. Now, in order to know whether the work is worth while, the owner should find out if his land could be let for a rent of 30 or 40 francs the hectare. If so, he will then have benefited since he will have a return of five or six per cent on his money.' Distinction was made, also, between the clearing of woodland, *landes* and grazing land and wise advice was given on the crops to be grown on cleared land.

The same circumspection is met with when the question of equipment is considered:

> If we wish to calculate the cost of dressing the land by hand we know that a man can do one hectare in nine or ten days: at 1 fr. 50 a day this comes to 14 or 15 francs the hectare.
>
> If, on the other hand, we use a horse-drawn hoe we shall pay out 2 francs for the horse, 2 francs for the man leading it, i.e. 4 francs a day plus 3 francs for the appliance. If we add to this amount the cost of three or four man-days for work by hand, we find we have saved the cost of dressing one hectare if it had been done by hand.

In dealing with agricultural instruments much emphasis is laid on the merits of the Dombasle plough. It combines 'three important and rare qualities, viz.

(1) reduction of motive power needed;
(2) increase in work produced;
(3) improved quality in work performed.'

Much attention was paid, also, to the harrow (particularly to the Valcour harrow) which seems to have been little used in the area, to the roller and to the horse-hoe which had been recently invented. All these instruments were considered indispensable and this was something quite new for this region at least, indicating the substitution of iron for wood, the penetration of large-scale industry in the shape of agricultural machinery into all rural farming. Other instruments were listed: the drill, the cultivator, the hoeing machine, the winnowing machine, the threshing machine – but without dwelling on them. 'They are not in the category of instruments essential to a farmer' (first year course, p. 48). On the other hand, long pages were devoted to the different ways of ploughing.

Fertilizers were classified in six categories:

(1) Straight dung
(2) Animal waste
(3) Vegetable fertilizer
(4) Mixed or liquid fertilizers (dung mixed with farm litter) (farmyard manure)
(5) Farm by-products (bone meal, grits)
(6) Composite fertilizers.

But only farmyard manure and its care was really dealt with. On the other hand, emphasis was placed on lime and its use without much attention seeming to be paid to the nature of the soil.

Finally, it is worth noting that the writer of the course stressed the need for artificial pastures and expanded on how to introduce them into the area.

Such as it was, the course was too generalized and too advanced to have much influence on the farming practice of the environs. But the fields at Petit-Chêne presented exactly the same problems as those of the neighbourhood and the example shown by the farm manager could be useful to nearby farmers.

M. Chabot, mayor of Saint-Romans, was instructed by the Prefect at Parthenay to enquire into the working of the farm school. His report, dated 27 November 1849, provides valuable information on the resources available and the work done:

Monsieur le Sous-Préfet,
I have the honour to present the result of the

inspection of the Petit-Chêne farm school made on
17 October by the commission of enquiry.

The members of the commission arrived unannounced.
They met there M. le Sous-Préfet of Parthenay who had
gone at the invitation of M. le Préfet.

The commission carried out their enquiry over the
whole farm both inside the buildings and outside. To
their great satisfaction, they found all the property in
excellent condition and well maintained.

We found the pupils engaged on various tasks, some
ploughing, others carting fertilizer.

Before proceeding to the fields, the commission
examined the equipment workshop: the instruments
are many and varied. The Principal is building a forge
where the pupils will be instructed in the repair of
implements.

The commission then moved to the fields where they
saw the produce of clean-weeded plots of cabbage,
beetroot and potatoes: then plots of green fodder crops.
They saw nothing else since the school was established
only on 6 May last.

They paid close attention to the ploughing and
watched some exercises under the direction of the
instructor. Ploughing is done with oxen and horses: the
Dombasle and La Rosé are the ploughs most often used.
The harrow and roller are used to complete the operation
over strips of land some 3 metres wide separated by a
drainage furrow.

The system of rotation followed at the farm of
Petit-Chêne is one of six years: first year, heavily
manured market garden crops; second year, spring
wheat; third year, clover; fourth year, winter wheat;
fifth year, green fodder with two applications of manure;
sixth year, winter wheat.

Eighty-eight hectares of land are worked; forty
stock – horses and oxen – are maintained in good
condition.

The commission watched a plot intended for winter
wheat being limed, the lime being mixed with earth
taken from ditches.

For those who are impatient for results there is little

to report: it could not be otherwise since the establishment dates only from 6 May. The market garden plots are well tended and will produce fairly abundantly in spite of the dryness of the past summer. Allowance must also be made for the nature of the soil; couch-grass, gorse and bracken are ever-present and frequent ploughing is needed to keep the land clean. Clover can only be grown for one year, after that time the couch grass takes over and renders the land unsuitable for another crop unless frequent ploughing, undertaken when weather permits, is capable of destroying it. It is a stubborn soil demanding much attention if it is to be brought into production.

Petit-Chêne lacks fertilizer; the Principal wishes to obtain some sheep whose manure will improve that from the other animals . . .

This short report will enable you, M. le Sous-Préfet, to judge the absurd rumours which have been spread concerning the state of affairs at Petit-Chêne. M. de Tusseau himself controls and directs affairs, no detail escapes him; he goes as far as to give practical demonstrations of ploughing to the pupils. With his good intentions and with the agricultural knowledge of M. Lebreton, I believe that the institution of Petit-Chêne is ready to render immense service to the *bocage*.

It is possible that this report, prepared deliberately as a defence of the farm school against accusations considered to be absurd, may be too flattering. Nevertheless, it brings out in sharp relief all the new ideas it was bringing into agricultural practice in the area: deep, frequent ploughing; the use of agricultural machines; planned rotation of crops, liming, etc.

An agricultural revolution

The farmers of the area could not all profit immediately from this example. They would have needed capital with which to buy implements and lime: and they would also have needed to possess a different mental attitude. But the better-off and alert farmers followed closely what was going on at the farm school and they adopted those methods which seemed most worthy of their attention. Their examples attracted the more timid, while the openings for sale of produce created by the improved means of communication led to new sources of funds becoming available almost everywhere.

Thus progress began to happen in this shut-in country of suspicious minds through the intermediary of local points of focus. This seems to me to fit in with everything I was able to observe later and the facts are confirmed by a precise detail from M. Bouet's agricultural monograph on the commune of Mazières-en-Gâtine.[7]

> Thanks to the experiments carried out at the farm school, the Dombasle iron plough was soon known and its worth appreciated.
>
> M. Massé de la Jaunelière was the first farmer to adopt the plough in 1856. This intelligent man told me that the first ploughing he did with a Dombasle was watched by more than two hundred people.

Ploughing done by a local man was more willingly visited and watched than that carried out at the farm school, but we may suppose that M. Massé de la Jaunelière had also paid visits to Petit-Chêne.

M. Bouet in his monograph adds:

> It must not be thought that the peasants had no misgivings in replacing the old by a new implement. Many held that it ploughed too deep and brought the poor subsoil to the surface with great disadvantage to crops.
>
> But when the good harvests obtained were seen the evidence had to be accepted. Another fact which contributed to the adoption of the iron plough was that deep ploughing did get rid of the bracken, the worst enemy of cereal crops at that time which the inferior performance of the wooden instrument completely failed to eradicate.

What then, were the chief items of progress in agriculture?

The peasants' efforts were first directed to land clearance which was performed in almost unbelievable conditions of toil and lack of resources, revealing extraordinary reserves of strength and energy in these Gâtine folk almost incomprehensible to us today. The peasants left home at sunrise; if their work was more than half a kilometre from the house they would not return before evening. They took their midday meal with them – and it was no more than a snack. I was told by the nephew of an old woman I used to know who, when she was young, had taken part in the clearing of her property, that she and her father used to take with them some bread and an egg to suffice for them both. Her case would have been quite normal.

Clearing must, moreover, have been very slow work. I remember very clearly, when I was a child around 1905, fields of broom which today are meadows. It is most probable that the clearing of woodland and heath did not begin before 1860 when the use of the Dombasle plough (as the farm school course tells us) allowed the deep roots to be cut. And it is worth noting that from that time the number of blacksmiths increased and many ploughs were fashioned. In 1864 the mayor of Mazières, when asked by the Sub-Prefect at Parthenay for the name of a farm in his commune worthy of a visit from the departmental committee responsible for the distribution of prizes and medals of honour to the best farmers, replied:

> There is in my commune no farm sufficiently well managed to deserve the award of 500 francs in the departmental agricultural competition.
> I can only mention some considerable and difficult clearing carried out by tenant-farmers Sanze and Baraton of Les Berthonnière and Petit-Chêne. These two farmers have added to the commune fields which have never been ploughed before.

At the same time the area sown to crops increased: the following table shows progress made in hectares sown:

	Wheat	Rye	Oats	Buckwheat	Potatoes	Beans
1849	17	75	55	35	55[8]	2
1853	18	75	80	35	10	1
1854	21	80	85	40	5	1
1857	30	90	95	40	20	1½
1867	80	90	140	30	15	–
1882	83	92	185	61	51	–

These marked increases, particularly in wheat and oats, reflect a progressive diminution in the time of fields lying fallow, thanks to the development of sown pasture which allowed more stock to be kept and consequently more manure produced.

In 1856 the mayor of Mazières in reply to a questionnaire from the Sub-Prefecture indicated that there were 'very few' sown pastures. But the fact that there were some was, in itself, something new.

Twenty-five years later in 1882 the following were grown: 20 hectares of vetch or *dravières*, 20 of red clover, 40 of fodder maize, 5 of cabbage, 5 of green rye, 160 of varieties of clover, 5 of lucerne, 46 of mangolds.

Extending the area devoted to cereals, the introduction of sown pasture, the growing of root crops such as swedes demanding more attention than potatoes, land clearance – all this pushed the farmers towards buying machines. So, little by little, ploughs, harrows, horse hoes were introduced into farms. But it is hardly before 1860 that one can see this evolution accelerate and even then it cannot be called rapid. Right up to 1880 sickles – not even scythes – were used for mowing and harvesting. It was back-breaking work, demanding a large labour force, which is why domestic servants cost more during the three summer months than during the nine months of winter.

'The first reaping machine to be used in the district,' writes M. Bouet, 'was tried out in 1875 in the testing grounds of the Ecole Normale at Parthenay where I was a student at the time. M. Launay, professor of agriculture, had invited several farmers to come and see the machine at work. But, either because it was imperfect or because it was badly operated, the work was ill done and the farmers departed, convinced that it could do nothing very useful. This put back for several years the adoption of an implement whose value is fully recognized today.'

The peasants, in fact, only adopted machines with the utmost reserve. It might be that they would reduce the amount of work but they were novelties and cost a lot of money. As for the farm workers, they viewed machines with fear. Later on one could often find stones mixed with the sheaves for threshing.

The use of lime, which was to be so beneficial for the heavy soils of Gâtine, seems to have spread more easily. According to M. Bouet's monograph it was used for the first time in 1858 on the Gobinière farm, and the results obtained were so conclusive that the practice of liming spread almost at once. That the date should be so precise is somewhat surprising to me. I have found among the statistics for October 1856 that there was at that time at Mazières a lime kiln which was not in existence in 1851 and which disappeared a few years later. It seems to me improbable that this ephemeral kiln should have been built solely to respond to the needs of the building industry. It appears likely that its owner sold the lime at a discount to farmers who had to fetch their lime from the neighbouring communes of Champeaux and Champdeniers. But at least we can stick to the oral tradition – unconfirmed but none the less invaluable – gathered by M. Bouet in 1880 and agree that the use of lime spread in the commune between 1855 and 1860.

It must have worked marvels. Its use was sometimes overdone: certain careless farmers would use lime without manuring the land later which resulted in exhausting the soil. So much so that the saying ran: Lime enriches the father but ruins the son.

Here was a real danger. Fortunately a chair of agriculture had been established in the *département*. The holder of the post, because of his close relation with many influential landowners, and because of a small book which, thanks to the school,[9] had a wide circulation, was able to direct and consequently to preserve the beneficial practice of liming. One essential point on which he insisted was the importance of never mixing manure and lime. The mixture gave an immediate result but the effect did not last long, the lime partly destroying the manure if it was dry and becoming sticky or forming into lumps if the manure was wet.[10]

Manure being more plentiful owing to the increase in the number of animals and to the greater length of time they spent in the stables, little by little the *pourriniers* disappeared. On all the larger farms at that time a poor person would be housed in a shed of some kind. His duties were to collect the dung and cow pats (*pourrin*) in the pastures. This *pourrin* was placed in heaps, hoed over and cut like the other manure. The crop obtained from the application of this fertilizer belonged half to the farmer, half to the *pourrinier*. By 1870 there were no more in the region.

two

Changes in society

Increase in the area of cultivated land through clearance and through the progressive shortening of the fallow period – thanks to the making of artificial pasture, a better economic return through the use of lime: all this had as end result the doubling and trebling of the value of land. Between 1850 and 1860 the following estates had been sold:

> The Forge farm at 31,000 francs for about 80 hectares of land which later became excellent, one of the best properties in the region;
> Pressigny – 90,000 francs for more than 100 hectares of varied land: woods, copses, full-grown timber and meadow (Pressigny had formerly been the residence of aristocrats); Les Gâts – 16 hectares of some of the poorest soil in the area, 6,000 francs.

In 1880 these properties had more than doubled in value (and by 1890 Les Gâts was reckoned worth more than 20,000 francs). An estate adjoining Forge, of smaller area and worse soil, was sold for 60,000 francs in 1879. Moreover, prices had a tendency to become uniform and one can say that arable land was worth between 1,500 and 2,000 francs a hectare in 1880, pasture a little more.

In the same way, the farm rents rose, although in a slightly smaller proportion, on the larger estates where greater capital became needed for the purchase of livestock and machinery. Thus the rent for the Les Brossardières farm had barely doubled (from 1,500 to 3,000 francs). According to the value of the land,

rents varied between 40 and 70 francs the hectare. The leases
were extremely long (for at least 9 years) and the same relations
between tenant and landlord seem to have prevailed.

But estates which had grown richer could be divided up into
smaller parcels and still yield a livelihood for a family. Also
many younger sons of better-off farmers or domestic servants,
having acquired a very modest capital sum by dint of self-
denial and thrift, would endeavour to rent *borderies* which were
easy to find – at a rental proportionately higher than larger
farms.

Information concerning farms of more than 50 hectares in
1860 and 1880 is fragmentary and often contradictory, but,
since the common practice in the region was to work or rent
land which formed part of one large estate (there were few
terres volantes as they were called), it is possible to find some
useful pointers by examining the figures for the changes in
estates, statistics which are full of other most valuable information.

First, estates tended to be divided up. The following table
summarizes changes which took place between 1860 and 1880:

	Residing in the commune		Outside the commune	
	1860	1880	1860	1880
Proprietors of less than 5 hectares	92	107	35	54
5–10 hectares	14	25	11	16
10–20 hectares	8	6	8	7
20–30 hectares	4	3	1	2
30–40 hectares	1	–	4	2
40–50 hectares	–	–	2	2
50–100 hectares	1	–	4	5
more than 100 hectares	1	3	–	1

It is impossible not to notice, on the one hand, the considerable increase in the number of small farms; 152 of less than
10 hectares in 1860 compared with 202 in 1880 and, on the other
hand, the increase in large estates: four owners of more than
100 hectares in 1880 as against only one in 1860. Rich town
dwellers could see that the best investment was still in land,
particularly when farms were increasing in value each year
thanks to the improvement in farming methods and easier

distribution of produce. Medium sized farms, on the contrary, tended to become fewer.

In addition, in 1860 there were 121 proprietors living in the commune. In 1880 the number had risen to 144. Similarly, 66 resided outside the commune in 1860; 89 in 1880. The increase is the same for each class but proportionately greater for those outside the commune.[1]

Evidence from the assessment of incomes corresponds with this. In 1852 there were 68 resident owners whose income was assessed at less than 50 francs per annum, 21 at between 50 and 200 francs and seven at more than 100 francs.

The following are the changes that I was able to discover:

	Owners living in the commune			Owners living outside the commune		
	Taxable income			Taxable income		
	−50 fr.	+50 fr.	+100 fr.	−50 fr.	+50 fr.	+100 fr.
1852	68	21	7	20	29	13
1860	95	23	8	31	22	13
1880	114	25	11	45	21	17

The total of taxable income was 11,100 francs in 1852, 11,193 francs in 1860 and 11,673 francs in 1880. What happy days they were when taxes increased with such sensible deliberation, when only new buildings seem to have been counted for increased assessment and when a very large house was reckoned at 30 francs for tax purposes. In these circumstances, the increase in tax assessment is quite marked – nearly 500 francs, whereas it had hardly varied at all since 1852 or even since 1842 when it stood at 10,960 francs.

It is also during this period that much house building was begun without reduction to be seen in taxes as a result of demolitions. Between 1853 and 1863 tax was levied on 32 new houses built between 1850 and 1860. Forty-eight houses (some of considerable size) were built between 1860 and 1870 and 45, including two châteaux and one *maison bourgeoise,* between 1870 and 1880.

Nothing demonstrates more clearly the prosperity of the region than this surge in building activity,[2] bringing with it changes in the social habits of the people.

Progress in the township

These changes can be measured by the progress of the township. In 1851 it held 210 inhabitants and we have seen that these inhabitants consisted of a few notables, a collector of taxes, a policeman, a teacher, a few artisans 'more often in the fields than in their workshops' and small farmers. In 1861 it had 237 inhabitants, in 1872, 252 and in 1881, 305. Leaving aside the figures for 1881 which show a sharp but fortuitous increase (due to the construction of the railway) let us look closely at the changes taking place in the town. First, there are eight personalities worthy of note: landowners living in town on the rent of their land with domestic servants. This was not something new but the number had risen.

Among the notabilities we still find the doctor, the health officer and the veterinary surgeon. But now there appears a lawyer (*notaire*), providing evidence of an increase in property deals in the district and showing that some of the peasants were making savings sufficiently large to need a lawyer for their investments. Then there was a bailiff. Not a few farmers would, no doubt, get into debt and a bailiff could make a good living collecting debts. And now the civil servants: the tax collector, the teacher and the gendarmes are still there as in 1846 but also, not one but two roadmen, a road foreman and – something quite new – three postmen. The time had long passed since a single man on foot sufficed to bring the mail from Parthenay to Mazières. What is more, this little chief town of a canton had become the seat of a justice of the peace: a judge and a clerk of the court had been appointed. The commune thought it should have a village constable – and appointed one.

Among the artisans, instead of one clog-maker, we find two, each with a workman; and we even find – a real novelty – a shoemaker who also had an assistant, which indicates that a relatively large number of people were beginning to wear not only clogs but also shoes. But, in fact, this cobbler had other ways of earning a living besides making and repairing shoes: he was, at the same time, a violinist and played at weddings and dances throughout the commune and even the region. His contorted figure – for cobblers in those days were often sick or misshapen – and his memory lived on in the minds of those born towards 1860. There were still washerwomen and dressmakers but now also a dyer, whose business probably consisted in rough dyeing local cloth.

If we move from clothing to food, more changes can be seen. There was still only one baker with his assistant. But there were no longer two 'merchants' (*marchands*) but, in their place, three grocers who conducted their trade as *colporteurs*, carrying their goods round the country on foot in large baskets. In 1880, one of them bought a cart. It was at that time that the use of coffee and sugar began to spread into the countryside. The grocers sold not only candles but also lucifer matches (one of them was known, for this reason, throughout his life as 'Father Lucifer'), which worked the miracle of being able to light a fire easily whenever one wanted to. It was around 1878–80 that two of these grocers added to their grocery-haberdashery business a small range of working clothes.

There were, also, not two but six café owners or innkeepers. This may be regrettable but it is a fair indication of the growing prosperity of the area.

The number of building workers had also increased greatly. There were no longer only one or two stonemason labourers but five masons with three labourers; no longer a single blacksmith but now three, of whom one employed as well as his son one workman and another, more skilled, who was also a locksmith. The appearance of three joiners is something new: people were beginning to make improvements to their houses. There was still only one wheelwright, one ropemaker and one pit-sawyer. The weaver had disappeared.

The number of day-labourers (seven men and two women) had not changed. Despite the increase in the number of those practising a trade, there were still destitutes in the town.

The larger villages still had their own craftsmen. All the weavers had moved out to them. None remained in the town, but there were two at Le Beugnon, one at La Texerie and one at La Blanchetière. There was also one joiner at L'Oucherie, another at La Forge; one mason at La Blanchetière and one each at La Chabirandière and La Touche. Also at La Touche, 200 yards from the town along the road from Niort to Parthenay, were to be found a chairmaker and a carrier who travelled every Wednesday to Parthenay and would take all those who wanted to go to the market at a fare of one franc. We should note, too – with reference to the presence of a lawyer in the town – that there was an estate agent at the large village of Mimaudière.

To summarize: all these changes were still not very noticeable. In the town there were still some eminent people whom all respected because they were wealthy and particularly because their wealth consisted of landed estates. But a lawyer, a bailiff and an estate agent had arrived on the scene. There were seven civil servants in 1850; there were fifteen in 1876. A justice of the peace and his clerk, two roadmen, three postmen and a village constable had been appointed.

Greater prosperity and the change in standards of living are seen in a new clog-maker and a cobbler setting up in business; in the increase in the number of grocers, innkeepers, masons, smiths and joiners.

The way of life

Let us try to imagine what these changes in the way of life meant in terms of physical conditions and, at the same time, what this entailed in mental attitudes.

All the evidence goes to show that the peasant farmers continued to live, as far as possible, within a semi-closed economy, purchasing as few things as possible. Everything that I have been able to gather from oral tradition confirms this view. People still spun yarn on the distaff; all linen came from local home weavers; local millers continued to grind grain brought to them by peasants in the neighbourhood, who still baked their own bread; there was still no butcher in the town; the only meat eaten was still the pork from pigs killed annually. Nevertheless, there are plenty of signs that the farmers were beginning to spend more money than usual on clothes (ready-made garments bought from the big stores as well as from the village shop began to be common), on shoes (remember there were two clog-makers and a shoemaker in the town instead of just one clog-maker), on food and on home comforts – it was at this time that crockery began to be used on the farms. On Sundays, and holidays, at first, later more often and finally every day, it became the custom for each person to be served food on a plate (one single plate, it goes without saying). The habit of drinking wine became more common, although it is true that wine, like coffee, was still a luxury reserved for holidays and Sundays.

At weddings it was not unusual for butcher's meat to be served as well as new delicacies such as asparagus and artichokes, provided with pride and joy to impress guests.[3]

Living conditions, too, began to improve very slightly. There was little change in the type of house being built but, as a general rule, ceilings were higher and wooden floors or red tiles replaced the old beaten earth floor. In particular, little by little, families began to live separately and the number of persons per house decreased. In 1851, in Mazières town, 40 houses contained 53 families and a total of 210 persons: that is to say, 13 houses held two families each. The average per house was 5 people. In the countryside 154 familes lived in 149 houses: that is, only 5 houses (although many consisted of only one room) held more than one family. The total population was 760 and the average per house was, therefore, a little more than 5 persons. In 1861 there were 58 houses in the town for 67 families and 237 persons (average 4 per house). In the countryside 144 houses for 146 families and a population of 706 (just under 5 persons per house). In 1872 in the town there were 64 houses for 75 families and 259 people (average, 4 persons per house): in the country-side, 153 houses for 163 families and 728 people (average, between 4 and 5 persons per house). In 1882, in the town the statistics reveal (not counting temporary residents) 78 houses for 84 families and 305 inhabitants (average, a little under 4 persons per house): in the countryside, 161 houses for 161 families and 781 people (average, under 5 persons per house).

The following table summarizes these changes:

	Town				Countryside			
	Houses	Families	People	Aver.	Houses	Families	People	Aver.
1851	40	53 (+13)	210	+5	149	160 (+11)	760	+5
1861	58	67 (+9)	237	4·09	144	146 (+2)	706	−5 (4·9)
1872	64	75 (+11)	259	4·04	153	163 (+10)	728	−5 (4·7)
1882	78	84 (+6)	305	3·9	161	161 (equal)	781	4·8

Generally speaking, therefore, there was a constant and noticeable decrease in the number of people living in each house, in spite of an increase in population. On this point it must be noted that the decrease of population in the villages shown for 1861, in spite of building activity, can only be accounted for by the abandonment of a certain number of hovels. We shall return to these figures, which seem to me to be very characteristic, in Part III, where I shall try to show how the prosperity of the commune and the increase in trade affected particularly the township which had grown and specialized and where the standard of living improved more than in the villages. But, for the moment, all that is advanced in this comparison is that the new material well-being of the commune is seen in a general improvement in housing.

By that time, too, the houses began to be better furnished. Even the poorest house began to have cupboards made by local carpenters – very simple wardrobes, lacking the ornamentation which was the glory of the fine rural furniture of the eighteenth century. They would have one or two doors, but nevertheless they were a mark of progress, both in themselves and in the household linen they were made to hold. This partly explains the increase in the number of carpenters. These men now began to buy their wood not only where it grew, having it sawn by pit-sawyers on the spot, but also to buy planks at Niort where important saw-mills were being developed.[4] Here we may note a clear sign of intelligence being put to use and of the practical value of a knowledge of symbols in the most humble trades: a clog-maker in the town, because he could read and write and because he knew how to measure timber, set up, in addition to his workshop, a timber yard.

All these steps in progress evidently did not take place spontaneously as part of a natural evolution in the commune nor independently of what was taking place in the country as a whole. They were largely a consequence of the improvement in the road network, which now allowed people to travel more readily to market at Champdeniers, or farmers to fetch their lime from Champeaux and Champdeniers, or blacksmiths, carpenters, shopkeepers to replenish their stocks of goods. They were also the result of the central government's efforts to improve agriculture,[5] subsidies for clearing land, agricultural shows and competitions, departmental professors of agriculture whose work we have already seen. All this progress in essence was part and parcel of the prosperity of France as a whole at the time and of the benefits of the easier transportation of the region's products towards Paris, owing to the construction of the railway from Poitiers to Rochelle, passing through Saint-Maixent and Niort. This was an aspect of the matter of which the mayor of Mazières was well aware. In 1864 he wrote to the Sub-Prefect at Parthenay: 'The price of the basic necessities is much higher than usual. I think they will remain at at least as high a level during the hard season not because the grain harvest has not been good but because there is always speculation in this basic commodity which raises the price. The extreme dryness of the summer has harmed the legume crop and has led to a drop in yield which is the cause of the high price of these products. Butter is scarce because pasture has been short: but I believe that this product as well as eggs, fruit, etc. will always hold a higher price *because of their being sent to Paris by rail.*'

Intervention by the State is more clearly seen in the appointment of the new officials whose appearance in 1876 we have already noted. That the upkeep of the new road system was a legitimate reason for the appointment of three roadworkers in the place of one is quite self-evident. But the presence of three postmen and a postmistress in a commune which, twenty years earlier, had not been thought worth the service of a mail delivery by horse indicates a remarkable change both in the attitude of government in agreeing more readily to new appointments and in the way of life and broadening horizons of some of the people. The post office served all the surrounding communes: Saint-Pardoux, Verruyes, Saint-Marc-la-Lande and even more distant ones such as Soutiers, Vouhe, les Groseillers, and Saint-Georges-de-Noisne, the centre of which is some eight or more kilometres from Mazières. From documents at the head office in Niort it appears that each postman covered an average of 30 kilometres a day on his rounds. They would use every possible dodge to shorten their journeys, the chief method being to arrive in the middle of the commune on Sundays as people were leaving the church, when they would hand to obliging neighbours letters which could not be delivered to the homes. In December 1879 one round which required a postman to go to Soutiers (5 kilometres), then to Saint-Pardoux (3 kilometres), to Château-Bourdin (3 kilometres) returning to Mazières (5 kilometres), not counting the distance covered in going to the ends of the communes and into the villages to deliver the letters, was halved. Some interesting details come out from the explanations given for this reduction in service. Postal revenue for the commune of Saint-Pardoux (pop. 1,898) was 690 francs; for Soutiers (pop. 277) it was 66 francs and 404 francs for Vouhe (pop. 705), or an average per head of 0 fr. 36, 0 fr. 24 and 0 fr. 57 respectively. A comparison of these different figures would have made an interesting study if I could have found all the details. It is enough to note that the least densely populated commune (Soutiers) made least use of the service while the most densely populated (Vouhe) used it most. It is probable that at Mazières-en-Gâtine the average was about equal to that of Saint-Pardoux, perhaps a little greater, bearing in mind the proximity of the post office. In any case it will not have exceeded 0 fr. 50 per person, letter postage being 0 fr. 20. We may conclude that many families hardly ever wrote any letters, hardly ever received any and that those who did use the postal service most would write and receive one or two letters a month.[6]

Another important innovation was the installation of a telegraph office for the canton of Mazières in 1866. It is evident that this action was not in response to the wishes, not merely of the people as a whole but even of their representatives. No resolution of the municipal council had requested it and a letter dated 1 June 1866 from the Sub-Prefect at Parthenay to the mayor of Mazières makes it clear that this was an initiative of the government applying to the whole district:

Parthenay, 1 June 1866

Monsieur le Maire,

Following discussion on the revised estimates for Mazières, the Prefect spoke to you concerning the establishment of a telegraph office in the chief town of every canton.

The costs of establishing this office at Mazières, after deducting half of the expenditure which is borne by the State, reach the sum of 1,860. 00

The department allocates to each canton assistance to the amount of 500. 00

There remains a sum of 1,360. 00
of which one-third is charged to your commune 453. 35

I have to ask you to call, as soon as possible, a meeting of your municipal council and induce it to vote this amount which is repayable in two annual instalments, i.e. in 1866 and 1867.

I have no doubt, M. le Maire, that the municipal council will hasten to vote so small a sum of so little significance in the commune's budget in order to gain the inestimable benefit of so swift a means of communication so necessary for the commercial and personal needs of all. I rely too much on the practical good sense of your elected representatives not to be convinced that they will warmly welcome this opportunity offered by Government of improving the general well-being in facilitating their relations with the rest of the Empire.

Yours etc.

Le Sous-Préfet
(signature illegible)

The municipal council, by a resolution of 24 June 1866, voted the necessary funds and, in its turn, described the installation of an electric telegraph office as 'an inestimable benefit'. It was the teacher who was appointed as operator on the recommendation of the mayor of Mazières, who wrote during August 1866 to the Postal Inspector at Niort:

Monsieur l'Inspecteur,

I have the honour to recommend to you as operator of the telegraph office at Mazières and as the person to be in charge of the cantonal system M. Popineau (Jean-Victor), aged 36, teacher at the commune school and municipal secretary. This man is very intelligent and of excellent moral character.

I recommend also that you appoint as assistant to take his place during absence Marie Giroire, his wife, aged 29, recognized teacher: she too is most intelligent and of good character.

As in the past, I expect that the telegraph service at Mazières will have but few messages to transmit, and I consider that to open the office from 9 a.m. to midday and from 2 to 3 p.m. will be quite sufficient.

I have found no documentation on the method of appointment of the justice of peace or his clerk, nor on what occasioned the appointments.

Material well-being and trade had, therefore, quite clearly increased through the peasants' efforts, assisted by improved communications, by the circumstances of the time and by initiatives of the central government. The town had changed a little: it was no longer just a village a little bigger than the others: it was beginning to be an administrative and economic centre. What changes in mental attitude may have accompanied these economic and social changes?

three

Mental attitudes

The mass of the people, still very poor, do not seem to have enlarged their outlook to any great extent. Many of them, poverty-stricken, continued to live a life restricted to a limited horizon, content with a few simple pleasures amid misfortunes which seemed to them to be the normal, natural way of life – the very stuff of existence. In the first part of this study I referred to those memorable portraits of Norman maidservants drawn by Flaubert around 1850. I now call to mind a man who used to work for my grandfather whom I knew in 1900 when he was about fifty years old. His name was Rocher and he was called 'Quatorze' because he was the fourteenth child in his family. In his childhood he had begged for bread. He himself had had six children: his wife and five children had died of tuberculosis and poverty. There remained one child, a little hunchback, a little older than I, very intelligent and of whom I was jealous because my grandfather, who loved to be read to aloud, would choose him as reader instead of me. This little hunchback, too, died. From every point of view, therefore, poor Quatorze's life was a lamentable one: and yet he had no feeling of being unhappy. Simple matters gave him pleasure: a word of praise from my grandfather, a glass of wine, permission to stay and warm himself by the great fire in winter. I remember, too, a poor old woman, named Marianne, who lived in a hovel in the village of Ternant and who my mother used to have in for a meal every Sunday after mass. From time to time, in order to earn a few sous she would bring heavy bundles of branches of broom for sweeping the courtyard. And how proud she was when one thanked or praised her! Sometimes, too, my mother would get her to sing in order, she said, that I should learn the 'fine old songs'. Thus I heard, sung in a rather shaky voice, the song of the 'Beau Gendarme' with whom the girls were in love. I did not dare say that it bored me: the old woman was so visibly happy and proud at knowing such lovely things and getting me to share in them. I never had the impression that old Marianne was unhappy: nor had she. Thus, in 1900 and even more so in 1880, there were many poor folk – but they were not conscious of their misery. Now and again the dark background of resignation would be lit up by flashes of simple pleasures.

In the same way, most of the people of Mazières allowed themselves to be governed in their daily routine by tradition and instinct. First, religion had remained a living force; most middle-aged men attended church regularly. If a few artisans in the town never attended even at Christmas and Easter – and they would be rare – all their children would nevertheless be baptized and make their first communion. All marriages and funerals were solemnized in church. Even the most convinced free-thinker of the area sent his sons to be choir-boys. And there was no house where meat was eaten on Fridays – or, at least, if it was eaten it would be with some hesitation and uneasiness. For long the story was told in the region of a certain Protestant teacher who wagered he would eat roast goose on Good Friday and died of it two months later.

The family remained completely under the authority of the father. Any wages earned by children or young men were handed over in full to their parents, at least until they reached the age of 21 and often until they married. When this happened, the father would pay for the wedding dress if it was a daughter, or the bridegroom's suit if it was a son: he would give them a chest, a bed, some household linen and would be thanked for his generosity.

Women were only too often regarded as inferior beings. If a mother, on the death of her husband, remained in her son's house, she would have great authority there. But the wife was looked upon rather as a servant. It would not be unusual to find houses where the women always ate standing up by the fireplace, seeing that nothing was lacking on the table where the men were seated. And everywhere it appeared normal and reasonable that women should be ordered about in a tone of voice which brooked no answer; if they did not obey, they would at least give the appearance of obedience in public: husbands who lacked authority were the laughing-stock of the country.[1]

The hierarchy of society remained extremely rigid. On the larger farms, for many years, the servants continued to eat at the foot of the table all from one dish and drinking from the same pot, while, at the other end of the table, the 'bourgeois' and sometimes the 'bourgeoise' with her daughters (the boys eating with the servants) were each provided with a plate and glass and enjoyed a less frugal meal.

Thus, the family – peasant or semi-peasant, traditional, religious, strongly hierarchical – remained firm and unchanged.

Some signs of change

Nevertheless, some cracks began to show themselves. Towards 1880, those young men born between 1855 and 1860 tended to neglect their religious observances; they no longer willingly attended mass on Sundays. Some of them, from the age of 15 or 16, would not even receive the Sacrament at Easter. Moreover, paternal authority, which all seemed to regard as legitimate, seemed tyranny to the more intelligent when it came up against the new forces which were beginning to transform this society. This was the time – we shall examine it more closely later – when the increase of small jobs (postmen, railway workers, village constables, etc.) began to give young men with a good primary education a chance to escape from the insecurity of their life. The two sons of the clog-maker who had added a timber business to his workshop had been, between 1865 and 1875, excellent pupils at the Mazières school. The elder, when called up in the army, was made a corporal at the end of six months. When his year of military service ended, it was suggested that he should re-engage with the rank of sergeant, and the prospect was held out to him of attendance at the Saint-Maixent school and, later, an officer's stripes. He was certainly tempted by the offer and at the same time frightened by this new prospect. He asked his father's advice. The answer was not long in coming: 'You are the elder: you must return home.' It was an order, and one which was not to be discussed. The younger boy wanted to join the railways: 'There is work for all with me,' declared the father and the boy stayed to be a clog-maker.

They were two excellent sons. They loved and respected their father but they hated paternal authority.

The school cannot be blamed in any way for these early signs of change in manners. Religion was still taught there and the teacher made no attempt to estrange the young people from their locality. He simply provided the means by preparing them for a new life which was thrusting itself from all sides upon this poor village.

It is possible, even probable, that the system of conscription, by taking away most of the young men for periods of one year, or some for five years (reduced to four by the law of 1872) to live far from home, had more influence in this matter than the school. It is true that most of the young soldiers were sent to nearby garrisons – at Parthenay and Saint-Maixent – but this was enough: they were living outside the family circle; they were getting to know another kind of life than that of their home village. As for those who did their service at Poitiers, or Tours, or Paris, they remained dazzled by the experience for the rest of their lives. When they came back many would try to talk the local patois no more (I have heard many racy stories on this point) and put on affected manners. Beneath the pleasure that they felt in recalling these memories of their youth, one could discover traces of the impression made on them by this new life in new surroundings, among friends who knew other lands than their own. All the stories they told bore witness, moreover, to their feelings for discipline and the respect they showed for all ranks: a warrant-officer, even a sergeant, remained important personages to them. Returning to their home district which, until then, had lived preoccupied with its own affairs in the midst of its fields of broom and its sunken lanes, isolated from the great centres of civilization, they brought with them something of the exciting atmosphere of the city and unconsciously – for a period of some years at least – an inclination to want to astonish with new ideas those who had never shifted from their homes.

If life continued, then, to be guided by tradition there were some signs of change and it was the same for that part of life which depends on instinct.

The increase in the number of inns in the town (six as against two in 1850) was a sure sign of the growing importance that the town was taking in the economy of the commune, of the rise in the standard of living in the district and, particularly, of the dominance among the peasants and the artisans of basic instincts over reason or the demands of a sublime religion. Innkeepers had increased faster than grocers or carpenters, which shows that their customers did not want first to improve the comfort of their homes and could not conceive of the possibility – or necessity – of ensuring the fragile security of their life before enjoying the only amusements the town had to offer them. The first effect of the rise in the standard of living was an increase in drunkenness. Few Sundays would pass without there being drunken fights in the town: few Mondays which the artisans did not spend at the inn. The lively horror which women of the district still have for men who are 'gourmands' is clear evidence of the poverty that many of their grandmothers knew so well.

The birth rate

The annual birth rate, too, remained relatively high as the following figures indicate.

1850	34		1865	32
1851	20		1866	23
1852	25		1867	33
1853	30		1868	30
1854	16		1869	22
	125			140
Average 25			Average 28	
1855	20		1870	30
1856	26		1871	20
1857	21		1872	23
1858	26		1873	22
1859	29		1874	39
	122			134
Average 24·4			Average 26·8	
1860	29		1875	31
1861	26		1876	41
1862	32		1877	38
1863	32		1878	43
1864	28		1879	29
	147			182
Average 29·4			Average 36·4	

The ratio of births to total population is as follows:

1850–55	25	:	970 or 257	:	10,000
1855–60	24·4	:	950 or 256	:	10,000
1860–65	29·4	:	952 or 308	:	10,000
1865–70	28	:	987 or 283	:	10,000
1870–75	26·8	:	1044 or 256	:	10,000
1875–80	36·4	:	1086 or 335	:	10,000

These figures represent relatively high coefficients, remembering that the present (1944) ratio in France is 140 : 10,000. Attention is drawn to one noticeable fact in these statistics: whereas the annual birth rate towards 1850 was practically uniform (for four years in succession from 1840 it remained at 29), subsequently there were abrupt variations, e.g. 1849 – 19, 1850 – 34, 1853 – 30, 1854 – 16, 1866 – 23, 1867 – 33, 1868 – 30, 1869 – 22.

It should be noted that the years of bad harvest, revealed from the correspondence of the mayor of Mazières, coincide almost exactly with the years of low birth rate. Similarly, when the various developments mentioned earlier took place and there was a marked rise in the general standard of living, the birth rate rose to over 30, and even to 41 in 1876 and 43 in 1878.

At the same time, where previously families of 10, 12 or 14 children had not been uncommon, there was now a tendency for a certain equilibrium to establish itself. In 1875 there was only one family of 10 children; there were many of three, four or five children among the poor, the artisans and the better-off farmers. Only the 'bourgeois' of Mazières had really small families: not one had more than two children. Their families have since died out or are represented only by one or two households with one or two children in each.

Thus, a temporary correlation can be seen between the good years and an increase in births and between the bad years and a decrease in births. Any conclusions which may be drawn from this must be only very tentative. It may be that the commune of Mazières was experiencing an optimum period of fertility. Religion, a living force in many minds, sanctioned and approved of large families, at least among the poor and humble.[2] Custom allowed the poorest families to send their children out to work for wages from the age of eight or ten – and there was work for them at that time; therefore the birth of a child, even when not desired, was not an alarming event. Few people had conceived of the possibility of change in society, and tradition joined with instinct in not wishing to restrict the size of families. Nevertheless, there was a perceptible concern not to have more children than could be fed. In support of this hypothesis are the facts which have already been deduced concerning the balance of mutual responsibility established between the poorer and better-off families.

Manners and customs of society, therefore, contained the germ of the factors of internal evolution relating to spontaneous change in the way of life of the people. But there were other more powerful evolutionary factors connected with external influences which were penetrating this rural environment.

Political movements

The most powerful of these external influences – political agitation – began to be felt between 1870 and 1880. Until 1870 the people of the commune seem to have shown little interest in politics. They were concerned only with those concrete manifestations which had a direct effect on their lives. They would go to the polling booth to vote for the official candidate with no thought of any debate. They would, on the contrary, at the fair or market or inn, discuss warmly the price of bread or freedom of trade. The profit gained by the baker from the revocation of the tax in 1863 certainly occupied their thoughts more than any intellectual speculation on changes in the Empire. This is what the Sub-Prefect at Parthenay wrote to the mayor of Mazières on 2 June 1864:

> Monsieur le Maire,
> Since the decree of 22 June 1863 concerning the bakery trade, the public have become more and more accustomed to the freedom from control which it authorized. In many respects, the bakers themselves after experience of the new system, have come back to charging the prices which the official tax would have fixed had it still been in force. . . .

But after this optimistic declaration on the efficacity of a measure which symbolized the new policy the Empire was embarking on, he asked what exactly were the local effects. The Mayor replied on 4 June 1864:

> The decree of 22 June 1863 concerning bakeries came into force on 1 September of the same year; the fixed price for bread was then 29 centimes per kilogramme. Immediately, the only baker in the commune raised the price to 30 centimes. This lasted until 1 November following when the price was reduced to 28 centimes at which figure it has since remained. I believe the freedom of trade to be good in places where there are several bakers and competition always brings about a reasonable price level, but in a small locality such as Mazières where there is but one baker there is no competition and one is bound to pay more for one's bread than the official price.
>
> As the price of bread has for a long time been low public opinion has not been aroused, but it is certain that, had the price been at a high level, it would have been necessary to fix the price at the level before the decree of 22 June was passed. Today, according to the market price of wheat, the fixed price ought to be 25 or 26 centimes, instead of which it is 28 centimes and the baker enjoys a good profit.

Such calculations must have exercised the minds of all purchasers of bread and even of the farmers who baked their own bread but could still envy the baker. Similar concern is shown in a letter from the Sub-Prefect at Parthenay on 26 November 1867 in which he expresses anxiety about possible disturbances at fairs and markets as a consequence of the rise in the market price of grain. The mayor's reply is missing. Probably it would have testified to disquiet and discontent among the peasants, but would have reassured the Sub-Prefect about public order.

The wars of the Second Empire passed almost unnoticed. A certain amount of enlistment in the army took place but very few were involved and the peace of the countryside was not troubled. The capture of Sebastopol, the victories of the Italian war and the union of Nice and Savoy to France were occasions for Te Deums to which officials and local notables were invited. The rest of the people of Mazières had no clear idea of the importance of these events. We can be sure that they left a favourable – but fleeting – impression concerning the Emperor and France and an added feeling of security, deeply felt and lasting, which was more important to them than anything else.

Nevertheless, in 1870, at the time of the plebiscite organized under the Empire, two votes were cast against 'Badinguet'. These two votes are significant: how can they be explained? One was cast by the master clog-maker/timber-merchant, whom we have mentioned earlier. He was a humble artisan, son of a ploughman of even more humble status in the neighbourhood. But he was extremely intelligent, very energetic and possessed all the qualities of a leader. How did it come about that he, a man who had lived all his life either in his native commune of Clave or at Mazières, could think of opposing the Empire? Was it that during his rare journeys to Parthenay or Niort he chanced to read an opposition newspaper like the *Mémorial des Deux-Sèvres*? Possibly, even probably. But I believe that something much more profound, relating to his character, is involved. I believe that, born a proud man among the humble and even so not imagining the possibility of, or indeed feeling, any desire to change the social system, an agnostic without fanaticism but resisting the influence of the priest, he was by nature suspicious of those born to wealth and authority. Above all, he could read; he loved reading and he loved ideas. In these two opposing votes we can see abstract ideas beginning to gain mastery in minds which were capable of thinking for themselves. It is undeniable that ability to read and the habit, thanks to this ability, of thinking about and handling ideas, must have played an important part in this evolution.[3] But the illiterate mass remained characterless, concerned only with concrete issues.

Important happenings, one national, the others local, were to accentuate this evolution. The first was the war of 1870.

I have spoken of the little notice taken by the peasants of Mazières of the victories of the Second Empire: all that these victories did was to strengthen in them that feeling of security which is the essential thing peasants require of governments. Now the 1870 war shook this feeling of security to its very roots. Men had been called to the colours far beyond the normal (very limited) call-up quota. Seven *gardes mobiles* from the commune had been killed; others had been wounded; all had suffered. And they had fought not far from the area; they declared that the Germans could – if they had wished – have come as far as Bordeaux and occupied the whole country.

Taxes had been levied. The town council, elected on 7 July, had met on 4 September and, by a singular irony at the time, had sworn obedience to the constitution and fidelity to the Emperor. It voted 1,374 fr. 16 for the clothing and equipment of the National Guards mobilized and 3,091 fr. 80 for their pay for three months: a total of 4,465 fr. 96. Since the commune had no available funds, the mayor, M. Pouzet, proposed a loan. The loan was approved by eight votes to five, those paying the most taxes having been called to the meeting. A supplement of 0 fr. 25 per franc was added to the assessments for the years 1871–4.

All the people of the commune had been seriously shaken by these events. Their sense of security had been broken; they had feared invasion; men had gone away to fight; additional taxes had been levied and all this for a war whose cause they did not, could not, understand. I do not believe that any distinction was made between the battles fought by the regular army of the Empire and the desperate resistance put up by the Republic. All accused the Empire of having wanted the war – and lost it.

A new municipal council was elected on 14 May 1871. The electoral list contained 289 names; 179 voted. M. Pouzet obtained 176 votes. According to the provisions of the Law of 14 April 1871 the councillors chose their mayor and M. Pouzet (Julien) was unanimously elected. Nothing, therefore, had apparently changed in the administration of the commune: but the spirit was very different. Men had begun to distrust those who governed them and who were out of touch with the people. This became clear soon after.

M. Julien Pouzet died and was replaced on the council by M. de Tusseau, squire of Petit-Chêne, heir of the Comtes de Breuillac, formerly the seigneurs of the parish and owners, for centuries, of many farms in the commune. M. de Tusseau was elected mayor on 29 October 1871, but only after three recounts and by 6 votes against 5 for M. Frère, a landowner living in the town. M. Frère had been on the council for a long time. He typified the careful approach to administration shown by

M. Pouzet, whose social conservatism, based on a perfect understanding of the affairs and people of the commune, had been
willingly accepted because he was well-known to them and
rather like a father. We should have to go back to 1840 to find
a squire of Petit-Chêne as mayor and over the thirty years
things had changed markedly. When the Vicomte de Laurencie
wished to compile some agricultural statistics, as we saw earlier,
he simply called the farmers to his château. He probably kept
all the commune's records there, for all the important documents are written in his hand.

By 1871 the administration of the commune had become
more complicated: there was a relief bureau, a budget encumbered with loans to balance, and a perpetual flow of letters
from the Sub-Prefect at Parthenay which required answers.
The Town Hall needed a secretary and this was the teacher.
A village constable was needed. An Assembly Hall had become
necessary. The Vicomte de Tusseau, grandson of the Vicomte
de Laurencie, after thirty years of administration by the
notables of the township, was going to find opposition among
the members of the council.

The irreconcilables, those who, by refusing to attend the
meeting of 8 March 1874 and thereby give tacit approval of the
nomination by the President of the Republic of M. de Tusseau
as mayor, were four in number: M. Frère – already mentioned –
two owner-farmers from the north of the commune and one
owner-farmer from Les Gâts near the château of Petit-Chêne
but independent of the château because he owned his own land
and was proud of the fact.

The date should be noted. It was 1874. The school, which
was to be blamed for having promoted the revolt against the
landed class, had been well run and enjoyed success only after
1860. There had been no time for it to have influenced more
than a very few electors. The opposition, therefore, could not
have sprung from its effect. It was an opposition of liberally
minded townsfolk, of artisans and of the better-off peasants,
good Catholics though they were, against the squire and an
authority out of touch with the common people and inclined
to manipulate them for ends of which they were ignorant.

The council which assembled on 27 December 1874 contained
no members of the opposition.[4] M. de Tusseau had managed to
get his friends and supporters elected: the notary, a property

owner in the town – M. Jorigné, whose father had resigned as mayor in 1848, one or two reliable men – owner-farmers from the north of the commune, and some tenant farmers from the south of the commune where he owned most of the land.

Only two actions of the council need be noted to show the way things were tending to go.

Since the commune had a population of over five hundred, it was called on to establish a school for girls in accordance with the provisions of the *Loi Duruy*. The municipal council, at a meeting held on 29 October 1876, refused to do so, arguing that its resources were inadequate. 'It is impossible,' it stated, 'to find in Mazières any house or site suitable for a school.' Asked to choose as teacher between a lay woman or a member of a religious order, it unanimously preferred the latter. Notice this unanimity. This was the moment in time when the campaigns of Jean Macé and the League for Education were preparing minds in France to accept the passing of laws a few years later which were to organize a system of free, compulsory and secular education. It was also the period when Monsignor Freppel was making every effort in Western France to maintain tradition in all its strength.

In 1876 the school teacher, Popineau, who we know was held in so high esteem by M. Pouzet and whose devotion to his work has been noted, asked for a transfer because of the mayor's hostility. He had too great an influence in the village and was too attached to the Pouzet family and the ideas it stood for.

M. de Tusseau's authority, based as it was on the firm support of his tenant farmers and on the great influence of the priest, might have held out even after the failure of Marshal Mac-Mahon's attempted coup in 1877 and in spite of the opposition of a section of the town and the rather timid disapproval of some of the farmers, had there not been within the commune itself as adversary a leading citizen, well-educated and deter-mined, who stood as a rallying point for the opposition. He was the son-in-law of Dr. Pouzet, M. Eugène Proust, who had married the doctor's only daughter in 1872. In Mazières he was heir to all the authority surrounding the Pouzet family, itself inheriting the authority of the family of the Health Officer Fraigneau. Sprung from a family of country gentry in Vienne, down in the plain, he was to use all his influence in the struggle with M. de Tusseau.

For thirty years the landed aristocracy had left their homes to live elsewhere: M. de Tusseau was born in Poitiers but lived in Paris. When they returned to their ancestral homes they found themselves confronted, even among the common people, by opponents springing from economic and social change and these opponents were united and led by a genuine figure of mark, heir to those who had taken their place during their absence.

This is not to say that M. Proust was a revolutionary character. On the contrary, as far as social reform went, he was strongly conservative. But, unlike his father-in-law, his was not a mind that saw things as they were and approved of them as long as people were content with them, distrustful of any theory which wished to bring about any abrupt change. He had a philosophy of man which he wanted to impose on those who lived near him. He was a passionate anti-clerical and he dreamed of improvement in the life of the poor and humble. Add to that the fact that he followed no profession, that he was an extremely active and pugnacious person, by nature authoritarian and even despotic, and you have force of character added to abstract ideas to create an implacable opponent of M. de Tusseau.

As far as it is possible to tell from a distance, they conducted the fight with the methods best suited to each. During the hard years of 1871 and 1872, M. de Tusseau used to distribute bread every Monday to the poor of the commune and he would give each two sous. Later, even when his wealth was beginning to diminish, at the end of the Sunday service he would send over to the café, where his followers were gathered, for all the copper coins in the place and, standing on the steps of the church, he would throw the coins to the crowd of poor people and urchins.

M. Proust's methods were different. He set up a news agency and I should imagine that it was thanks to him that Gambetta's fiery speeches penetrated into this poor land, and that the orator won such fame and notoriety that his portrait was to be found in many houses, and that one blind man (whom I knew) was called Gambetta the whole of his life. M. Proust also built for himself in the commune of Saint-Marc-la-Lands, but barely 200 yards from Mazières township, a country house on which all the local workmen were employed; he laid out and planted a park, providing work for all the manual labourers.

On the one hand, then, we have generous gifts but gifts which sometimes might humiliate those who received them and, in any case, were considered by them to be their due. On the other, propaganda based on a motive whose stimulus was beginning to be felt – i.e. work.

The forces of tradition were balanced. On the one side was the noble aristocrat, supported by the priest – a sure and solid tradition; on the other side was the genuine bourgeois with no 'de' to his name, inheriting the influence gained by his father-in-law during the absence of the aristocrats. The bourgeois was going to win; but he would not win without a struggle.

In 1878, no fewer than four elections were required before the council could be formed. On 6 January, M. de Tusseau and all the candidates on his list were elected.[5] But he was suspended from fulfilling his functions as mayor and the election declared invalid by order of the Prefect on 24 January. He had had his ballot papers printed on special paper (lined blotting paper) which was easily recognizable and the constable had withheld the opposing list of candidates.

On 10 February 274 electors voted: M. de Tusseau obtained 164 votes and M. Proust 107. Eight candidates from the Petit-Chêne squire's list were elected; four from that of the notables of Mazières. But thirteen ballot papers were invalidated on the grounds that they bore strange and recognizable signs and the election was declared void. On 24 March fresh elections were held and 274 voters returned eight councillors from M. de Tusseau's party, five from M. Proust's. The Prefect's office appointed as mayor and deputy mayor two farmers from M. de Tusseau's party. One – the Mayor – was a well-to-do land-owner from the north of the commune, named M. Guichard. There were seven councillors from M. de Tusseau's party (M. de Tusseau himself and six farmers, of whom only one came from the north of the commune) and five belonging to M. Proust's. In 1879, following supplementary elections, two candidates from M. Proust's party were elected and M. Guichard resigned as mayor.

By official order dated 2 December 1879 M. Proust was appointed mayor. M. de Tusseau remained on the council and did all he could to make things difficult. M. Proust refused to discuss any of the motions he proposed. On 9 January 1881 fresh elections were held. M. de Tusseau was not re-elected: all

M. Proust's candidates, except one, were successful. We now find on the council artisans and shopkeepers from the township, more important tenant-farmers and owner-farmers judiciously shared by both the north and south of the commune. Joy was unconfined in the town: a firework display was held and an effigy of the Comte de Tusseau was burnt.

four

The school

What had happened to the school during these thirty years? What effect had all these events had on it to assist or slow down its progress? What part had it been able to take in them?

In 1848 the mayor of Mazières considered, as we have seen, that the most urgent work to be undertaken was the construction of roads and the repair of the presbytery: the school could wait. However, in 1853, when the Emperor had made available a grant of two million francs as an encouragement for the communes to undertake schemes in aid of the unemployed, there was talk of building a school at Mazières. Plans and estimates were drawn up and on 8 January 1854 the council

> in consideration of the fact that it is absolutely essential to build a school at Mazières as promptly as possible because the building in use at the moment as a school and which the commune rents at high cost is most inconvenient, quite inadequate in accommodation and that there is no possibility of finding alternative accommodation,
>
> And considering that the commune owns land suitable for the building of a school,
>
> approved unanimously the plan and provisional estimate of 9,000 fr. presented by the Departmental Architect dated 19 December.

On 14 March 1854 the council requested financial aid towards the cost of building the school. In this way it would be able to offer work for the needy on preliminary operations pending the

final formalities of approval. A list of their earlier efforts was
provided:

2,500 fr. for the presbytery
12,000 fr. for the church
400 fr. for the clock
1,800 fr. as assistance to the poor during the winter.

6,000 francs was voted for the school. Construction began
during 1855. A resolution of 16 October 1855 states that it was
almost completed. A further resolution of 25 October 1857
considers that the work has been well and truly done and that
the building offers every guarantee of permanence and solidity.
The vote had been overspent by 2,500 francs but this excess was
considered justifiable.

This school still exists. It stands half-way up the slope on the
road to Parthenay. The school house consists of two large
rooms on the ground floor, one of which serves as a kitchen/
dining-room: there is a bedroom on the first floor. The teacher
also had the use of a large woodshed and an immense garden.[1]
Today all this seems very small and ill-arranged: in 1856 the
peasants must have looked on it as almost a palace. The school
itself comprised a small playground and one classroom which
the pupils reached (and still reach) only by passing in front of
the teacher's house.

Teacher Thébault occupied it for only one year, because he
left in 1856.

The enrolment: its geographical and social distribution

The year 1856–7 will serve us as a convenient starting-point.
The material progress that we have been noting had not yet
begun; only the roads had been built. The teacher was a
village man and we know about him.

In 1856 there were 48 pupils on the school register, attending
for periods varying from two months to a year.

17 were children of artisans or shopkeepers in the town;
1 the son of a carter living in a village;
6 sons of day labourers;
3 sons of millers;

1 son of a weaver;
20 sons of farmers, all from villages in the north of the
commune or from the borders of the town.

Now, in the commune there were 174 children of school age
(94 boys and 80 girls); only 42 attended school – more or less[2] –
34 boys, 8 girls. Thus 132 had never set foot inside the school –
60 boys, 72 girls. A certain amount of importance was therefore
attached to the education of boys since a good proportion of
them had attended school, even if for only a couple of months.
Little importance was given to girls' education. The eight little
girls who did go to school may be listed as follows:

1 daughter of a baker in the town;
1 daughter of a ropemaker in the town;
1 daughter of a blacksmith in the town;
1 daughter of a poor day labourer from Beugnon village;
1 daughter of a farmer living in a place called Petite Ville;
2 daughters of a miller;
1 daughter of a roadman living at Ternant village.

Thus only one daughter from among the farmers.[3]

We will now make a closer study of the distribution of the
boys according to the places where they lived and the work of
their parents.

In the town there were 16 boys of school age. Two were not
enrolled at the school: they were the sons of the justice of the
peace and a wealthy landowner and must have been brought
up in Niort or Parthenay. The 14 others were all enrolled and
attended very regularly *for the whole year*. They were all children
of artisans or small shopkeepers, except for two from very poor
families and who were admitted to school without fees. Thus,
the attendance of boys from the town was excellent.

In the villages to the north of the commune there were 35
boys: 11 attended school, 25 did not. Of the 11 at school three
were admitted free (two were sons of day labourers, one of a
wheelwright); one was the son of a carpenter/farmer; the rest
were the sons of peasant farmers. The registration was, therefore, over 30 per cent but most of them attended very irregularly and then only during the winter months.

In the villages and farms in the south-west of the commune
there were 43 boys of school age: only nine went to school.

Of these nine, one was the son of a well-to-do landowner, two were sons of road-workers (at Ternant) and one the son of a carpenter. The remaining five came from peasant families.

Admittedly the southern villages and farms were a little further from the town than the northern villages but I have already pointed out that we need to bear in mind the concept of distance at that time. Moreover, from the villages nearest to the school, like Roulières, only one boy (out of three) was enrolled.

Also, it can be shown that this contrast in school attendance, as between children from the town or northern villages and those from the south, depended on the attitude of the parents rather than on economic position.

In 1858, the mayor of Mazières opened a subscription fund in aid of the poor of the commune. All the well-off people made it a duty to subscribe. M. Pouzet headed the list with a gift of 1,000 livres of bread and was followed in this by his predecessor in office, now his deputy, M. Jorigné, and by the squire (no longer resident) of Petit-Chêne, M. de Tusseau. Apart from the mayor and his deputy, the town provided only seven subscribers: the tax inspector (400 livres of bread); the justice of the peace (300 livres); the notary (200 livres); the veterinary surgeon (200 livres); the police sergeant (50 livres); one gendarme (50 livres); a shopkeeper (50 livres); the rope-maker (40 livres); a grocer (40 livres).

Of these subscribers only three had children of school age; the two grocers and the rope-maker. Their children went to school.

The villages in the upper part of the commune provided ten donors, all peasant farmers, giving between 100 and 50 livres each. In the villages and farms in the southern part there were 27 subscribers but none gave more than 100 livres: many offered only 50 or even 30 livres.

Only one of the independent farmers from the north, Guichard of La Mimaudière (who gave 500 livres of bread), had children of school age: he had a son aged 11 who never missed school except at harvest and ploughing time – July, August, September and October – and a 12-year-old daughter who attended school for the whole year.

Fourteen prosperous farmers from the south of the commune who had given bread had children but only four families sent them to school and then only for seven or three months; none for the whole year.

This is the significant point: all children in the town, from rich or poor families, attended school and for the full year; the children of a prosperous landowner in the north also went to school for nearly the whole year; but only a few children of the prosperous farmers in the south were enrolled – most did not attend at all.

A close study of the military conscript lists and the way in which the illiterate were separated from those who could read leads to similar conclusions. From 1859 to 1869 92 conscripts were called up in the Mazières commune: 39 were illiterate, all being peasant farmers or farm labourers, except one – a ropemaker. Among those who could read, write and count there were 14 artisans and 39 peasant farmers. From 1871 onwards illiterates are the exception and they are all peasants or farm labourers.

Nevertheless, as we have already seen, new economic and social forces were about to transform this old countryside in the 1860s.

A farm school was in operation at Petit-Chêne. It only accepted youths with some education ... What went on there and what was spoken about was not for poor peasants. And yet Masse from La Jaunelière and others went to see what went on and to hear what was said about it. A small, new wind coming from afar was beginning to blow over the country.

Land clearance was beginning. But it is not enough just to clear land: one must work out whether the clearance brings in a good return. New farm implements were being bought and they were costly. In the end it would perhaps be an economy but how could one be certain if one did not know how to reason things out and do one's sums? The most ignorant, that is to say the majority, evidently relied on the experience of the more prosperous and better educated. They copied them full of wonder at their knowledge and began to think that, even in their own sphere of activity, it would be a good thing to be able to think things over, pen in hand. Some of them, still very few – those who could read – obtained employment as postmen or road-workers and, among large families, this meant more room for the children.

Also, since that terrible year of 1855 when there had been

almost complete destitution, people began to hope, despite a mediocre harvest in 1859, that they would be able one day to rise out of their poverty. They had more things to sell. The markets at Champdeniers and Parthenay from whence produce was sent to Paris by the railway at Niort and Saint-Maixent were very busy. The roads were good. People travelled often to market where they met many folk and could chat with them. Those who could read the notices were much admired: those who could read the *almanach* and books on agriculture which gave good advice were envied. Little by little, everyone came to accept the idea that it would be useful to know how to read and count and also that it is a good thing in itself. After all, it might not be impossible, if a little trouble was taken, for the children to gain these benefits.

All this might have remained a vain hope or, at least, have come about only very slowly, despite the fine new school, if there had not been a change of teacher. But the authorities were beginning to be worried at the slackness of M. Thébault. The report on the schools in the Parthenay *arrondissement* for 1855 notes: 'The teacher at Mazières is a man of little energy; the local authority requests his transfer.'

In 1856 M. Thébault was moved to Saint-Georges-de-Noisne and was replaced by a young teacher named Bertout who had just qualified from the *Ecole Normale* at Parthenay. He was not to stay long at Mazières – for barely eighteen months – at the end of which time he resigned. He must have found, in common with many other teachers, more lucrative employment.

A good schoolmaster

On 29 April 1858 the mayor of Mazières was advised that 'by a Departmental Minute dated 28 of this month, M. le Préfet de Deux-Sèvres had appointed as schoolmaster for the commune of Mazières-en-Gâtine le sieur Popineau (Jean-Victor), schoolmaster in the commune of Marigny'.

On 4 May M. Popineau came to Mazières, where he 'swore obedience to the constitution and loyalty to the Emperor' and was installed as teacher for the commune. He was to remain at Mazières until 1876 and all his pupils would remember him with gratitude, admiration and affection. It can be said that, thanks to him, the latent forces then ripening in the area which would sooner or later have compelled the establishment of an efficient school came into full bloom at once, at the right moment.

He was born in 1831, the son of an artisan at Saint-Maixent named Isaac Popineau. He was a student at the Parthenay *école normale* from 1847 to 1850,[4] and this is a point which should be noted. The *Loi Guizot* in 1833 had made provision, together with primary schools in the communes, for teacher training institutions in each *département*. We have seen that this provision had had no noticeable effect as far as the school at Mazières was concerned. But in 1835 the *département* of Deux-Sèvres had established an *école normale* at the only suitable place – Parthenay – and now this training college was about to permit, in 1858, the realization at Mazières of the intentions of the law of 1833.

Furthermore, M. Popineau was born at Saint-Maixent, that is to say, in a small town in the plain of Deux-Sèvres where the presence of a certain number of Protestants among a majority of Catholics had, because of the controversies to which this led, maintained a certain activity of mind and often a certain moderation in belief.

It happened, too, that he was a student at the training college from 1847 to 1850, that is, during a revolutionary period when staff and students were in a kind of ferment. In particular there had been difficulty in maintaining morning and evening prayers and it was only because they were compelled to that the students continued to repeat their Paternoster.[5]

It seems, therefore, highly probable that, together with the professional competence which would soon show itself and the intellectual and moral qualities which would win him the esteem of the whole population and particularly that of the mayor,[6] M. Popineau brought to Mazières a certain independence of mind. Remember that M. de Tusseau was to cause him to leave in 1876.

He performed his duties meticulously. I have found in the school log-book, which he kept most carefully, many references to religious education. He took his pupils to church on Sundays: he sang mass. He would never have inspired confidence in the parents if he had done otherwise: and his success was complete.

Eighty pupils had been enrolled in 1856 under M. Thébault. In 1857 the number rose to 98 with M. Bertout, and fell to 83 in 1858 with M. Bertout and M. Popineau. But it became 105 in

1859, 135 in 1860 and remained around that level until 1870. The following are the figures of school enrolment for these ten years:

1860	135 including 10 indigent			
1861	128	,,	12	,,
1862	137	,,	17	,,
1863	140	,,	18	,,
1864	125	,,	14	,,
1865	126	,,	17	,,
1866	129	,,	17	,,
1867	137	,,	17	,,
1868	133	,,	19	,,
1869	140	,,	23	,,

The efforts made by Duruy at the Ministry of Education this time had immediate and direct effect at Mazières. The teaching of history and geography was introduced: I have found records of marks given to pupils in history and geography from 1867 onwards.

Most importantly, classes for adults were started following a letter from the Sub-Prefect to the Mayor, dated 11 October 1866 – a curious letter by its 'democratic' tone:

Monsieur le Maire,

A circular from M. le Préfet dated 19 July, included in No. 16 of the prefecture gazette, has drawn our attention to classes for adults.

In France, in the near future, it will behove our dignity as premier nation in the world that every citizen should know how to fill in his voting paper, that every workman should be able to keep his own accounts and, indeed, that all should be in a position to be able to read some work of value to his profession or to his mind. Adult classes alone can fulfil this magnificent aim by permitting all who have grown to manhood and were deprived during their childhood of any primary education to remain no longer disinherited of all its benefits.

I draw your closest attention once again, M. le Maire, to the encouragement which should be given to these evening classes during the long winter nights; and I invite you to call a meeting of the Council as early as possible for this purpose and to call upon the members to vote the necessary funds as indicated in the circular from the prefecture referred to above.

The Emperor's government attaches the greatest importance to the success and development of classes for adults.

The Municipal Council resolved as follows:

Adult Classes.

Today, 21 October 1866, the members of the Municipal Council of the commune of Mazières have held a special meeting at their usual venue, the Town Hall, under the chairmanship of M. le Maire for the purpose of drawing the attention of the Council to the value of classes for adults and to vote the funds necessary for the success and development of these classes.

Present: Mm. Jorigné, Dupond, Cathelineau, Chabauty, Guichard, Girard and Pouzet, mayor.

The Mayor, as chairman, submitted to the Council the letter from the Sub-Prefect of 11 inst. and explained that, immediately after receiving the letter, he discussed this course for adults with the communal schoolmaster, that the latter, whose zeal for all that might improve public education is beyond all praise, has assured him that the course would commence at Mazières on 1 November next, that it would be open from 6 p.m. to 9 p.m. and that he requested no subsidy from the commune for it but that, if the Municipal Council was willing to vote 30 francs, the amount required for heating and lighting for the class, he would admit without fee those indigent pupils whom the communal administration would like to send to him.

The Council, sensible of the great benefit which must result for all from popular education widely spread throughout the countryside, recognizing moreover how M. Popineau, the communal schoolmaster, carries out all his functions with zeal and devotion, as testified by the ever-growing success of his flourishing school, is of the unanimous opinion to grant M. Popineau a subsidy of 30 francs to meet the cost of lighting and heating for the class and to raise this sum from the funds of the commune.

This resolution has a very local accent. The Council is very 'sensible of the great benefit which must result for all from popular education widely spread throughout the countryside'; but particularly it 'recognizes how M. Popineau, the communal schoolmaster, carries out his functions with zeal . . .'. Its opinion would certainly have been very different if, instead of a first-rate teacher, they had had to deal with an idle or incompetent or even an average teacher. Thus it is that liberal and *abstract* ideas as conceived by politicians cannot be translated into action unless there are men on the spot who enjoy the esteem and trust of the people upon whom these ideas are intended to operate, first to explain their purpose and then to apply them. This is to say that progress could not be swift: it was in part due to the *Loi Guizot*, partly to the creation of the *Ecole Normale* at Parthenay and also because economic and social conditions in the Mazières commune were ripe for this new step, that the adult classes envisaged by Duruy in 1866 could be brought into operation.

The Law of 10 April 1867 made the establishment of girls' schools compulsory and required the Departmental Council to fix their number according to communes. The same law created 'hamlet schools' in those communes covering a very extensive area: these schools would be in the charge of assistant teachers, male or female. It also broadened the scope for free education for 'all children whose parents are unable to meet the cost of the monthly school fee'.

The Municipal Council at Mazières resolved as follows:

The School and Adult Classes.
In the year 1867, on 28 July, the Municipal Council of the commune of Mazières met under the chairmanship of the Mayor in special session as required by the Sub-Prefect on 12th of this month.

Present: Mm. Chabauty, Jorigné, Guichard, Dupond, Girard, Rougier and Pouzet, Mayor.

The chairman explained that, in order to ensure as from 1 January 1868 the implementation of the Law of 10 April last concerning primary education, it is necessary for the Municipal Council to decide at once on the following points: (1) the number of boys' schools, mixed schools and girls' schools; hamlet schools; and adult classes which should be opened or retained in each commune.

The Council, being of the opinion that the requirements of primary education can be fully satisfied by the establishment of separate institutions for each sex and by the continuation of adult classes, expresses the wish that a separate school for girls be established after an interval of a period of two years since, by that time, the loan raised for the building of the present school will have been redeemed.

(2) The amount of allowances to be granted to the headmasters and headmistresses of communal adult classes. By reason of the services rendered by the teacher during the last adult course in admitting several pupils voluntarily without fee and animated with the desire of maintaining the success of the course, the Council allocates to the teacher, as an allowance, the sum of 30 francs for the cost of lighting and heating the class.

(3) The fixing of a rate of school fees to determine the final salary of the master or mistress. The Council approves a fee of 10 francs p.a. for each exempted pupil but would prefer an annual fee which would be more convenient for payment at monthly rates.

It is worth noting that the number of pupils exempted from fees rose from 17 in 1867 to 19 in 1868 and 23 in 1869. The Municipal Council was parsimonious in implementing the Ministry's instructions. The girls' school was not to be built until much later. Nevertheless the number of pupils at the school after 1870 increased continually:

1869	140	1873	209
1870	151	1874	221
1871	160	1875	234
1872	189	1876	250

The fee revenue from this kind of enrolment, modest though it was, gave the schoolmaster a reasonable salary. Already in 1860 M. Popineau received 1,123 francs: by 1875 this had risen to 2,325 francs. The regard in which he was held in the countryside must have contained something of the respect paid to success, to those who have managed to make money and find themselves a really good job. This is the tone, it seems to me, of the resolution passed on 21 October 1866 confirming the continuing success of M. Popineau's school 'which is thriving'. He was a shopkeeper whose trade was of a rather special nature, something like a chemist, who had done well in his business.

A sharp increase in numbers after 1870

We will now try to explain why the enrolment increased rapidly after 1870. First, material prosperity, the causes and first signs of which we noticed between 1860 and 1870, showed itself in a more marked fashion. Through the consequences of this material prosperity, through the development of trade, through the effect of more frequent visits to market, people's attitudes changed and became more favourable to the school. I have attempted to show this in explanation of the success of M. Popineau's school between 1860 and 1870.

From 1872 compulsory military service, by removing many young men from their homes, by obliging the illiterate – both parents and soldiers – to correspond with each other only through a third party who could write and read their letters, drew everyone's attention to the value of education.

The increase in the number of minor jobs and the possibility for anyone who had successfully completed primary education to obtain them, the practical use made by some of the knowledge gained at school, on the spot and in their own trade, in improving their circumstances carried a good deal of weight in this sudden increase in school enrolment.

We have just seen the significance of the fact that from 1858 on all the town children went to school and that children from the countryside attended only rarely. Here is something even more significant: the children from town families who attended a school were all able to use what they had learnt in earning a living.

One son of the rope-maker remained a rope-maker like his father; but, towards 1880, he added to his earnings as an artisan the income from an insurance agency which he took on. The other son left the village between 1872 and 1875 to join the railways and returned to die in Mazières in the house inherited from his father.

Of the two sons of the village *marchand*, one stayed a dealer like his father; but he added to his trade a small tinsmith work-shop; the other was killed fighting in the Jura as a lieutenant in the *gardes mobiles*.

The grocer's son carried on the grocery business, but there is no need to emphasize that a shopkeeper, no matter how small his shop may be, must be able to read and keep accounts, especially as his trade develops and if he finds he needs to extend credit to his customers. The innkeeper's son became a captain in the army. Young Guichard (Eusèbe) from La Mimaudière who went to school in 1858 became the estate agent we have mentioned earlier.

On the other hand, none of the children from prosperous farming families in the south of the commune who did not go to school or, if they did, attended very irregularly, changed their situation. Only one, one of those who attended regularly, did stay on in the army where he finished his career as warrant officer.

If now we pass from the list of names of those who made gifts of bread[7] to the list of unfortunates who received them, we find a number of children, some of whom came to school as paupers who did not pay fees. One of them, one of the poorest (his name was Det and he was called Champagne, why I don't know), was to become a railway employee at Paris, like the son of the prosperous rope-maker who had subscribed forty livres of bread – and at the same time as he.

And so, this humble village school at Mazières was making it possible for the most impoverished, as well as the more prosper-ous, to obtain some of those many minor posts of employment which the economic, social and political development of France was causing to multiply and, what is more, to take their place in them on terms of equality. This double take-off must have been the subject of conversation for many years in the village and in the farms of Mazières. Its effect could only have been to add to the prestige of the school in the township: the peasants' indifference was broken down.

Furthermore, the frequent elections held between 1870 and 1880 and the burning political debates of the time which had their echo in Mazières certainly aroused among the electors whose votes were now being solicited a greater sense of their dignity. Those who could read were listened to with close attention.

M. de Tusseau's council does not seem to have discouraged this enthusiasm for the school – quite to the contrary, for the number of pupils admitted without fee rose from 23 in 1870 (Dr. Pouzet's council) to 24 in 1871, 30 in 1872, 33 in 1873, 43 in 1874 (de Tusseau's council). It is true that it returned to 39 in 1875 and to 30 in 1876 at the time when the *République des Ducs* was threatened and was on the defensive. I have been unable to discover the number of pupils not paying fees who were admitted in 1877 at the moment of acute crisis, the new teacher's arrival being accompanied by some disorder in the school records.

The impetus had been given and, with education being more widespread, it became a matter of shame not to be educated.

In 1863 of 69 persons called upon to sign as witnesses at the registry of births, marriages and deaths, 37 could write their name i.e. 58 per cent. In 1873 the figure was 56 in 81 i.e. 69 per cent: in 1883 63 out of 88 i.e. 70 per cent.

In 1853 out of eight conscripts, five were classed as completely illiterate; in 1863 out of 11 conscripts, five were classed as completely illiterate; in 1873 out of 11 conscripts, one was classed as completely illiterate; in 1883 out of nine conscripts, one was classed as completely illiterate and four who could not read.

Parents began slowly to feel guilty if they did not see that their children went regularly to school. All of which goes to explain why, in 1876, M. Popineau had 250 pupils on his school register.

Teaching methods

We may ask how he – the only teacher – could possibly teach so many pupils at one time. In fact, he had as assistant his wife who, under his supervision, looked after the girls while he gave his close and personal attention to the boys.[8] The teaching he gave was very mechanical: it could not have been otherwise since his class usually contained more than 100 pupils, taking into account the absentees owing to such an irregular attendance. He used Noel and Chapsal's grammar which, like a catechism, consisted of a series of rules to be learnt by heart, the only exercises it contained being in the form of question and answer. In geography the pupils had to learn by heart the names of the principal countries with their capitals and chief towns: an old man who was once his pupil could still, a few years ago, recite to me what he had learnt in this way 70 years earlier. It was the same method for history and religious education. In addition he set many problems and gave much dictation and, for the brighter children, plenty of French composition. Thus, a very mechanical kind of teaching. Nevertheless, because it was given regularly and carefully supervised, clever pupils who attended regularly and, after leaving school, continued in the adult classes, reached a standard of knowledge and culture equal to that of the *Brevet Elémentaire*.

M. Popineau does not seem to have bothered to adapt his teaching to the environment, that is to say, to give an agricultural bias. In this matter he limited himself to giving his pupils, as reading book, a work on agriculture edited for the Département of Deux-Sèvres by M. Guillemot, departmental professor of agriculture. In 1845 Jacques Bugeaud had wanted farmers to learn to read so that they might be able to read such works and thereby be led to improve their farming methods. In actual fact, it does not seem that the reading of M. Guillemot's book at school had any remarkable, or even noticeable, effect. Not one of the old peasants whom I interrogated on this point had preserved any precise memory of what they had read. It must be remembered that the most regular attenders at the school were the sons of artisans or shopkeepers in the town: agriculture did not interest them directly. And I cannot imagine that the farmers sent their children to school to learn how to farm better than they themselves. All that has been said earlier leads one to the conclusion that, on the contrary, they sent them because gradually they began to see the importance that words and figures held, and necessarily held, even in a half-closed society like their own and because education allowed a man's dignity to rise: but more because to be ignorant became a mark of inferiority.

M. Popineau was replaced, in 1876, by a teacher named Sausseau. Public opinion was not long in declaring that he was not the equal of his predecessor, and the number of pupils dropped rapidly: 188 in 1877, 183 in 1878, 169 in 1879.

If it went up again to 198 in 1880, this was owing to a rapid increase in the number of fee-free pupils enrolled: 34 in 1878, 41 in 1879, 72 in 1880. This was still far below the global figure of 60 per cent of 'free pupils' for France as a whole, quoted by Jules Ferry in a speech to the Chamber of Deputies on 20 January 1880: 72 out of 198 comes to approximately 36 per cent. As far as Mazières-en-Gâtine was concerned, in spite of the progress that we have seen made over thirty years, it was perhaps too much to hope, as did Jules Ferry for the nation, that 'the attitudes and opinions of the general public would have completely solved, within a period of ten or fifteen years, this question of free education which is as much a philosophical problem as a financial problem', and something which seemed to him to be no more than 'a memory of a state of things condemned by the whole of society'. The sharp increase in the number of free pupils in 1880 was most probably the result of M. Proust's election as mayor. But ingrained habits of economy in the minds of the authorities and of price in the 'customers' of the school would soon have been a brake on the impulse forward.

It is noteworthy, nevertheless, that M. de Tusseau had paid fees for more than twice as many pupils as M. Pouzet – even three times as many in 1874 – and that M. Proust who, with certain differences that have been remarked, reflected M. Pouzet's ideas, accepted almost six times as many (74 as against 13) – and this at a time when there was a good deal more general prosperity. It is a clear indication that the school was beginning to be an accepted part of life and custom. This was so true that a teacher of average ability was still able to enrol 126 fee-paying pupils and that several better-off families, both artisans and farmers, wishing to find a better teacher for their sons, sent them to boarding schools in Parthenay.[9]

Conclusion

A number of influences had thus combined to ensure that the school would be a success: economic and social changes which modified the original indifference of the peasants; the arrival at Mazières in 1858, just at the moment when these changes were beginning to make themselves felt, of an excellent teacher trained at an *école normale*. The unforeseen coincidence of a number of laws and a whole variety of events made their weight felt also: the 1833 law for primary education which required the *Département* to establish training colleges; the 1836 law which organized the French road system; agricultural shows;

the introduction of machinery into agriculture; the building of a railway in the region; the increase in the openings for employment; the 1870 war; the 1872 law on recruitment; the political ferment between 1875 and 1878. The success of the school was the result of all these laws, all these events and many others too.

Before 1860 attendance had been extremely irregular, which means that its first pupils reached adulthood in any numbers only between 1875 and 1880. But after that date it was to take its full place in the course of events. So, having attempted to analyse in this chapter the reasons for its success which we have seen to be much more a consequence than a cause, we will now examine in the next chapter the extent of its influence in the commune between 1880 and 1914.

part three

From 1882 to 1914
The school: the cause
of economic, social
and moral development

one

Economic development

Work on the construction of the railway line from Bordeaux to Paris via Salutes, Thouars and Chartres came within the boundaries of Mazières commune in 1881. As might be expected, this was a most important date in the history of the commune.

Many resolutions since 1860 had demonstrated the interest taken in the region in the building of a railway. In particular, in 1866, the Mazières-en-Gâtine town council had been asked to associate itself with the request of the Parthenay council for the construction of a line between Poitiers and Nantes. The Parthenay council resolution emphasized the progress made in agriculture and the difficulties experienced in transporting produce. The opening of the lines between Saumur and Nantes and between Poitiers and La Rochelle 'had destroyed the natural pattern of communication'. The previously busy traffic between Nantes and Poitiers, Saumur and Niort had been ruined and Parthenay, which was at the centre of this traffic, was suffering considerably from this. The remedy was to build a line between Poitiers and Nantes through Parthenay and Cholet. It would then be possible to send out through Nantes cattle, grain, flour and wool and, through Poitiers timber, cattle feed and foodstuff. Mazières, of course, associated itself with this plan which would put the nearest station – Parthenay – only 15 kilometres from the town.[1]

On 6 February 1870 we learn from a council resolution that the railway from Poitiers to Nantes may be regarded as an accomplished fact. The council supported the request of the

Deux-Sèvres departmental council for a line from Niort to Le Mans.

On 14 May 1871 there was fresh discussion on the same subject: the line from Niort to Le Mans having been abandoned, a request was made for a line between Niort and Parthenay via Champdeniers and Mazières. A good many local interests must have been concealed in these successive requests. The construction of a double-track main line would satisfy even the most exacting demands.

Construction work between Champdeniers and Mazières, particularly on the borders of Mazières, presented difficulty. Cuttings had to be excavated to reduce slopes; bridges had to be built across the many streams flowing through the countryside. For more than two years the town and villages near the line were crowded with labourers. The meanest hovels were rented as lodgings for the men and the cafés did a roaring trade. It was a time of great excitement for the whole area. The Sunday walk was an occasion to go and see the line being built. The uncouthness, constant drunkenness and habits of the workers (several of whom were not French) shocked the local people.[2]

The station was built just over a kilometre from the town, in spite of the expressed wish of the council[3] that it should be closer, where the Niorteau level crossing now is. A road had to be made to reach the station and this was some time in being done. On several occasions the council protested at the delay.[4] After getting the road they asked for express trains to be stopped at Mazières[5] – something out of the normal, but a happy chance for us since because of it we are able to learn that Mazières–Verruyes station had sold 4,500 tickets in its first year, producing a revenue of 8,713 fr. 65. This opportunity of travelling quickly (it took only 25 minutes to reach Parthenay instead of two hours) and comfortably – and, it should be added, cheaply for the cost of a third-class return ticket from Mazières to Parthenay was 1 fr. 10 – was to bring about a profound change in the peasants' attitudes. I have collected many stories of their marvelling at the engines, of their fear of getting into a train and of their general apprehension.

Meanwhile, on 10 February, the council had asked for the station to be opened for slow trains. On 19 May 1886 it requested and was granted the building of a goods yard and a loading bay for cattle. 'If there is one station on the Niort-Saumur line,' read the resolution, 'where cattle loading facilities are essential, it is most certainly at Mazières, the centre for the production of the important Parthenay breed.' The station became a focus of activity; by 1886 two cafés had been – or were being – built.

The opportunities for export created by this railway line brought about an economic transformation in the country, a transformation aided (it should be noted) by improvement in the secondary roads. A resolution of the town council on 20 May 1883 classed no fewer than five roads as *chemins communaux*. Right up to 1895 every year relatively important sums were voted for the improvement and upkeep of the roads. All the villages served by these roads were thereby able to participate more easily in the growing commercial activity.

As early as 1890 one of the station café-owners and a work-man in the town, gifted with energy and possessing enough primary education, set up as apple merchants. Until that time the many orchards of the region had hardly constituted a source of revenue. The peasants made cider from the fruit or fed it to the pigs, selling only the best at market – they were *pommes clochard*, highly prized in the district. But there were very few outlets and most of the fruit was lost. Now it was possible to send their apples by train as far as Paris or Bordeaux, where the better fruit fetched as much as 20 fr. or 30 fr. per 100 kilogram. Thirty tons of dried or fresh fruit were despatched from the Mazières station in 1885.[6]

A co-operative dairy

Later, an event of major importance – on 1 January 1895 a co-operative dairy was opened near the station. Until then the only use made of the cows' milk was to feed the calves. It is true that a certain amount of butter was made by stirring cream for a long, long time in stone pots. This inferior kind of butter and eggs were sold to a poultry trader who visited the villages at fixed times during the week: but there was little profit in it. There was only a small quantity for sale, and as the butter still contained plenty of whey and quickly went rancid, it fetched only a low price. These resources could only be developed through a concentration of production and an industrialization of processing.

Now, several years earlier, co-operative butter dairies had

been established in the surrounding lowlands at Surgères, in the Charentes country at Beauvoir and in the Niort plain. The number of cows in the region had risen. The permanent use of lime gradually rid the grazing of the wild garlic which gave an unpleasant taste to the butter. The station offered good facilities for export. M. Proust, whose authority was now undisputed, determined in the nineties to profit from all these favourable circumstances by establishing a co-operative dairy which would still further increase his influence and bring more prosperity to the region.

It was not an easy undertaking: forty years earlier it would have been impossible to contemplate. In 1849 the government was anxious to organize throughout France 'Philanthropic or Mutual Aid Societies'. 'The considerable benefits which have been gained from these societies in the towns endowed with them,' wrote the Sub-Prefect at Parthenay to the mayor of Mazières on 26 July 1849, 'prove conclusively that they contribute naturally to the improvement of the workers' lot. The trial made in the town of Parthenay has been crowned with success and today it is recognized that the society renders great service.' The mayor of Mazières, having omitted to reply, received a reminder on 17 October 1849. He wrote three days later, saying:

> On returning after a few days' absence, I have found your letter of 17 inst. in which you request a reply to your letter of 26 July concerning the establishment of a Mutual Aid Society in Mazières.
>
> I asked the Deputy Mayor in my absence to call a meeting of the town council, which he did. But, after submitting your letter of 26 July to the council, he did not frame any resolution although the council was unanimous in rejecting the proposal because the country people, being still too ignorant, are unable to understand the value of such an association.
>
> If you wish for a resolution in this sense, would you please be good enough to write to me again and I will at once call a meeting of the council.

The central government made a fresh effort in 1854: 'The Sub-Prefect of Parthenay reminds[7] the mayor of Mazières of the letter which he had the honour to write to him on 31 August last concerning the creation of a Mutual Aid Society for his commune and would be grateful for an immediate reply.'

Dr. Pouzet replied on 2 January as follows:

> Yesterday I consulted the Municipal Council for the third time on the subject of the creation at Mazières of a Mutual Aid Society. It remains of the same opinion that there is no point in organizing such a society since the essential bases are completely lacking in Mazières commune. The rural workers do not understand the advantages of these associations. I have spoken to several persons who have replied that they would not wish to have anything to do with one. I have been able to find only a few honorary members who will agree to subscribe 50 centimes a month: I do not feel that we could achieve anything of value with such small resources. This is also the opinion of M. le Juge de Paix. If, however, M. le Sous-Préfet, you feel that we should make further efforts, with the support of M. le Curé, we will do what you think fit.

In 1890 the situation was quite different. People were now buying and selling more; they had the habit of dealing with money; their outlook had broadened; many had been to school. The initiative which was to lead to the setting up of a co-operative butter dairy instead of coming from on high at a far distance from people unknown, now began within the district itself – not indeed from the peasants but from a person of repute in the district whose word carried great weight.

Nevertheless, there was much prejudice to overcome among these peasants who mistrusted and were jealous of each other. They would provide the milk and carry it to the roadside where the milk-carts would pick it up – agreed: they could understand that butter made by machine would be better than their own home-made butter and that it could fetch a higher price; the idea that the milk-carts would bring back the whey which they could use to fatten their pigs was very attractive. But – who would guarantee that all that money from the butter would go to the people who had provided the milk? Doubtless there would be representatives who would supervise the accounts and M. Proust was rich enough not to be tempted to rob them. But, then, one never knows. . . . Moreover, politics were involved.

M. Proust's opponents went round saying that he was doing all this in his own interests. Nevertheless, rules were drawn up, revised and adopted at a general meeting on 11 February 1894 attended by the first 140 members of the co-operative. A board of management, with M. Proust as chairman, was constituted, composed of leading figures in the region and delegates elected from among the farmers in whom they could trust. The necessary capital was lent by M. Proust and the better-off farmers. A suitably large site was purchased close to the station. Building could begin and, indeed, was started at once. The greatest difficulty was to find water, for the building was on the fault covered by the alluvial deposit mentioned at the beginning of this study.[8] There remained one essential problem to be solved: where to find a man capable of managing the works, of drawing up and keeping a complicated system of accounts, of controlling the milk transporters and of inspiring confidence among the members. M. Proust – and in this he faithfully reflected the feelings of his constituents – distrusted 'foreigners'. He looked for his man among those in the town who, thanks to M. Popineau's teaching, had acquired twenty years earlier an adequate education, and he offered the post to the clog-maker's son who had been stopped from joining the railways by his father's veto. This man worked with his father, but he felt the trade offered no future[9] and regretted having stayed in Mazières: he was no longer only twenty years old. He quarrelled with his father and became the managing director of the dairy.

Similarly, for the collection of milk in the surrounding communes, ten milkmen were found in the area, each owning a horse and cart and able to write down on a form the number of litres of milk supplied daily by each member,[10] together with a butter-maker and a stoker but, for the post of inspector,[11] they had to have recourse to a former gendarme and, later, to a man who had been coachman to M. Goirand, the squire of Petit-Chêne.

Success was immediate. From the first year the number of members (originally 140) rose to 558, owning 1,700 cows. 1,700,000 litres of milk were treated; 85,000 kilogrammes of butter made; net receipts rose to 230,000 francs, of which nearly 150,000 were shared out to members. In 1896 the membership was 713; in 1897, 902; in 1898, 950; in 1899, 990. In that year the number of cows supplying milk to the dairy was 3,950 and 3,665,311 litres of milk were treated; 173,466 kilogrammes of butter were sold at 2 fr. 58 the kilo. The members received 0 fr. 109 per litre of milk supplied, a total of 388,651 francs.[12] The carriers received 37,493 francs and the employees at the dairy 5,959 francs. The remainder of the receipts was devoted to the maintenance of the machinery and building and to the repayment of loans. This was real wealth for the country.

Many of the members enrolled did not share M. Proust's politics but those of the Marquis de Maussabré, his political opponent who was now Député for Parthenay. In 1899 they formed the majority and, with the Marquis opening two dairies in the district, they forced the calling of a general meeting, which decided on the dissolution of the co-operative dairy.

It was relatively easy to gather together the faithful members and continue with fresh regulations on a more modest basis. But there was a certain Article 26 which reads: 'The dissolution of the union of milk suppliers may only be decided at a general meeting by the majority of members enrolled; in this case, each member will share in the assets and the liabilities in the ratio of the amount of milk which he shall have supplied from the commencement.'

Nothing could apparently be more reasonable – or, in reality, more dangerous. In the face of the number of members who demanded their share, the dairy nearly had to be sold. Fortunately M. Proust was wealthy: he set an example of financial aid to the young society and it was able to meet its liabilities. But endless calculations were necessary. Everyone in the town who could count got to work. Throughout a whole winter relays of teams from 8 o'clock to midnight set down the figures; among them the teachers were foremost. It was clearly a matter of unpaid labour and those who devoted their evenings for the benefit of the co-operative dairy had little personal interest in saving it. The peasants, who were so deeply involved, could take no part in this accounting work. For those who undertook it, it was an act of faith which, for a whole year, stirred the emotions of this poor village and for years after those who were its humble heroes loved to talk about it. Their efforts, moreover, were to be crowned with success. In 1900, 2,070,000 litres of milk were treated and, three years later, 3,080,000 litres. In 1904, the price of butter having risen from the 2 fr. 58 per kilo.

in 1899 to 2 fr. 71, sales beat all records, reaching 425,000 francs. The co-operative dairy was saved and, thanks to it, prosperity spread through the countryside. Many *bordiers* and tenant-farmers paid their rents from the price of their milk and with the whey they fattened their pigs. Near to the dairy – as might be expected – a café had been built and, in the town (as we shall see) artisans and shopkeepers profited from the milk-carrier trade. For all this to happen there was needed, in addition to facilities created by roads and railway, the persistent drive and authority of a leading figure who occupied his leisure time in the development of republican ideas, and the presence in the country of a certain number of farmers capable of thinking things over who would not be frightened by the presentation of ideas containing an element of novelty – and, also, some intelligent and warm-hearted men of the common people, sufficiently educated to be able to organize, set in motion and manage as important and complicated a business as this. In short, this country still covered with broom and heath needed what was called in the eighteenth century 'the progress of enlightenment'.[13]

Changes in agriculture and cattle husbandry

In 1850, as we have seen, this Gâtine country had remained, from the point of view of economics, in much the same state as it was in the eighteenth century – that is, a land of slovenly agriculture living chiefly on cattle rearing. The main efforts of farmers, up to 1900, had been on the improvement of crop growing. By that time they had practically completed the clearing of land and had given up the custom of leaving land fallow. The country was in the full flow of agricultural development.

The following figures, taken from statistics compiled in 1903 with quite exceptional care by the teacher/town clerk with the aid of his pupils, are significant:

Out of the total area of 1,904 hectares in the commune, 1,118 were under the plough (under crops or as sown pasture); natural pasture had an area of 225 hectares, rough grazing 317 hectares and woodland 120 hectares. The 1,118 hectares of plough were comprised as shown at the top of the following page.

wheat	290 hectares	potatoes	90 hectares	
maslin	40 ,,	jerusalem		
rye	8 ,,	artichokes	30	,,
barley	10 ,,	mangolds	80	,,
buckwheat	40 ,,	clover	50	,,
oats	160 ,,	lucerne	150	,,
maize	6 ,,	grass	20	,,
beans	2 ,,	fodder crops	30	,,
		(vetch, peas, red clover)		

Compare these with the figures for 1849 quoted on page 84.

wheat	17	hectares
rye	75	,,
oats	55	,,
buckwheat	35	,,
potatoes	55	,,
Total:	237	hectares

A veritable transformation; in fifty years the cultivated area in the commune had quadrupled. Unrewarding crops like rye had been practically abandoned whereas wheat had undergone prodigious expansion and oats, too, had increased enormously. This is clear evidence of a transformation in the economy and in the way of life of the peasants. But there is something still more noteworthy – and this, to a certain extent, provided the basis for the progress in grain growing. New crops (Jerusalem artichokes, mangolds, clover, lucerne, etc.) completely unknown to the farmers of 1850 had been introduced. They opened the door to the stall-feeding, in winter, of animals which formerly had had to find their own food in the fields. They led to this poor land of shepherds changing into a land of farmers and stock-raisers devoting their efforts to improving the yield from their stock. A comparison of the numbers of animals in 1850 and 1903 is illuminating. (See next page.)

The decrease in the number of horses in 1903 (117 instead of 150) is striking: one no longer saw saddle horses ambling along the road – the opportunities for travel offered by the railway enabled the farmers to do without a carriage. Only the more wealthy kept, along with a brood mare, a pony for the trap.

Also, there were far fewer bulls and oxen. Most probably this was a consequence of the sub-division of land and the increase in the number of farms being worked. By 1900, in fact, only the larger farmers bred bulls which they sold at the age of two years as *doublons* for use as working oxen. The *bordiers* mostly raised heifers. The tenant-farmers, too, were the only ones to own oxen; the *bordiers* or small landowners working their own land used their milch cows for ploughing and as draft beasts. In 1850 there were fewer small farms and, moreover, on the one hand the bad state of the roads and, on the other, the difficulties of ploughing with heavy wooden ploughs, meant the almost universal use of draft oxen.

	1850	1903
horses and mares	150	117
		plus 9 mules
		and 6 donkeys
bulls	120	56
oxen	220	144
cows	350	592
heifers	100	532
ewes	400	140
sheep	500	59
he-goats	3	–
goats	50	226
boars	3	5
sows	250	138
pigs	400	346

But in 1903, in spite of the decrease in area given over to stock, there were many more milch cows (592 as against 350) and more than five times the number of heifers and calves (218 of one year and over, 314 of less than one year, according to the statistics). The economic influence of the co-operative dairy made itself felt in this marked increase in milch cows, an increase which was to continue to rise since, in 1913, if the figures for that year are to be believed, there were 608. It was particularly felt in the method of feeding calves, which were separated from their mothers at three months at the most and fed on whey and meal bought in the neighbouring town. The decrease in the number of sheep is accounted for by the disappearance of the *landes* and common pasture land. The increase in goats was due to better communications enabling cheese to be sold at a good price in the Parthenay and Champdeniers markets.

Agricultural machinery

Since 1880, too, working conditions had changed. Until that time the peasants had stuck to using only a sickle for reaping. They sowed their wheat and rye in the furrows: the heavy Gâtine soil drained better that way and the grain was better protected from frost. With a sickle the stalks could be cut close to the ground even in the furrows which would have been impossible with a scythe. But reaping with a sickle was an extremely slow and difficult task and, gradually, the peasants gave up sowing in the furrows and the use of the scythe began to spread. But old men have told me that, right up to 1895, they still reaped with a sickle.

The first machines to be introduced were, it seems, threshing machines. By 1885 the flail or *manège*[14] was in use only in the poorer *borderies*. Contractors, often blacksmiths, had bought threshing machines and had, not without difficulty, persuaded their customers to co-operate and even – which was much more difficult – to agree to a roster. The one who was first to use the machine in one year would be the last on the list the next: rain falls on one or the other purely by chance and so the peasants came to accept taking their turn with the same fatalism.

The first reaping machines became current in the district about 1890. There was still some hesitation in spending large sums of money to undertake work which could be performed in another way and the farmers found the most varied and ingenious pretexts to convince themselves that this kind of expenditure would be useless: the reapers cut only irregularly; they could only be used on very flat land – which was seldom found in Gâtine; they were dangerous – a great stir was caused by an accident to a farm worker who fell off a machine while it was working and cut his foot. For a long time, the smaller tenant-farmers and *bordiers* betook themselves to blacksmiths who owned reapers and who, for an agreed price, would come and cut and harvest their crops for them. It was not until 1904 or 1905 that all harvesting on farms of any size was done by machine, and on the eve of the 1914–18 War there were still only two binders in the district.

The introduction of the Brabant plough, encouraged by numerous practical demonstrations, was comparatively swift. It made the drover redundant and meant one person less to feed. Also around 1900 many trench ploughs and hoeing-machines were bought for the purpose of breaking up the sub-soil without bringing it to the surface; also many root-cutters to lessen the work of the cowmen tending the cattle in the fields during winter.

Fertilizers

The need to rid the fields of wild garlic meant continual and more intense liming of the pasture. The longer stay of the animals in the byres enabled great heaps of manure to be carefully maintained in every farmyard. In addition, it became quite customary to use artificial fertilizers: to begin with, bone meal from the factory at Parthenay or Champdeniers and, later, superphosphates, potash and nitrates. This custom was greatly encouraged by the establishment in 1901 at Mazières of a branch of the Deux-Sèvres Farmers' Union. This powerful organization, which counted among its most fervent members many of M. Proust's political opponents, was cold-shouldered by many farmers. Gradually, however, because no trader in Mazières itself stocked fertilizers, the majority joined the Union and trade increased to such an extent that the grocer/cobbler who at first undertook the management of the depôt found himself obliged to give up his earlier trade and devote himself entirely to the work of the Farmers' Union. This depôt would have had a less rapid success had the manager not been a man of the district possessing the confidence of the local farmers and sufficiently intelligent and educated to be able to keep a relatively complicated set of accounts very competently.

During this period, then, agricultural progress had been quite remarkable and the semi-closed peasant economy that we have been studying was now transformed.

Railway traffic

The exercise of their calling meant that henceforth the farmers were obliged to buy and sell – a change which can be measured fairly precisely from the increase in traffic at Mazières–Verruyes railway station.[15]

The following tables summarize goods traffic for the years 1885, 1890, 1900 and 1910:

Year	Express trains		Slow trains	
	Departures	Arrivals	Departures	Arrivals
1885	6 tons	n.a.	1,208 tons	2,482 tons
1890	33 ,,	(global figure)	1,405 ,,	4,312 ,,
1900	181 ,,	77 tons	2,304 ,,	4,807 ,,
1910	324 ,,	83 ,,	2,867 ,,	6,195 ,,

If the details of this traffic are examined, the tonnage of timber and, particularly, grain despatched can be seen to rise annually:

Year	Timber	Grain
1885	152 tons 500	731 tons
1890	129 ,,	1,006 ,,
1900	300 ,,	1,303 ,,
1910	306 ,,	2,038 ,,

The highest figures among the receipts – and very significantly – are those for fertilizers:

1885	969 tons 500
1890	1,908 ,, 700
1900	1,494 ,,
1910	2,389 ,,

Finally, the following are the figures of receipts of 'manufactured iron and metal and machines' reaching Mazières–Verruyes by slow train:

1885	11 tons 500
1890	11 ,, 200
1900	163 ,,
1910	129 ,,

This was at one and the same time a sign and a cause of changes in the state of mind of the peasants. The school had played its part in this transformation: it was now to profit from it.

Changes in society

Poverty

The incidence of poverty had decreased. Only the farm labourers continued to live a hard life and for years their wages remained very low. In 1865 they received 1 fr. 50 a day during harvest time and 1 fr. at other times. That is for those who were fed at the farm: others were paid an extra 0 fr. 50 a day.[16]

In 1880 an unmarried worker who was hired for the year, was fed at the farm and had his washing done there received 450 francs per annum. In 1900 these rates had not changed. A married worker would hire himself out only during the three summer months, when wages were high. He would receive about three francs for a day's work which began at four o'clock in the morning and ended at ten o'clock at night. In winter he would work by the day or take on piece work – cutting and laying hedges, felling and splitting wood, making bundles of faggots, digging gardens. One of the grimmest of his tasks would be stripping cabbages on those grey, damp, icy days of which there are so many in Gâtine. He received an average of two francs a day and his food. He lived in a humble dwelling in the town or in a village. If his family was large – as was often the case – he found it hard to feed them properly. Ernest Perochon's fine but cruel novel, *Les creux de maisons*, is as true a picture of the farm workers of Gâtine as it is of those of the Bocage.

Towards 1910 wages had risen: an unmarried worker received 600 francs a year, with food, and the farmers were beginning to complain of a shortage of labour which led them to increase their outlay on equipment.[17]

Property ownership

Farm rentals were also rising but less fast than the income of the farmers, except in the case of the small *borderies* which were in great demand. As a result, for example, a farm of seven hectares was leased for 900 francs in 1900 and another of six hectares for 800 francs whilst one of 60 hectares, consisting of pasture land of poor quality and partly covered by woodland, did not reach 3,000 francs. A smaller estate of 40 hectares, but of better soil, was rented for 3,200 francs. The capital value of land rose in similar proportions. The value per hectare of arable land which, as we have seen, was between 1,500 and 2,000 francs in 1880, had mounted to 2,500 or 3,000 in 1910. Land near the station or the town was even more expensive: Mazières market-place, covering one and a half hectares, cost 15,000 francs in 1900.

This meant that the farmers, although less poor than before, were forced to devote most of their resources to maintaining their stock and to purchasing implements, the cost of which was continually rising. They could rarely afford to buy property outright. In fact, only isolated fields or properties of less than five hectares found purchasers. The following table summarizes the changes in landed property between 1880 and 1914:

| | *Owners* | | | | | |
| | Resident in the commune | | | Non-resident | | |
	1880	1900	1913	1880	1900	1913
5 hectares	107	99	101	54	71	85
5–10 hectares	25	16	21	16	20	22
10–20 hectares	6	9	11	7	14	13
20–30 hectares	3	1	3	2	2	1
30–40 hectares	–	1	1	2	4	4
40–50 hectares	–	–	–	2	2	3
50–100 hectares	3	–	–	5	6	4
Over 100 hectares	–	–	–	1	1	1
Total:	144	126	137	89	120	133

This table shows the growth in the number of owners and, consequently, the subdivision of land: in 1880, 233 owners, in 1900, 246 and in 1913, 270. It was the number of small owners that had increased, as shown by the following table:

	1880	1900	1913
5 hectares	161	170	186
5–10 hectares	41	36	43
10–20 hectares	13	23	24
20–30 hectares	5	3	4
30–40 hectares	2	3	5
40–50 hectares	2	2	3
50–100 hectares	8	6	4
Over 100 hectares	1	1	1

The number of owners of more than 20 hectares had hardly decreased from 18 in 1880, 15 in 1900 to 17 in 1913. On the other hand, ownership of land of less than five hectares had greatly increased and similarly the numbers of owners of properties of 10 to 20 hectares (the area of a typical *borderie*). It should also be noted that, although the total number of landowners living in the commune remained more or less the same (144 in 1880, 126 in 1900, 137 in 1913), there were many more owners living outside the commune (89 in 1880, 120 in 1900, 133 in 1913). This is explained partly by the sale of estates (which will be studied below) but also, and above all, it is a sign that medium-sized properties were being subdivided, thereby becoming too small to provide a living for a family and forcing the heirs to depart to live elsewhere.

But all these figures, however significant they may be, still lack the breath of life.

The sale of M. de Tusseau's estate

The sale, between 1881 and 1886, by M. de Tusseau of the properties he owned in the commune permits a more telling analysis of the evolution of rural ownership.

The estates of the De Breuillac family referred to in the first part of this work, the ownership of which went back to at least the sixteenth century, had passed by inheritance at the beginning of the nineteenth century to the Comte de Laurencie and then, almost entirely, to his son-in-law M. de Tusseau. In 1881, only 30 hectares were owned by M. de la Laurencie, grandson of the mayor of Mazières who bore this name and who so meticulously collected statistics of the agricultural resources of the commune, as we have seen in 1826.

It happened that these estates were crossed by the railway line and, in 1882, nearly all were sold to the State. The remainder, about 11 hectares, were bought in 1886 by a Niort lawyer named Feu (Jean-Jacques).

M. Charles de Tusseau had inherited, in 1865, nearly 600 hectares from his father Eusèbe de Tusseau who held them through his wife, *née* de la Laurencie. His father had sold about 200 hectares in 1863 (farms or *borderies* of L'Oucherie. La Soultière, L'Angevinière, Le Moulin de Ternan, Les Brethommières, Le Petit Moulin) to the Chebrou de la Rouillière family living at the house of the Bâton chapel. He bought back part of these lands between 1874 and 1881, so that, by 1884 and 1886, when he decided to sell up what he owned in Mazières, he had almost 600 hectares. In 1884 a small farm, La Soultière (about 50 hectares of good land), was sold to M. Chauvet, a landowner at Contremarche in Petit-Brisse commune. In 1885 a *borderie*,

La Fertière, was sold to M. Nargeot, grocer at Mazières (one of those who had learnt to read in 1858).

In 1886 there was a large sale (nearly 300 hectares) of a whole collection of adjoining farms: Le Chêne-Billon, Le Moulin de l'Oucherie, L'Oucherie, Egray, L'Angevinière. They were bought by M. Dupond, a landowner at Niort. In 1892 the farm and château of Petit-Chêne, former residence of the lords of Mazières, were sold in their turn (about 80 hectares). The purchaser was M. Goirand, a Paris lawyer, *député* for Deux-Sèvres – the son of a humble saddler from Melle – and a former bursar at the Niort lycée. Then, in 1894, M. de Tusseau finally sold the last farm remaining in his possession – Les Brethommières – to MM. Tèze of Thouars.

The aristocracy, owning these estates and passing them down through the line of inheritance, had almost all lived at Petit-Chêne and had interested themselves in the development of agriculture. M. de Tusseau himself, although he was born at Poitiers and lived most of the time in Paris, had founded the farm school. The *procès-verbal* drawn up in the hand of M. de la Laurencie and quoted on p. 28 is evidence of a keen interest in matters concerning the land. It is most probable, too, that the Comtes de Breuillac had personally concerned themselves in former days with the lot of their peasants. The new owners understood nothing of farming. For the most part they lived in towns some way off: what their farmer tenants did could be of no particular concern to them.

The personal links, a legacy from feudal times, which bound the owners to a land which they no longer worked themselves and to the people who undertook this work, were now stretched or broken.

One might consider this to be a step towards the emancipation of the peasantry if the new owners had been less demanding than the old but it was the opposite that happened. M. Dupont is known for having managed his property very much more closely than did M. de Tusseau, and it is worth mentioning that the Petite Soultière estate, which passed by inheritance in 1914 to a big farmer in the commune, very well up in farming matters, was at once put out to *métayage* by the latter. As far as I know, this is the only land in the commune under share-cropping.

Despite the progress made in relative prosperity that we

have noted among the farmers of the commune, in 1885 and 1895 (a century after the Revolution and the sale of national estates, and forty years after the area had been opened to an exchange economy) not one found himself rich enough to participate in this liquidation of property which had belonged for at least three hundred years to the local aristocrat. Only two of the purchasers can be said to have come from the common people: one, M. Nargeot, the son of a well-to-do farming family, had made his money as a grocer; the other, M. Goirand, had by his intelligence been able to move up into the world of business. Both had only been able to arrive at owning land – which is the thing most prized by man and which, despite all appearances, remains the basis of all things – because they had left the land and because, in various degrees, they had gained proficiency in the manipulation of symbols and men.

Progress and specialization in the town

The people who could be seen to have benefited most from the economic evolution were the town-dwellers, those who lived detached from the land as non-producers. This is already clear in the population figures. In 1876 the town had a population of 267 and we have seen how it was beginning to specialize in activities. At five-year intervals it grew as follows:

1881	305
1886	353
1891	373
1896	336
1901	350
1906	362
1911	378[18]

The town had gained more than a hundred inhabitants in thirty years. It had almost doubled since 1851 (378 against 210). Whereas at that time it had been little more than a village rather larger than the rest, it had now become both more important than and, more particularly, very different from the surrounding villages.

On the other hand, the population of the villages and farms had remained practically static.

1876	777
1881	781
1886	835
1891	799
1896	810
1901	816
1906	795
1911	800

In 1851, it should be remembered, the population of these villages and farms was already 760.

The number of landowners in the town living on dividends and rent from their land had decreased: in 1886 there were only seven, in 1896 six and in 1911 three. The doctor was still there but the veterinary surgeon had died around 1900 and his place had been taken by a *vétérinaire empirique,* i.e. unqualified.

Business activity was reflected in the practice of the solicitor whom we find, in 1896, employing a clerk. But the solicitor was soon to be confronted with a serious rival in the same town in the person of a peasant who had made himself an expert in property. Married to the schoolmistress and taught by her, intelligent, industrious and thrifty, he was to become comparatively wealthy. 'Here begins his second million,' people murmured when they saw him buy himself a motor-car.

The number of civil servants increased. In 1886 there were no fewer than six postmen and a postmistress living in the town. In 1896 the number of postmen had fallen to four and, by 1906, to three. But this was because post-offices had been set up or postal-clerk/postmen had been appointed in all the surrounding townships. Any large village composed of twenty houses and a population of sixty served only three times a week could then claim a post-box which would be cleared daily. Nothing illustrates better than this how trade and communications had developed and how the people's horizons had been broadened.

There were still three roadworkers (two roadmen and a foreman), but an inspector of roads had been added. There were still a justice of peace and his clerk, three gendarmes and a sergeant, a tax-collector and a priest. But instead of only one schoolmaster there were three masters and two mistresses. In 1896 three private mistresses appeared on the scene. In that year, too, the name of a registrar appears in the Mazières records. After then only one new public servant was added: in 1911 the tax-collector was given a clerk.

There was a constant increase in the number of workers in the building trade but not of masons. In 1886 there were four masons and eleven labourers; in 1896 four masons and seven labourers; in 1906 five masons and eight labourers; in 1911 six masons and four labourers. There was thus an increase in the number of men setting up on their own account, a sure indication of increased prosperity and also a sign of progress in education. Each master-builder had become a small contractor able to draw up estimates, to carry on business correspondence and keep simple accounts. One of them – and this is a sign of the times – more enterprising than others and possessing a certain amount of capital, had even undertaken the building of houses on land that he had divided into building plots for sale as purchasers presented themselves – a speculative builder, in fact. His enterprise was crowned with success: a small collection of houses halfway between the town and the station provided him with a living. This was a kind of undertaking which would have been impossible to think of 30 years earlier. But the number of building labourers remained constant or decreased. At the same time the houses that were built were of improved design. Other kinds of workmen set themselves up in Mazières. Between 1890 and 1896 a stonecutter came to live near the station, where he had delivered from the Echiré quarries slabs of that fine freestone which embellished the new houses in the town or were carved into tombstones gleaming pure and white among the humble wooden crosses of the old cemetery.

In 1886 a tinsmith had set up business in Mazières. In 1896 he had a workman and also a competitor who, a few years later, employed three workmen. These artisans did not confine themselves to tinning saucepans or laying slabs and fixing drainpipes in the houses: they also installed pumps – which were gradually taking the place of wells – and, in particular, roofed the houses with slates instead of tiles. Because there was a railway station nearby, house building no longer needed to rely only on local material.[19]

With larger houses being built, more openings offered themselves and the number of carpenters and joiners tended to grow. In 1886 three master carpenters employed five workmen; in 1896 there were four employers and five workmen; in 1906 five and six and in 1911 five and seven. It was a splendid time for their trade. They made frames, floors, even staircases, doors, windows, shutters,[20] and there was still not a single piece of furniture in the district (except in the houses of some civil servants or notabilities) which had not been made by their own hands. In ten years, one of them – who employed two workmen – made 40 wardrobes, 40 beds, 50 tables, 10 sideboards, without counting, of course, wall cupboards and corner cupboards, etc. There were still two pit-sawyers at Mazières, two brothers whose sons were to leave them one by one to go as shop-assistants or join the railway; but most of the planks came from the Parthenay sawmill.

It was in 1886 that the registers carried the first reference to a 'grocery and cotton goods merchant' and, in 1896, to a draper. The small shopkeepers, whose first hesitant steps we have noted and who had begun by selling a few pairs of ready-made trousers here and there, now travelled all over the countryside in covered carts piled up with all sorts of goods: groceries, soap, coffee (tea did not come in until later), sugar, cakes, pasta, salt, pepper, haberdashery, writing paper, needles, thread, wool, cotton goods, ribbons, cloth, ready-made clothes, etc.

On the front of the carts, like flags celebrating the victory of imported products over local products, of an exchange economy over a closed economy, were fastened long, light brooms made of millet – a temptation to housewives long condemned to using the old implements made from the local broom plant.

Shops in the town now boasted glass window fronts. A paraffin lamp stood there during the long winter evenings; when the shop door was opened a chime sounded or a little bell tinkled, to be heard at the back. But they were to suffer; after 1905, as far as their customers in the town were concerned, there was competition from the big Paris stores, from the dress-makers, tailors and merchants of Parthenay.

In this way, money from the countryside created work and wealth in the township and, from there, repeated the same action in the larger towns.

In 1886 we still find a clog-maker working on his own and another with three assistants. But the hunchback cobbler mentioned earlier now had a workman and another had set up business, also with an assistant. In 1896 the master clog-maker had only two helpers and by 1906 there were only two clog-makers left, neither employing any workmen. They no longer made the old heavy wooden clogs from start to finish in their own workshop: they now made fancy clogs with uppers made of leather in Parthenay or Niort. Their living came from selling ready-made clogs, slippers . . . and hats. By contrast, the cobblers were on the crest of the wave of prosperity. In 1906 three had established themselves, two with workmen. They not only sold and repaired old shoes but made new footwear for practically the whole of the commune. By 1911 a slight decline had set in. The triumph of factory and town was made manifest in the sight of ready-made shoes on show in the front of the cobbler's shop. He himself had transformed his workroom into a shop and had taken refuge in the corner of his courtyard where he went on repairing shoes.

There were still dressmakers and seamstresses to be found in the township but now, in 1911, a modiste appeared on the scene. This was the sign of a considerable change in the way of dressing. Only the old women continued to wear bonnets and coifs and gradually their dress began to resemble that of the town women. They hardly ever wore *caracos* or cloaks but dresses and costumes instead.

Nearly every woman born after 1880 had given up wearing caps.[21] Most of the time they went bare-headed and on Sundays, for church, wore hats ordered in Mazières from the town, sometimes even from the *grands magasins* in Paris. A modiste and milliner could, therefore, make a good living.

Changes in food habits were no less important. In 1886 there was still only one baker, but a wine-merchant,[22] a butcher and a pork-butcher had set up. In 1896 a beer merchant came along. By 1906 there were two bakers, one with two workmen, the other with one. The peasants had, by this time, practically entirely given up making their own bread. In 1911 we even find a fishmonger at Mazières: she did not sell much first-quality fish but plenty of sardines, mussels or oysters and, in season, melons and grapes.

In 1898 one of the tinsmiths had opened a fine ironmonger's shop. He sold paraffin, coal and wood cooking stoves, coal, buckets, jugs, etc. He was soon copied by his rival – the other tinsmith – and the two shops did well. In 1905 a watchmaker came to live in the town. He tried to increase his income by adding a photography studio, but this was premature. Also, a fellow watchmaker from Parthenay came every Sunday looking for watches and clocks to repair and, after a few years, the former had to give up. On the other hand, a hairdresser (*perruquier*) made a good living.

These are all signs of great change in the way of life of the people of the commune, but progress in agriculture was also reflected in the development of the township. First, there was the appearance by 1886 of wheelwrights whose yards did good business until 1911. In that year all of them employed a workman. The peasants' and milk-carters' vehicles were continually growing in numbers: a harness-maker who started up in 1886 employed a workman in 1896 and two in 1906. Only blacksmiths' numbers went down: in 1886 there were nine, of whom four were their own masters; in 1896 still four masters but only three assistants; by 1906 only two with assistants, the other two worked on their own. The reason for this was probably the presence in a village in the south of the commune of a first-class smith employing several workmen, who also undertook threshing on contract.

In this evolution of the township the most significant fact, both as regards economic development and as regards the part played by the school, is the setting up and development of a grain and seed business by a local young man.[23] Around 1885 the elder son of the clog-maker who, in obedience to his father's wishes, had given up the idea of a military career, had – while continuing to work in the family business – started a small fire insurance office, this being the only form of insurance which could attract clients at the time. This brought him into contact with many farmers and, seeing the progress being made in agriculture and the many facilities provided by the railway, he had the idea of starting a grain and seed business. Because he was an extremely intelligent man he was able to place his orders well, bought first-class stock and found customers throughout the neighbourhood.

Moreover, he was a man who used his brain and never stopped learning more: consequently he gained the confidence of the farmers and became their counsellor and friend to such an extent that often, when they were puzzled about something, they would come to him for advice: 'My wheat hasn't done well. I'm thinking of sowing spring wheat. What do you say?' Or: 'What ought I to plant in that field? It's always very wet.'

Accordingly by 1895 he had to devote himself entirely to insurance and this grain trade. It was partly owing to his influence and to his deep understanding of men and local affairs that the growing of root crops, clover and lucerne made such rapid progress. Towards 1905 he introduced into the district new strains of selected wheat seed which gave a markedly increased yield. Also, in this ancient land formerly so inward looking, he sold groundnut flour, cattle cake and rice from Indochina by the van load. Everyone thought highly of him. It is probable that he rendered more service to his country by staying in his native commune and using his education, of which he had gained the first elements at the primary school, and his rare gifts of intelligence and character than if he had stayed in the army and risen to the rank of officer.

The township, then, had developed and become more specialized. Hardly anyone lived there who was not a public servant, an artisan or a trader. In contrast practically no artisans were left in the villages. In 1911 there was only one carpenter in the big village of Le Beugnon in the north of the commune and one blacksmith (with two assistants) at Petit-Chêne. Only a few craftsmen whose trade was dying out as a consequence of economic development still carried on: one weaver and a pit-sawyer at Le Beugnon, another weaver at La Guittonnière, and they could only exist by adding a bit of agriculture to their own trade.

Living standards

Contrasts between township and countryside

The standard of living of the farmers had seen great changes. The last chapter shows the considerable progress made in housing, furniture, dress and food between 1850 and 1880 – progress which continued and even accelerated, particularly after 1900. But to the extent that it enabled the peasants to buy things from the towns it also at the same time contributed to an increase in wealth in the towns and, in a more tangible way, to the specialization and enrichment of the tiny urban centre that the Mazières township was becoming. In this way it created a marked contrast between the inhabitants of the township and those living in the villages and farms.

There was great building activity in the commune. Eight new buildings were assessed for tax in 1882; 2 in 1883; 6 in 1885; 7 in 1887; 4 in 1888; 10 in 1889 after a new assessment; 18 in 1890; 11 in 1891, 1892 and 1893; 4 in 1894. It is not possible to follow details of construction work after 1895 but the net taxable income rose from 19,213 fr. 75 in 1895 to 22,917 fr. in 1905 and to 25,059 fr. in 1911. This building work included barns, stables and many new houses, particularly in the township.

Here the changes had been so many that the whole appearance of the commune was altered. The road surveyor had drawn up the town plan in 1880. A few years later, some hovels whose presence prevented a central public square from assuming its final – or at least its present – aspect were demolished. In 1885 the mayor failed – for what reason will be seen later – to remove the cemetery which ran alongside the presbytery: he was to succeed in 1905. Earlier he had had the market hall just below the town hall changed into an assembly room.[24] In 1892 he had a communal clock installed whose chimes could be heard all over the township. A pump was set up in front of the town hall with branch canals leading the water to three wall fountains serving the three principal 'quarters'.

In the twenty-five years between 1885 and 1910 more than twenty-five houses – some of considerable size – were erected. Some were built on the site of old houses which had been pulled down, others on vacant sites. The importance of roads could now be seen: all these houses – except one – were built facing each other along the roads or the edges of public squares. Some of them – the doctor's, the solicitor's and one leading citizen's – contained reception rooms; others, like those of prosperous tradesmen, had a kitchen *and* a dining-room, sometimes even an office. No one who had rebuilding done during these years thought it remotely possible to eat, or even to sleep, in their work-room or shop as they had been used to doing until then. On the other hand, in the countryside, although the rooms were larger and better lit, the peasants continued – more often than not – to eat and sleep in the same room where meals were cooked. If there were other rooms in the house, they consisted of 'bedrooms' – well-furnished and kept very tidy but entered only rarely and then with an almost religious reverence.

The few young women of the township who followed fashion as far as to use eau de Cologne, rice powder and toothpaste, ordered their requirements from the big departmental stores where they also obtained finer material than could be found in the Mazières shops. They received mail order catalogues, well-illustrated and very tempting, from which they made their orders. The stores also sent their catalogues to farms but, except very occasionally, the farmers' wives ordered very little. Their daughters might well know how to read and write but, to place an order with a big store, one needs to have a certain level of familiarity with symbols – pictures and writing – and a certain confidence in them which these girls lacked. They would only buy materials and things which they had seen, touched and felt in their hands.

A man's tailor from Parthenay came each month to take orders in the township, bringing with him samples of cloth. He would take measurements and his customers would go for fittings if they happened to go to Parthenay on Wednesdays, or they would not bother with a fitting. However, they nearly always found that the suits fitted well.

The most marked contrasts between the town way of living and that of the country are to be seen in their diet. The presence of a butcher and the twice-weekly visit of a pork-butcher is clear evidence that the townsfolk bought meat regularly. The bakers were now selling one-kilogramme (more often two-kilogramme) loaves. Finally, fish and fruits foreign to the region now formed part of the normal diet of artisans and tradesmen, just as it was of the notables. In a good many houses, by 1910, knives were used at table and a fresh plate for each course of a meal.

Nothing like this was happening as yet in the country where one rarely ate butcher's meat; where – if, after 1910, hardly anyone bothered to bake his own bread – one bought from the baker only enormous round loaves weighing five kilogrammes which lasted a whole week; where – even if the custom of eating from one dish had gone – only one plate for each guest (except on special occasions) was used; where table knives were unknown – the farmer's attachment to his sheath knife was quite significant as were the local sayings like: 'A sharp knife is the knife of a man who likes his food; a blunt knife is the knife of a layabout.' In fact, changes in the peasants' diet related chiefly to the introduction of wine into every farm and to the use of items of grocery and more varied vegetables. About 1900 they began to grow radishes, asparagus and artichokes in their gardens: tomatoes came later, towards 1910. The farmers had also begun to eat chicken and rabbit raised on the farm, some-times – but very seldom – even geese and turkeys, which previously they had denied themselves in order to sell them. But they still lived as far as it was at all possible for them on what they produced themselves, buying as few articles as they could. They participated fully in the exchange economy through what they were forced to purchase or pay for in the exercise of their calling (all kinds of implements, feed for their animals, fertilizers, bills from the threshing contractor, the wheelwright, the blacksmith, etc.) and through the constant sale of produce from their poultry, their cattle and their crops.

The peasants had remained more closely attached to their trade and to their milieu than had the inhabitants of the town-ship and they were more hesitant in letting their children follow any other calling than theirs.

The young men leave

During the period of time covered in the previous chapter several instances of young men leaving the district to become civil servants have been mentioned. In actual fact, they were very few.[25]

Between 1880 and 1900 these departures became much more frequent. A certain number of young men of the commune, many of whom could have looked forward only to a poor exist-ence, obtained better paid posts thanks to their education. The bright ones made their way immediately on leaving the primary school to the teacher training college. There were many reasons for this: first, the influence of the schoolmaster and the esteem and respect he enjoyed – more will be said on this later; secondly, the fact that the *Ecole Normale* at Parthenay was only 15 kilometres away; the fact that success in the entrance examination to the college at the age of sixteen or seventeen ensured a respectable position after three further years of free study. And this entrance examination could be prepared for almost entirely at the Mazières school: one or two years of further study at the senior primary school at Bressuire was amply sufficient. Finally, and above all, was the contagious example set by the early successes, the close relations linking one family closely with another and the strength of the current of opinion thus created. It was in this way that, in 1884, the son of a gendarme entered the *Ecole Normale*: he was following the example given by the postman's son mentioned earlier. Two years later, a well-to-do farmer in the neighbourhood sent his son there. This, on the face of it, was a surprising decision but this man had a large family – three sons and two daughters. Two of the boys became civil servants (both teachers), the two girls married and the third boy remained on the land. In 1893 the son of a prosperous blacksmith in the township followed his neighbour, the farmer's son, at the *Ecole Normale*. This blacksmith – who also owned some land – had sent his three sons away to boarding school. The first two had not done very well, the third, the youngest, proved himself to be an excellent pupil and was accepted at the *Ecole Normale*.

A few years later the girls began to leave home to look for work. In 1900 much discussion took place in several families. A carpenter, whose business was doing well, decided to send his only daughter to the senior primary school at Secondigny, 13 kilometres from Mazières, to prepare for the entrance examination for the *Ecole Normale* at Niort. What probably led him to take this decision was the feeling that, having married the daughter of a public servant (the road foreman) who – what is more – was the cousin of the schoolmaster, he was no longer quite in tune with the tradition of the region which consisted in trusting in what the future might hold and in opportunities which might present themselves locally in the way of work for their children, particularly for the girls. His decision must have influenced the manager of the co-operative dairy whose elder daughter was also very bright and who was a man too accustomed to thinking things over not to be concerned with preparing his three daughters for a better future – or one which he hoped would be better. Both these decisions must have carried weight with one of their friends, a small local independent farmer, whose younger son had come to the notice of the schoolmaster in the adult classes. In spite of all the advice given by the teacher, this man would never have made the sacrifices involved in sending his son away to a boarding school if he had not had the example of his two best friends – the carpenter and the co-operative dairy manager – to follow. Now the impetus had been given and, from 1900 to 1914, a dozen girls were to become teachers or train for the profession. But of these twelve girls, eleven came from the township, from families of artisans, tradesmen or public servants: only one from the country and, most probably, she took this course solely because one of her aunts – on her mother's side – was herself a teacher. Six other young men – only one among them the son of a farmer (and related to the farmer who set the example in 1886) – became teachers. Of the boys and girls of the commune who continued their education only very few escaped to climb the ladder of the senior primary school and the *Ecole Normale*. Three girls only, all from the township, went to the girls' Lycée at Niort and one of them – the daughter of the teacher, became a teacher while waiting to get married. Five boys only, all from the town – one a bursar – underwent secondary education. Others were sent to boarding school but were not capable of benefiting from their studies.

Thus, the children from a number of families of artisans, shopkeepers and public servants in the town continued with their education; the brighter ones became, for the most part, teachers – imitated in this by just one or two children of the better-off farmers. Other young men left the commune on completing their military service. After leaving the primary school and until they reached the age of twenty they did any kind of work they could find, either with their parents or as paid employees. When they had finished their military service, they looked for permanent employment.

It was in this way that two sons of pit-sawyers, cousins, became railway workers. The older, on a visit to a sawmill while he was a soldier, saw that his father's trade was bound to disappear. His departure led not only his cousin to follow him but also his younger brother who became a shop assistant. A postman's son and two farmers' sons also joined the railways. It is not surprising that the son of a postman should have sought and obtained a post under the Government but the departure of farmers at that time *is* surprising. One was the son of a well-to-do independent farmer in the north-west of the commune. He was a handsome lad with very refined manners and had been a very good pupil at the school. He found peasant life hard and dismal and he was drawn to try to use his education in finding a different way of life away from home. The other came from a very large family. He had learnt to be a carpenter before joining the army and liked the trade: but he did not have even the small amount of capital needed to set himself up in business. He, too, had been a good pupil at Mazières school. His military service had separated him from his family and from the surroundings in which he had grown up. He preferred the security of paid employment to the freer and, perhaps happier but less secure life of a rural craftsman. Others used military service itself as a way of finding employment: they became gendarmes, *gardes républicains* and non-commissioned officers in the army.

Here, too, the town provided more than half of those who left the area. Research reveals only two gendarmes, three N.C.O.s and two railway workers who were born on the farms. Old peasants consulted on the matter, moreover, attached little importance to the exodus. On the other hand, they set great emphasis on the astonishing career of two farm-workers who went into the business world. One, on his return from military service, took a job as a waiter in a café. At twenty-five he had become manager of a hotel near the station at Niort: by dint of hard work and careful living he had made a fortune. All his brothers – four of them – followed each other in the hotel. Only ten years were needed before they had saved enough capital to live on the interest for the rest of their lives.

The second man, when he had finished military service, became a traveller for a big draper's shop in the district. He was a likeable person, extremely intelligent and trustworthy. The large van loaded with goods which he took round the local fairs and to the Parthenay markets nearly always came back empty. He, too, was a very handsome young man. His employer's daughter fell in love with him and he married her, to become one of the most important traders in the district. These two young men would never have been able to carve out such a career, whatever gifts they posssesed, had they not received at the school a solid grounding of primary education.

The young men from the town migrated in greater numbers. The sons of the minor civil servants (postmen, railway workers, roadmen) could find no work at home. The sons of craftsmen and shopkeepers could not all follow their fathers. On leaving school they learnt a trade and then went off as workmen; or those who had more ambition and had done a little better at school tried their luck as shop assistants or bank clerks. To tell the story of all of them would be too long and tedious a task – the carrier's son who became (a sign of the times) a motor mechanic and then a garage owner; the mason's son who became, through his marriage, hotel keeper in a neighbouring town; the two sons of the postman, one of whom was employed in an arsenal and the other became an N.C.O.; the sons of a foreman platelayer who became motor mechanics at Parthenay, etc., etc.

It should be borne in mind, at least, that this commune, which we have seen in 1850 to be overpopulated, was hiving off many of its young people throughout the surrounding region. They could make a living away from their homes by reason of the increase in employment openings in Government, and those resulting from the transport of goods and people and the trade this brought and from industrial development. Their father's trade – clog-making, pit-sawing – might die but they were saved: they were of use to the community and could make a living. They could have done this less easily – some of them never – had they not been adapted by the primary school to the conditions of a changing society. It is understandable that children from the town should have adapted themselves more quickly than country children, more rooted in and attached to old customs and the old economy.

New growth in the population

In 1872, as we have seen, very few of the people living in the commune had not been born there or in the immediate vicinity. In 1906, in the town, there were twenty heads of family – workers or civil servants who had not been born even in the *département;* eighteen others had been born in various communes of Deux-Sèvres *département*, quite distant from Mazières. At the station all the employees had been born outside the *département*. In the countryside practically all the farmers were natives of the commune or of neighbouring communes: only one tenant farmer had been born outside the *département*. Two others had come from fairly distant communes; three day-labourers had been born beyond the immediate neighbourhood;

one road-worker living in a village (Ternand) came from Vienne *département*.

There was, then, a certain reconstitution of the population much more noticeable in the township than in the country.

Mental attitudes

A broadened horizon

The broadening of people's outlook brought about by this immigration from outside was helped by more frequent travelling. We have already seen that, in its first year, the Mazières railway station sold 4,500 tickets. A few years later, every weekly market at Parthenay (Wednesdays) and every monthly market at Niort (the first Thursday in the month) meant crowded trains – even relief trains had to be run. In 1885, 13,046 travellers bought tickets at Mazières station. 19,089 passengers passed through in 1890; 33,724 in 1900 and 42,360 in 1909.[26] In addition, horse-drawn vehicles had increased in number and in 1890 the first bicycles appeared, to begin with in the town, later in the country.[27] The young now made a habit of going for rambles in the countryside, thereby getting to know each other better. The custom of inter-communal fights between the youths died out.[28]

The everyday world had become much vaster: it was no longer just the commune but the whole region. Only the land beyond Parthenay and beyond Niort remained foreign and far-off. Nearly everyone who had relatives living at a distance (and they were many) allowed themselves to be tempted by the demon of adventure and would arrange to go and visit them – *en famille* – at least once in their life if they were old, more often if they were young. Proper expeditions used to set out like this for the distant homes of gendarmes, postmen or railway-workers. They were discussed long beforehand and long after.

Neighbours, too, became interested in these distant places where, after all, people lived just as they did at Mazières. They placed them in their mind not according to their knowledge of geography, which was poor, but according to their relations with the people who lived there: 'Rivarenne? It's near Tours.'

This meant nothing: the fear of the unknown, which leaves a name in which one is interested in one's mind but without the power of being able to place it, persisted in the one who sought information. But . . . 'You know: where M . . .'s son was first posted as a gendarme.' Then the face lit up. Rivarenne was placed and for ever after it was where M . . .'s son had lived.

So, in the world outside, in those lands beyond Parthenay and Niort there were names that were known and placed in one's mind, places of interest to one: and one knew – dimly as yet – that wherever French was spoken, a peasant born and bred in Mazières-en-Gâtine could fit in and live his life.

The habit of letter writing had become general: old grandmothers bewailed the fact that they were unable to read when they received news from their far-off sons and daughters. They had their letters read to them two or three times over and praised the style and the handwriting: 'Isn't he clever? Doesn't he write nicely?' Then they would carefully lock away those scraps of magic paper which had brought them – black on white – news of their absent ones, enabling them to conjure up a picture of them. They were the first to get angry with the little ones who, preferring to go and play or herd the oxen, played truant from school.

Thus, through the interplay of economic forces, the attitudes of the people began imperceptibly to change and the homogeneity of the region to be broken, the town becoming separate from the countryside and taking a clear lead in this evolution.

Old ways die hard

But one must not think that, even in the township, people's minds were completely emancipated or their eyes fully opened. In point of fact they still belonged to their own little world and the way in which those who came to live there were assimilated into it is significant.

The justice of peace, the registrar, the tax inspector, even the gendarmes were regarded rather as outsiders: one hardly knew them except when they were carrying out their duties. In any case, they were only birds of passage.

But the masons, the tinsmiths, the blacksmiths, the innkeepers, the 'quack' veterinary surgeon, the railway-workers and the postmen soon became part of the community. The wives went to the public washplace near the spring. There they heard all the local news, became involved in it and passed it round. It was not long before, for them and their families, it was clear that Mazières was no longer just another village like any other but the centre of their existence, a standpoint from which the outside world was judged. When this happened, those who had left were forgotten and the newcomers were accepted as belonging. In the country memories are long; for years after one would talk about neighbours who had gone away and newcomers were received with suspicion.

Any comparisons made were in relation to things known to all within the community. A 'fine house' would be such-and-such a house in the township or nearby; so-and-so was thought to be comfortably off because he had an income of 1,500 francs; another was rich because he had more than 3,000 francs. M. Proust was much richer, but then he belonged to a different social class to which one would not compare oneself.

One day in 1905, some children picked up close to the town some hotel bills dropped by a passing motorist on his way from Biarritz. These bills passed from hand to hand and people were amazed: 'How could anyone pay this much for a room?' They felt neither envy nor indignation; they were just amazed and their astonishment had not the slightest effect on the feeling of comfort and security that they experienced when they went home to find a good cabbage soup steaming on a table covered with oilcloth.

It is clear that modern civilization had not touched them – or corrupted them as Rousseau would have said. They had no idea of what constituted luxury; they knew nothing of art. They had had their own art form – that of telling spicy stories in patois and many a peasant was rightly celebrated for excellence in this. But this intimate art form died out when everyone had his own fireside, when everyone had light at home, when things which used to be made at home in the evening could be bought in shops, when there were fewer evening gatherings in common. The city art form reached them in the shape only of sentimental romances (which, moreover, were very much to their taste), of melodramas acted at village fêtes, of monologues recited at wedding banquets when the most *risqué* were the most appreciated, of penny novels and detective stories. A brass band had been formed[29] in 1884 on the initiative of M. Proust and from

1893 to 1912 it was under the direction of a teacher who was an excellent musician. Praiseworthy efforts were made to play well-known compositions, but it consisted of only twenty players blowing brass instruments and its audience would have preferred the rhythm of military marches.

Thus, the people were too ignorant, as a whole, of the world beyond Parthenay and Niort and of a social world different from their own not to remain deeply attached to the things they saw around them, the only ones they knew and loved.

National politics

Signs of this ignorance of the outside world and this narrow local patriotism can be seen in the form taken by new ideas which tended to reshape people's attitudes of mind. These new ideas came through the medium of newspapers. From 1880 onwards one of the town cafés had a bookstall. From the start it sold *Le Petit Patriote* and *Le Petit Journal*; a little later *Le Petit Parisien*, *La France de Bordeaux et du Sud-Ouest* and *La Petite Gironde* were added. The bookstall had about forty regular subscribers and a certain number of casual customers, usually people from the countryside. In addition, some of the town notables subscribed directly to various daily papers. The exact number I could not discover, but the records of the Mazières postmen's rounds show that the almost entirely rural commune of Saint-Marc-la-Lande contained ten subscribers in 1906. This is few enough and of the ten perhaps not less than five only took a paper because they received it free. From 1895 to 1914, in fact local political journals were sent free to persons who were thought to be influential. The radical republican paper was called *Le Bocage et La Plaine* and was published at Thouars: the conservative republican paper was *Le Memorial des Deux-Sèvres*, published at Niort. A good number of Catholic journals, especially *La Croix et Le Pélerin*, were also provided.

But none of these papers had any deep effect. The *affaire Dreyfus* which aroused so much passion throughout France left Mazières practically unmoved. It was too complicated and confusing and too many matters unknown in this corner of the land were involved for even the most enlightened to become really excited. Those who did take an interest were too few to work each other up by arguing fiercely. Only a few notables and civil servants and their closest friends, through contact with them, took sides in the matter. In Mazières there were only a few Dreyfusards and a few anti-Dreyfusards – and they were relatively cool and indifferent.

Surprisingly, however – and this is something that will be dealt with in more detail later – foreign affairs had a much greater effect. Political ideas did not spread as a result of arguments; political convictions did not – for most – grow from careful reflection. They came from the influence of some- one in whom one had confidence or from mass suggestion. I was once able to catch a lifelike glimpse of how the conflict of opinion was conducted between peasants at the time of a general election. I was chatting with a very shrewd old man, a friend of mine, when one of his neighbours happened to pass by. He asked him in to take a glass of wine. 'You know,' he said, 'I have asked you in because I think you are going to vote for D . . . If I thought you weren't going to vote for him I'd wish this wine would poison you.' The other said nothing but drank his wine and went off. 'Will he vote for D . . . ?' I asked. 'I'm not sure,' he answered, 'they are all *chouans* in his village.' There had been no attempt at argument, merely a friendly gesture aimed at appeasing prejudice and the suggestion of a mind firmly made up. Moreover, it would have been very hard for that peasant, shrewd as he was, to explain his thoughts clearly or justify them. He was not capable of handling theoreti- cal ideas.[30]

In 1876, when M. de Tusseau was mayor, 251 out of the 307 registered electors voted at the general election; the conserva- tive candidate – General Allard, the retiring deputy – received 207 votes, the republican candidate – M. Ganne – 40. At the election which followed the dissolution of parliament in 1877, M. Taudière – the conservative candidate – obtained 202 votes at the first ballot and M. Ganne 51. 260 votes (9 more than in 1876) had been cast and the swing was insignificant. At the second ballot, with the victory of the left becoming evident, there was a much more definite swing: M. Taudière received 190 votes instead of 202 and M. Ganne had 71 – i.e. 20 more. Moreover, M. Ganne had a majority in the Parthenay *arrondisse- ment:* 8,408 votes against M. Taudière's 8,176.

At the 1881 election M. Ganne was in his turn the out-going member. M. de Tusseau was no longer mayor of the commune, having been replaced by M. Proust. Of the 309 registered electors, 264 voted: M. Ganne obtained 153 votes, or 81 more than in 1877. M. Garran de Balzan received 8 and M. Taudière 99, or 91 fewer than in 1877. At the second ballot M. Ganne had 168 votes, M. Taudière 99. The swing, this time, was considerable. It must be attributed mainly to mass suggestion by the local victory won by the republican party in the person of M. Proust.

After that time the number of votes for the conservatives remained roughly the same (110 in 1881; 109 in 1889; 110 in 1898; 120 in 1902; 112 in 1906; 96 in 1911; 100 in 1914). Votes for the republicans increased sharply as the electoral roll grew and the age of the voters decreased (175 in 1881; 170 in 1889; 185 in 1893; 188 in 1898; 200 in 1902, 231 in 1906; 242 in 1910; 231 in 1914). This increase was probably due much less, after 1900, to the influence of M. Proust – who was growing old and who was beginning to be criticized – than to the infiltration everywhere of the republican spirit and belief, the elements of which will be analysed later, and partly, too, to the influence of the school. It is all the more remarkable that, after 1906, the republican candidate was no longer a Progressive Republican – M. A. Lebon, Minister for the Colonies in the Meline administration – but a Radical Socialist, M. Louis Demellier. It is true that M. Demellier was a local man, and it is no doubt owing to this that he obtained in the commune about the same number of votes as the best supported candidates at the time of the municipal elections. To this extent the republican faith of the people of Mazières was affected by their restricted environment.

Local politics: new ideas and old habits

The same situation is found when one moves from national to local politics. While a general election, whose importance was indeed realized, aroused people's feelings without inflaming them, municipal elections and anything which touched on local politics released a flood of passion.

M. Proust, as we have seen, was appointed mayor of the commune in 1881. One of the first actions of the council of which he was president was to build a new boys' school and he met no opposition to this, in spite of the large sum of money involved. In 1881 he had the washplace rebuilt. In 1886 he had

a hamlet school built in a large village in the south of the commune: L'Hirondelle. In 1889 he had the girls' school building
repaired and enlarged – that building which before had seemed
so fine was now clearly too small. Every year he included
relatively large amounts in the budget for the construction of
new secondary roads. All this went quite smoothly, but as soon
as the mayor's activity touched custom and belief, the whole
country erupted. This comes out clearly in the attempt to move
the cemetery and the 'affair of the bells'.

The cemetery, as was usual in many parts at the time, was
next to the church, in the middle of the township. It was full,
for the commune's dead had always been buried there. There
was only one empty spot left, planted with walnut trees, and
this was the place that had been reserved for protestants and
suicides. No one wanted to bury their dead there. M. Proust,
who had ideas of town planning, wanted to move the cemetery.
His choice was a plot of land on the way to the station and he
made a provision of 2,000 francs for its purchase. But the
enquiry of *comodo* and *incomodo* revealed opposition. The
meeting of 7 April 1881 recorded: 'It is more according to their
political party than to the promptings of their conscience that
most of the supporters have been moved.' And M. Proust
mortgaged the cemetery, which could not be sold for twenty
years, in order to pay for the new site. Feelings in the commune
ran high. Many were shocked by the idea that their dead might
be exhumed and moved away from the spot where they had
been laid for their last rest. The priest lent his support to their
indignation; the cemetery next to the church was something
that belonged to him and rather like a symbol of his power. So
the town council had to bow before the wishes of – if not the
majority – at least an important part of the community. It had
to abandon the plans it had formulated while, at the same time,
suggesting that 'an administration more detached than it itself
could be from local influences might find a solution suited to the
prime interests of public health' (Resolution of 9 June 1882).
The mayor accused the priest of being the engineer of his
defeat. The latter was not one to abandon his responsibilities:
he was a courageous and violent man, authoritarian, with a
burning, even intolerant, faith, intelligent and well-educated –
a man who was reluctant to see the country escape from the
power of his influence. On Sundays he preached fiery sermons in

which hell and the fear of hell figured largely. 'My word! Wasn't he in a temper!' said the peasant women after mass. It was inevitable that there should be a violent conflict between this priest and the mayor whose anti-clericalism and taste for authority we already know. The storm burst over the 'affair of the bells'.

The Vestry Board wanted to hang three bells in the church belfry. The departmental architect was of the opinion that the tower was not strong enough to bear their weight but all fear of danger would disappear if it were strengthened. The Vestry undertook to meet all the costs. At a meeting on 5 May 1883 the town council observed:

- that the cost may very well not stop there;
- that if the belfry did collapse, the responsibility on the commune would be great;
- that no explanation has been given why three bells are now required whereas in the past one has sufficed.

By six votes to five it rejected the Vestry's proposal.

The mayor had used all his influence to obtain this result and, despite all his authority, he obtained a majority of only one. In a letter dated 14 May 1883 the senior priest of Mazières protested and asked the council to reconsider its decision. On 20 May the council met again and by eight votes to four maintained its opposition to the project.

In August the town was in a ferment. In spite of the town council's opposition, alterations were made to the church's fabric and the blessing of the bells was announced. A meeting of the council was hastily called for 14 August when, by nine votes to two, it was resolved to oppose the work being undertaken.

The priest then decided to take down the old bell and the tower, still bearing the marks of the work already begun, became silent. The people launched strong protests against this quarrelling which was disturbing their accustomed tenor of life.

At a meeting on 26 November 1883 the council raised its voice against the priest's attitude. 'His summary and totally insulting actions place the Council under the necessity of opposing him unless it is to appear, in the eyes of the population, ready to abdicate its functions in the face of clerical pretension. Should this episode in a perpetual quarrel be settled, the pretensions of the priest, the leading spirit of the Vestry, will nevertheless reappear in another guise and, consequently, it is impossible to expect any truce or respite on the part of so intransigent a man.'

By eight votes to one the council refused to reconsider its decision on the proposal made to it. On 10 February of the following year it agreed to discuss the matter for the fifth time (at the head of the agenda the secretary had written: *Question des cloches* with an exclamation mark) but only to reaffirm its refusal by seven votes to one.

Meanwhile, feelings remaining high, M. Proust wished to submit his attitude to the judgment of the electors. He resigned, together with all the council, and the teacher was delegated to carry out the mayoral functions. On 18 May 1884, M. Proust returned to the council with nine of his supporters. He controlled ten votes out of twelve: he was re-elected mayor.

The question of the bells came up again. The council refused by five out of the six votes cast to associate itself with the Vestry project and declared that it would in no way 'renounce its indefeasible right to be consulted whenever the Vestry wished to carry out the work at its expense'.

But everyone was tired of the strife and M. Proust ended by agreeing to the erection of the three bells, which have remained the glory of the church and are the life and joy of the town. It must be remembered that in all this violent quarrel the electors of the commune supported M. Proust because he was wealthy, intelligent and a man of authority; but when his actions did violence to their customary way of life they knew how to show their disapproval. It is very significant that at the final discussion in a council under his control he could obtain only five votes; five of his faithful supporters had abstained, and that must have taken a good deal of courage.

The years that followed were relatively calm with no major rows. The priest still campaigned against the mayor and the latter would not agree to urgent repairs to the presbytery. But war broke out again in 1895 over the opening of a Church school for girls. The mayor had suffered defeat in 1884 because he had shown himself intolerant and sectarian. In 1895 it was the priest who was beaten because, in his turn, he tried to misuse his moral authority.

A resolution of the council at a meeting on 19 December 1895 speaks of 'the decision taken by M. le Curé to no longer allow the girls from the State school to sit in the pews they usually occupy which will be reserved for girls from the Church school in future'. It was proposed 'to rent sufficient accommodation in the church for the girls from the State school, the commune to meet the cost thereof'. Such steps were to turn the people away from the priest who, moreover, refused absolution to mothers who were unwilling to send their daughters to the Church school. In so doing he kept from the confessional, for many long years, some good Christian women.

When, in 1901, the Prefect of Deux-Sèvres asked the council to express its opinion on the advisability of granting permission to the Sisters of Saint-André to teach at Mazières, the council answered in a long resolution which merits being quoted in full:

29 December 1901
Opinion of the Council on the advisability of permitting the Sisters of Saint-André to teach at Mazières.

The Council, called upon to give its opinion on the advisability of the establishment in the commune of Mazières of the Church school for girls of the Croix de Saint-André.

Considering that this undertaking which has already been functioning, without permission, for two years has yielded results which might have been expected, viz. that it has caused dissension in families compelled by the priest (patron of the concern) to choose between supposedly Christian education and what is called 'godless' provided in the lay, State school;

Considering that, from this fact, a deep breach, previously unknown, exists today between parents and will divide the children even more if this state of affairs continues;

Considering that the ever-growing importance of woman's role in modern society renders the question of her education of absorbing interest; and that it is necessary that, as man's companion and partner in life, she should share his opinions and not become, in the hands of the priesthood, an instrument of discord and domination;

Considering furthermore, as shown in periodic examinations, that the education given in this kind of establishment, lacking competent teachers, at least in sufficient numbers, cannot compare with that given in the State institutions and that, in any case, it is well-known that children are brought up there to hate and despise their friends at other schools;

Considering that this education is liable to inflame citizens one against the other, to the great injury of society but to the great advantage of people who, having no well defined fatherland, aspire to universal domination;

Considering that this danger, which is indeed great, has compelled the State recently to adopt energetic safeguarding measures which must be pursued vigorously: if not, public opinion will demand it be done;

Is of the opinion, by a majority of eight votes to two of the ten members present, that the permission requested by the ladies of the Saint-André community to continue to maintain the youth of Mazières in ignorance and in the practice of feelings of hate and discord, be absolutely rejected.

In spite of this resolution, however, the Sisters of Saint-André continued to teach and were able, through their kindness and tolerance, to gain the affectionate respect of a large part of the population, even of families who did not send their children to them to be taught. The strife between the two schools – Church and State – will be discussed elsewhere.

To summarize: the changes which had taken place in the people's way of living had had their effect on their minds but without separating them from the world of reality in which they lived. That this was still a very restricted world is seen in the way in which they received the new ideas which were seeking to make their way into their milieu. They did not become excited over ideas or events which were taking place far away; they were, indeed, interested only in the local repercussions of those ideological struggles of which France was the stage, and the customs that they held dear were sometimes opposed to the ideas that their elected leaders would have liked to impose on them.

Nevertheless, there was a gradual change to be seen in the moral basis of the life of many of the people.

The decline of religion

First and foremost, amid all the disputes in which religion was involved, and of which it was often the cause, piety and religious observation decreased. This was very visible at the time of the separation of Church and State.

As we have seen, the major events of French internal politics had passed almost unperceived in this corner of the land. But the plans of Separation caused an enormous stir. At first everyone experienced a kind of anxious confusion. The faithful were furious and the shopkeepers said: 'If there is no longer a priest in the town what will happen to us?' Then, gradually, people began to get used to the idea that the priests might no longer be paid by the State . . . especially when it became known that all those already appointed would retain their salary. When the time came to take an inventory of the Church's vestments and treasures, M. Proust, the anti-clerical mayor, was no longer at the town hall. His place had been taken by a doctor in Mazières who had married a Mlle Pouzet. Proton, the priest who was M. Proust's great foe, had died. Mazières had given him a worthy funeral. He had been replaced temporarily by a young priest, born in the neighbourhood and who, consequently, was not greatly respected and who tried to gain this respect by talking incessantly about his recent pilgrimage to Jerusalem. This impetuous young priest decided to resist, as best he might, the taking of the inventory and the mayor was unable to make him change his mind. In the end Mazières awoke, one fine day in 1906, to find itself full of soldiers. A company of infantry surrounded the Church square; officials stood trembling on the steps of the Church; they made – in vain – the customary summons; and the church doors were forced. The faithful who had shut themselves inside came out a little sheepishly, it seemed, and filed off under the eyes of the curious onlookers. There were not many of them: a dozen women and two or three men only. Strength rested in the law and, as always, most people felt – in all sincerity – that those who were strongest were those in the right. 'Did you see that great fellow X . . .? He looked pretty silly,' said the gossips and for days after they talked of nothing other than these events. For many years the church doors bore traces of their wounds. On the white wooden planks with which the sacristan/carpenter had patched the holes, the priest had had painted in large black letters: '1 March 1906. Sacrilege! 1 March 1906. Liberty!' The priest who took Abbé Proton's place permanently – the priest who was so violently vindictive – was a gentle old man who visited the sick and comforted the suffering. The only use he made of the 'liberty' proclaimed on his church door was to give lessons in tolerance and charity. Everyone loved him, except for a few rabid Catholics who found him too lukewarm and whom he had to calm down. He counted for a great deal in the religious peace which reigned for fifteen years in the commune and in the respect for religion held by all the young men who knew him.

But the country as a whole was slipping into indifference over religious matters. One by one the practices which served as props for religion were disappearing. No longer did one put branches of consecrated boxwood in the corner of the fields to ensure a good harvest or in the cowshed to ward off disease. People began to eat meat on Fridays from time to time. They went less often to mass and many no longer took the Easter communion.

A new faith

The Catholic religion lost ground in men's minds all the more as a new religion was born, a religion whose dogmas had not been put clearly before the people of Mazières, a religion with no priest but which circumstances and the general climate of opinion in the country had brought into being and which, through a thousand obscure little pathways, took possession of most men's consciences. Its manifestation can only be glimpsed in brief, but extremely significant, flashes.

Belief in progress

Try to imagine the state of mind of people who, born in 1830 in a country without roads, without trade, poor and overpopulated, now saw around them in 1885 or 1890 a network of safe roads, a railway station at their door, houses full of light and a countryside beginning to enjoy prosperity. They could only feel amazement. Or those, too, born around 1860, who had grown up in poverty and who could now see, at the age of 25 or 30, that they were eating better, their clothes were better and that they could look forward to the future with confidence; their horizon was more clearly defined and it had widened. The heavy skies which had crushed them had lifted: they could dream for themselves, and especially for their children, of an even better time to come, of endless progress.

Some time in 1895, Pascal Chaignon, the postman, was busy one evening after his rounds raking the paths in M. Proust's park. He had been born 30 or 35 years earlier on a small piece of land which his father worked some ten kilometres from Mazières. He had grown up with his two brothers and his sisters in a small, dark house isolated from the village. He had been a remarkable pupil at the school in the neighbouring township and had left able to read well and also to write and count. He continued reading anything he came across when working as a domestic servant – for he had had to hire himself out in order to earn a living. He could have stayed on in the army as a non-commissioned officer, but he was too fond of his independence and preferred the post of postman that the squire of his village had obtained for him. He earned only a modest salary, but it was regular and he added to it by taking on piece work after he had finished his daily rounds. He lived in the township, where he rented a house much larger and brighter than the one he had grown up in. His wife stayed at home to do the housework and he returned every evening to find her clean and happy. Pascal Chaignon, when he compared his present situation with his childhood, could feel full of confidence and pride. He read the newspapers – the one he bought for himself and those he took round to the subscribers. He thought things over and argued about them with his friends. His opinions were listened to attentively and of this he was proud. He felt himself to be living quite another life, infinitely richer and on a level altogether higher than that lived by his father and to which his two brothers who had remained on the land appeared to be condemned. His son – an only son – was doing well at school. Pascal Chaignon dreamt of sending him to the *collège* at Saint-Maixent and he was not worried over what he would become.

His ambition was limited by his personal experience: his son would become an employee in the higher grades of the Post Office. This would be the prolongation, the full flowering of his own career. But to do it he needed a bursary. Ah! if only M. Proust would help. . . . All this was always in the back of the postman's mind, thoughts that he returned to continually while on his long rounds during the day and while he was raking the paths in the park. . . .

At that moment M. Proust came out of his château – a small man, well-fed, self-confident in bearing, sure of himself and of his wealth. 'Hallo, Pascal, how are things?' 'All going well, M. Proust' . . . and, taking his courage in both hands, the postman added: 'Since you are here, may I ask you something?' 'What is it?' 'My son is doing well at school; he is 12 and I should like to send him on to the *collège*.' 'To the *collège*? What do you want to make him? A misfit?' M. Proust had a horror of children from the common people going on to secondary education: primary schools as many as you like, but he was very conscious of the fears of the bourgeoisie in the face of the rising tide of unemployed lads who had passed their *Baccalauréat*.[31] All Pascal Chaignon's pride rose up in arms. The battles he had won and those he still dreamt of winning through his son made him draw himself up to his full height. 'I don't know if I shall make him a misfit, but I very much hope I shall turn him into someone better than his father.'[32]

The story went right round the commune: I heard it told 15 years later. It only had such an effect because it reflected a general feeling. When I was a child I often heard of similar incidents from many different sources. Whereas formerly families which had managed to improve their material circumstances used their authority to keep their children at home, the time had now come when the idea of progress had become planted in men's minds. The most loving fathers of families agreed to their children leaving home, to deprive themselves of their presence and to make considerable financial sacrifices to ensure for them a different future from their own and one that they thought would be a better one. They did so, indeed, because they thought that in this way they were securing their children's happiness; but it also seemed to them to be in accordance with an important law which they must obey under penalty of appearing unworthy parents: the son must do better than the father and thereby raise as high as possible the family name.

And what importance was attached to these names! In families well on the way climbing the social ladder, male heirs were impatiently expected; at their baptism they had more peals of bells and they were much more spoiled than were girl children. From their infancy they were told everything that would make them proud of the name they bore, the merit acquired by such-and-such a forebear, the respect that they had enjoyed in the region. 'A Dumont never lies. A Dumont has never gone bankrupt,' said Grandfather La France in *Le Roman d'un Brave Homme*. Such phrases were often spoken in Mazières at that time. It was expected of the boys, particularly if they did well at school, that they should raise high and afar, as high and as far as was possible, the good name of the family. They owed it to themselves, to their parents and to their ancestors that they should have male heirs to carry on the line. All their efforts were received and supported by the special attention and affection of all, even of aunts and uncles. It could be said that the vague and sometimes unconscious hopes of untold generations who had struggled hard with no expectations from fate, suddenly came to full bloom in them; and the best of them felt themselves responsible for their lives in the presence of all their ancestors.

This belief in progress had all the characteristics of a religion. It had that amount of generality on which the power of a religion depends and an element of mingled intellectualism and sentimentality. It also had religion's intolerance. I happened to cast doubts on this and even, on one evening at the beginning of the 1914 war, on the whole idea of human progress. I was soon brought up short: I was amazed at the anger and the vehemence of the protests I had provoked; I had a feeling of having touched on the very foundations of my listeners' moral code.

In 1850 the commune of Mazières was covered in broom. In 1880 a railway line was built there. In 1900 everyone – or almost everyone – could read and write and lived with no fear of the future; all the fields sang of man's glory. The first feature of this religion was, therefore, faith in progress.

Republican sentiment

A second feature was republicanism. People attributed to the governments that had preceded the Republic all the misery that the overpopulated Gâtine, lacking trade or industry, had experienced. All the credit for the progress they could see around them was given to the republican régime.[33]

People were proud of being able, through the vote, to take part in the conduct of the affairs of State – of which they knew little, which the *député* knew better and which the Ministers knew perfectly. Nothing in the world would have induced them to give up their right to share in the conduct of the affairs of the commune through their vote and their almost continual approaches to their town councillors. Election campaigns were keenly followed, when the struggle was on, and were like ceremonies at which faith was renewed. Every year, on 14 July, a great republican ceremony was celebrated amid scenes of joy. The public square – in the middle of which a greasy pole was erected – was turned into a fairground. Competitions – of which the least popular were never the *concours aux grimaces* or the sack race – were organized and prizes presented. Nearly all the children in the township and many from the country – even the *chouans* – took part in the games and races. In the evening never fewer than a hundred guests sat down to a subscription banquet in the great reception hall at the town hall, although the peasants might still hesitate to subscribe because of the cost. A speech was made in which reference was invariably made to the Bastille. Everyone applauded. A torchlight parade, a great firework display at which the crowd would spontaneously break into singing the Marseillaise, and a public ball ended the fête.

In this way the republican sentiment was maintained.

It was so widely felt that, in this old country which in former times had been so often fought over by the armies of the Vendée against the armies of the Republic, even those who were considered to be reactionaries did not dare to call themselves royalists. Right-wing candidates at general elections were for a long time aristocrats from the other side of Parthenay: the Marquis de Maussabré, the Comte de Beauregard, the Baron de Vissocq. They were mistrusted. It was partly because they were aristocrats that the peasants would not vote for them; they preferred the local notable whom the radical party put up to oppose them. It is probable that, if in 1906 (the date of their defeat in the *arrondissement*), the parties of the right had put up against the radical candidate not an aristocrat – the Marquis de Maussabré – but, as they were to do later on, an intelligent and sincere man of the people, they would have won and strengthened their hold for many years. People mistrusted all who had any kind of connection with a past which was hated on account of the misery suffered by the forebears who had lived through it. This mistrust was so strong that the new squire at Petit-Chêne, even though he had come up from the common people, was never elected to the town council by more than a narrow majority. And yet he was a remarkable man whose position as Senator and whose success in business gained him a considerable influence. But the château of Petit-Chêne was too grand; it recalled in too many ways the power of the nobility who had occupied it for the new owner to be regarded as a good republican in whom one could trust. M. Proust's château, La Ménardière, much smaller and quite new, did not share in this mistrust.

The Republic as conceived by the Mazières electors was, then, a republic of ordinary people within their own comparatively restricted world, governed by notables of moderate consequence, separated from the common people through their origins and their wealth but nevertheless closely related to them through the interest they took in what concerned them directly, and above all with no connections with an authoritarian régime.

The essential qualities that they demanded of their elected representatives were honesty and decisiveness. Their idea of honesty was that of ordinary people, that is to say, any sign of being mixed up in financial dealings seemed to them inexcusable.[34] They were a little more indulgent, while remaining strict, where morality was concerned. This is evidenced in the loyalty they gave to their mayors, even when the latter shocked their feelings sometimes, in order to demonstrate that they liked to know there was someone in command.[35] The prestige enjoyed by Thiers and Gambetta for years in the region goes to show that these folk needed, at bottom, to feel able to trust in someone to whom they could hand over the conduct of affairs and that no politician in the Republic could meet this need because not one of them was able to stay long enough in office and was never free from criticism. Moreover, politicians were judged less by their deeds, the value of which was seldom assessed, than by their private life. Gossip about Joseph Caillaux in 1914 disillusioned his strongest supporters.

Belief in progress and a firm attachment to the Republic, which was credited with all the evidences of progress the people could see and which was believed to have the capacity of ensuring endless advance: these were the first two elements of this religion which came into being around 1880. By 1893 it was a religion with solid roots. The peasants, artisans and tradesmen of Mazières and the surrounding district preferred people who would defend ideas which they could understand and which were close to their hearts rather than those who put themselves forward only to defend their own interests.

M. Lebon was the Progressive Republican candidate at the election in that year, opposing M. Taudière, Conservative Republican, the retiring member. The election campaign was extremely lively. The Republican party emphasized ideas, the Conservatives material interest. This is what the voters could read in the *Echo de Parthenay* (the Republican paper) on 20 August 1893: 'We are now in the month of August 1893. Time has moved forward and with it the strength of France; breaking with the traditions and legends which were the source of its glory and greatness in other times and against other enemies, our nation has set itself resolutely to the task and from that nation whom we have seen shattered like a piece of glass, gripped by the throat and choking like a child has arisen a virile, enlightened, learned generation, ready for any sacrifice and equally fitted for the long, patient tasks of peace as for the manly hardships of war.'

A circular signed by the members of the Republican Committee of Thenezay is even more indicative of the ideas spreading among the people. 'Let us not look backwards but let us think of the future of our children. Let us grasp fully the idea that the Republic is the government of the workers. Why do the nobility and the clergy fight against the Republic? It is because, under this government, which offers education to all without exception and by so doing is destroying ignorance, they are no longer able, as they were in former times, to make slaves of us.[36]

Here, on the other hand, is what the *Petit-Gâtinois* (Conservative paper) provided for its readers on 30 July 1893:

The refusal of the Government and the Republican
majority to agree to reduce the tax on land is important
to the electorate in other ways than the form of
government and goes beyond politics.

It is a matter of hunger, ruin and poverty.

It is the battle joined between the starving people of
the countryside and the Republicans who starve them.

The only friends of agriculture are the conservatives;
its worst enemies are the opportunists.[37]

These arguments must have carried weight in 1893 at a time
when many peasants had a close knowledge of poverty. But
these are the results of the elections:

	Mazières-en-Gâtine		*Parthenay arrondissement*
M. Lebon	1889 :	170 votes	8,918 votes
	1893 :	185 ,,	10,465 ,, (elected)
		+15	+1,547
M. Taudière	1889 :	109 votes	11,344 votes (elected)
	1893 :	98 ,,	10,093 ,,
		−11	−1,251

The influence of the school, just as was seen in 1881, still
amounted to very little in these results. M. Bouet (whose work
we shall be examining closely) had been there hardly ten years.
Many of the communes in the *arrondissement* still had teachers
whose methods of teaching had hardly changed since the days
of the Empire. But the conditions of living had changed: most
peasants could read and a few simple ideas were working in
them.

Patriotism

The extract from the *Echo de Parthenay* quoted above was
appealing to a third element in this religion which was widespread among the people around 1880: patriotism.

The 1870 War and the bitterness of defeat were still recent.
Newspapers and politicians spoke about them. In many households, Gambetta – the Defender of the Fatherland – and
Thiers – the Liberator of the Land – were well-known and
loved names. Portraits of the two great men were hung on the

wall, each, in his own way, symbolizing the national feeling. By their side were hung engravings showing Alsace and Lorraine as young women in mourning, holding hands and looking sadly towards France. No theatrical performance was given without one of the amateur actors coming forward to declaim a poem by Paul Déroulède. And it was this that received the greatest applause. In particular, 'Le Clairon' had a tremendous success because it was a song accompanied by fanfares of trumpets, giving the audience the impression of being present on a real field of battle and of sharing, in their own bodies, in the death of a hero.

> L'air est pur, la route est large.
> Le clairon sonne la charge
> Et les Zouaves vont chantant. . . .

In the wings a trumpet sounded loud and clear: all the men rose at attention: women's eyes became moist and the children's began to shine. The last trumpet call, slow and mournful, proclaiming the soldier's death, aroused so deep an emotion that it was hard for anyone to clap.

At this point of time in civilization's progress, violence and men of violence were no longer admired. People did not want war, they even feared it greatly; but they remained very responsive to deeds of heroism in war. What Péguy wrote of the people of France in *Notre Patrie* in 1906 was completely valid for Mazières-en-Gâtine.[38]

Right up to the end of the century, all the soldiers returning from their military service brought back with them the pride of having seen new things and a pride of having served with the regiment. All who had got the stripes of corporal or sergeant were extremely proud of them and, because of them, enjoyed a certain prestige in their circle for the rest of their lives. The officers seemed to almost everyone to belong to a superior race of beings, infallible in all they did. They figured large in all the stories told of the regiment – stories which unconsciously but very strikingly revealed the respect in which they were held. In many regiments the men received a veritable education in patriotism. The atmosphere of the time would allow a captain to address his company in these terms: 'My children, if we have to go to war, we shall all go together; I shall be at your head, and I shall be the first to be killed.' Among other souvenirs brought back from their time in the regiment by soldiers of that time, I found an enormous handkerchief of military instruction devoted to the assembling and taking to pieces of the 1874 model rifle. The border was full of pictures relating to the duties of a sentry and ends with these moral precepts:

> It is the duty of all of us to defend against the foreigner the soil which gave us birth. If all Frenchmen are volunteers when the Fatherland is in danger, then all these volunteers must be real soldiers.
> Let us work, then, without stopping; let us learn all we can.
> Let us not forget that in the eyes of the Master of us all, in the eyes of God, Right and Justice are superior to Might.
> Let us be patient, let us work hard, united by the sacred love of the Fatherland and soon our dear and well-beloved France will rise again more beautiful, more glorious than ever before.
> Vive la France.

Between 1900 and 1905 the feeling of patriotism seems to have weakened and lost some of its earlier strength. The generations who had known 1870 were disappearing. People travelled more widely, the standard of living was rising and minds were becoming more 'free': the regiment and military service no longer had the same influence. The stories the men brought back showed a quite different attitude. Jokes and ridicule did not spare officers: after all, they were no cleverer than others; they were doing a job like anyone else. The soldiers knew some who had been born and grown up in the district and who were not exceptionally intelligent. As for the N.C.O.s, they were 'poor types' who came from nowhere and puffed themselves up because they wore stripes. The young men who came back from the regiment with a corporal's stripes were no longer very proud of them; they would almost apologize for them among their friends. But with countries as with individuals, there are moments in their lives when the most unforeseen events combine to lead them towards the goal which they had fixed for themselves: the blind faith which people settled on Russia, thanks to a not entirely disinterested propaganda and the extraordinary feeling of security that the

Franco-Russian alliance gave to the peasants, breathed a new life into French patriotism.

The feeling of danger that had been felt at the time of the 1870 war had been so keen that everyone who could read – and who read the newspapers – had been particularly eager to follow what was said about foreign affairs. I can clearly remember my grandfather talking to me about Fachoda. I can still see in my mind's eye, stuck in a corner of the big fireplace, a coloured picture from the *Petit Journal* issued at the time of the Boer War: it showed a tall, very thin Englishman bent double over the blows delivered at his stomach by a Boer, much shorter but stocky and determined. The Franco-Russian alliance brought a great feeling of relief. Decorated cake dishes, illustrating Russia, the Kronstadt meeting, the visit of Russian sailors to Paris, were often to be found in the houses and much discussed at holiday or family mealtimes. Portraits of Tsar Nicholas and the Empress on the walls replaced Gambetta and Thiers who were now forgotten.

These feelings, it is hardly necessary to say, were stirred up and sustained by the Press, by all the papers. They became more firmly rooted as many people with modest capital lent money to this immense new land with infinite resources, to this friendly country whose alliance stood as a guarantee against all risk of war with Germany and whose aid – if war broke out – was an assurance of victory for us. Certainly, it was well-known, if confusedly, that the Russian people were poor and that the Tsar was an autocrat . . . but, after all, everyone is entitled to arrange his own affairs as he wishes, and the Russian peasants who adored their Tsar were quite happily assumed to enjoy their poverty. I never knew one Republican at Mazières who was really deeply disturbed by the alliance between Republican France and Tsarist Russia.

These, then, were the three essential features of this religion: Progress, Republic, Fatherland. It is very necessary to remember that it was so solid and widespread only because it was deeply rooted in everyone. All, even the poorest, had a lively and precise feeling of enormous material progress – verifiable in the recent memory of the older and even in the middle-aged.

They had an equally clear impression of great social progress, of limitless evolution towards greater freedom and equality, thanks to a suffrage which allowed one to share in a concrete fashion in the affairs of the commune and in those of the nation. And this evolution proceeded smoothly without anything changing in people's habits. They hoped that, if they themselves were not happy and educated, that at least their children would be. Their close, deep family affection in this way cemented the alliance of their faith in progress and their belief in the Republic.

Finally, they had a very keen feeling of love for their native land which was identified with the small countryside they saw every day and with the old traditions so dear to them.

The birth rate drops

This new religion, in which the thought of progress and the rise of the family played an important role, had a natural and very serious consequence. It strengthened and gave a certain nobility to the arguments of those who, daily more numerous, replaced instinct by calculated thought in the conduct of their lives. As one's possessions became greater, one began to learn to save.

People did not go down to the inn so often; the young men went off, on Sundays, on their bicycles on trips to more distant places. They took part in shooting competitions; the older men played *boules*; there was much less drunkenness. All this was excellent.

But the voluntary limitation of the number of children was a serious matter. 'There are your shillings turned into sixpences' (*Voilà tes pièces de 20 sous qui sont devenues des pièces de 10 sous*), said an old peasant to his grandson on the birth of a second child. When one owned some land one did one's best not to divide the land up. Because one hoped for a better future for one's family, one made careful reckonings: one could increase the chances of upward mobility for one's family if one limited the number of one's children. Families of average prosperity, but without reserves of property or money, who had only one or two children were able to send them away to boarding school – something they could not have done if the children had been more numerous. Finally, attitudes having changed, the poorest felt ashamed if they had to send their children out to work while still young; they sent them to school until they reached the age of thirteen and afterwards hesitated to take their wages from them, as was the former custom. After 1895–1900 the father usually opened savings accounts in the name of their children who were working as domestic servants into which they paid all the wages earned, after deducting the cost of clothes and pocket money. So the children no longer brought money into the home: they began to cost money instead, and gradually they began to get an idea of their parents' duties to them.

In fact, the danger of a fall in population did not show itself in any striking fashion before 1914. Only a few symptoms – but quite significant – can be seen if one looks very closely. The total population of the commune rose from 1,086 in 1881 to 1,162 in 1911, an increase of nearly 100 in 30 years or 20 to 25 families more. Life was becoming easier but the number of births tended to decrease.

From 1880 to 1885 people's attitudes had still changed very little. More land was cultivated but machines were not used. There was plenty of work for everyone. Work on the railway created a level of prosperity hitherto unknown and a liveliness, almost insouciance, in the village people and their surroundings. Each year more than 40 children were born: 1880, 45; 1881, 44; 1882, 42; 1883, 42; 1884, 42 – a total for the five years of 215 children. This is an exceptionally high figure and, at the same time, the death rate decreased – only 100 deaths in five years. In 1884 the figure was the abnormally low one of eight.

In the years 1885 to 1890 there were 168 births: 1885, 36; 1886, 30; 1887, 36; 1888, 38; 1889, 28. The decrease is marked and became more so during the five following years during which there were only 155 births: 1890, 37; 1891, 35; 1892, 32; 1893, 25; 1894, 26. It is noteworthy that the year 1893, which saw only a very low figure of births, was a year of extremely bad harvests – the lowest recorded figure of births since 1857 (21 births) which was also a year of hunger and poverty. From 1895 to 1900 the birth rate continued to decrease: 1895, 28; 1896, 26; 1897, 31; 1898, 25; 1899, 33 – a total of 143. Between 1900 and 1905 the total was 126: 1900, 21; 1901, 30; 1902, 20; 1903, 24; 1904, 31.

To summarize

1880–5	215 births
1885–90	168 ,,
1890–5	155 ,,
1895–1900	143 ,,
1900–5	126 ,,

The decrease was constant, but from 1905 to 1910 there was a recovery and the number of births rose again to 150 (1905, 33; 1906, 29; 1907, 28; 1908, 35; 1909, 25). But the recovery was of short duration. From 1910 to 1915 the figure returned to 136 (1910, 31; 1911, 33; 1912, 29; 1913, 20; 1914, 23). The years 1913 and 1914, which were a time of prosperity, produced (in a commune whose total population had increased by over a hundred souls) a number of children born hardly equal to what was known during bad years at a time when people were not concerned at ordering their lives on a basis of reason (1855, 20 births; 1857, 21 births).

The reason for the increase in the total population was a fall in the death rate.

	Births	Deaths	Difference
1880–4	215	100	115
1885–9	168	117	51
1890–4	155	99	56
1895–9	143	72	71
1900–4	126	74	52
1905–9	150	104	46
1910–14	136	92	44

The average age of the population was, therefore, rising appreciably as can be seen from the following table which summarizes the changes over the years 1881 to 1901:

Age	1–10 years	11–20 years	21–30 years	31–40 years	
1881	305 (28·2%)	186 (17·2%)	161 (15%)	153 (14·07%)	

Age	41–50 years	51–60 years	61–70 years	Over 70 years	Total
1881 (contd)	103 (9·4%)	77 (7·09%)	73 (6·8%)	28 (2·5%)	1,086

Age	1–10 years	11–20 years	21–30 years	31–40 years		
1901	231 (19·8%)	253 (21·5%)	179 (15·4%)	145 (12·4%)		

1901 (contd)	41–50 years	51–60 years	61–70 years	Over 70 years	Total
	141 (12·1%)	120 (10·3%)	67 (5·7%)	39 (3·3%)	1,751

The proportion of the population under 31 years of age was 60·4 per cent in 1881 and 56·7 per cent in 1901: those under 41 years were 74·8 per cent in 1881 and 69 per cent in 1901.

As in everything, the township was ahead of the countryside in this development also. Taking 1901 as an example from the middle of the period we are examining, there were only six families in the town with more than three children: a farm worker, a mason, a blacksmith, a postman, a carrier and a harness-maker. Eight families had three children and were to have no more: 16 had two each and 37 had only one child (and would have no more). The public servants were in the van of this move towards barrenness. Among them were an old bachelor (the tax inspector), an old spinster (the postmistress), two families (teachers) who had only one child and would have no more: the roads surveyor had none, likewise the magistrate's clerk (married to a teacher) and the justice of peace; the police sergeant had one child; two gendarmes had one each and another had none; one roadman had one child, another had three . . . Seventeen civil service families living in Mazières in 1901, therefore, had (and would have no more) only 17 children, with one postman accounting for four and one roadman for three. The 15 other families had ten children between them. Among the notables the lawyer had two children, the doctor one, two *rentier* households had one each and the mayor was childless.

In the country, two families had seven or more than seven children; three had six each, eight had five each, 16 had four; 28 had three; 51 had two, 36 had one and 12 had none.[39] The following table shows the differences between town and country:

Number of children	0	1	2	3	4	5	6	7 or more
Town	14	37	16	8	3	1	2	–
Country	12	36	51	28	16	8	3	2

Of the 81 families in the town, 51 (or more than half) had either no child or only one; only 30 had two or more. In the country, of 156 families, only 48 (or less than one-third) had none or only one; 108 had two or more. And it must be emphasized that in the country itself the birth rate tended to decrease. In 1881, twenty years earlier, the commune could show 14 families (instead of two) with seven or more children; 12 families (instead of five) with six children; 22 (instead of nine) with five; 26 (instead of 19) with four.[40]

two

The school
The legislature's objectives

By 1880, at the same time that the moral and intellectual evolution that we have noticed was slowly and somewhat hesitatingly taking place in this rural commune, eminent men, representative of all the great ideas and traditions of France, were debating the educational problems of France. Important laws governing the primary education system had been passed. The passionate arguments that they gave rise to are worthy of a close study: they shed vivid light on a decisive moment in the history of contemporary France, one of those moments when its whole soul in all its strength and weaknesses becomes evident.

There was never any thought of glossing over in silence the fundamental problem, of reducing the teachers' rôle to one of acting as mere instructors in techniques which modern life rendered indispensable for all. French schools intended for the masses had grown up in the shade of the Church and those established before 1833 were usually in furtherance of a plan for religious proselytization; we have seen how Guizot in the development of popular education wanted above all to have the aid of the Church in guiding minds. The success of the elementary schools in 1880 may well have derived, judging from my native commune, from the economic rôle they were called upon to play among a people whose way of life was swiftly changing, but they could never cut themselves off from their traditional rôle which, in everyone's eyes, remained fundamental: the provision of a broad, liberal education. Emotions were too closely engaged for any other concept to be considered.

Not for a moment, either, was any serious thought given to decentralizing education, to stimulate or encourage any local initiative. Two general philosophies of life, two principles of universal application were in opposition: from now on it was inevitable that they should lead to impassioned debate in the Chamber of Deputies and in the Senate.[1]

The defenders of tradition

Among the speakers were those who represented Tradition: men who were devoted to religion, to the village and its church, who cherished the peasant family firmly bound together under the authority of the father and of the priest. They had a passionate love of country; they distrusted the town and the men who worked there; they distrusted new ideas and, beyond them, the education which propagated new ideas. They did not want the peasants to be too much or too quickly educated, thinking that in this way they could stop them from going to the towns. They objected to being compelled by law to send their children to school; they wanted this school, since it existed, to stay within the commune since it would thus be closer to the family; they wanted those parents who could afford to pay for their children's education to continue to pay; above all, they wanted the school to remain a church institution and the teacher to continue to be the priest's auxiliary.

To the defence of these ideas they brought a passionate obstinacy. It is possible to accuse them of wishing to keep the people in a state of ignorance within the Faith in order more easily to maintain a social system from which, in different degrees, they profited and in which they believed. For some of them at least, there is a grain of truth in this accusation. But for many, and certainly for the best of them, it was indeed a matter of something very worthy, much more profound than a mere defence of social privileges. It was a question of their view of mankind and the world as a whole, a pessimistic view within which came the notion of original sin, mistrust of man delivered over to his own powers, the idea of the necessity, in order to ensure a firm morality, of seeing that he was controlled by a religious faith and, in order to maintain his own happiness, to leave him tightly bound in his old customs. They were able to love the peasants quite sincerely – as they were – and felt that since many of them, like the workers or old Marianne, whose story I told earlier, were happy, it would be cruel and dangerous to make them conscious of their misery.

I imagine that Dr. Pouzet at Mazières, who in all good faith in 1850 saw no reason to change the peasants' habits and thought that their houses needed only a coat of whitewash to be made quite suitable, would have agreed, liberal-minded though he was and devoted to the people he administered.

And it should be added that, if those who sent their children to school had been consulted, most of them would have felt the same.[2]

These ideas could probably never have enjoyed more than a brief or, at least, partial success. Roads and railways were encouraging the development of a mobile society based on an exchange economy in which the education of the school became indispensable for everyone and in which a general feeling of the dignity of man was beginning to dawn in each man's mind. Already, as we have seen, the sons of better-off families in the commune were leaving a school run by a teacher whose teaching seemed unsatisfactory to go and finish their education in schools in Parthenay. Twenty years later, if the school had not been well run, poor people who were unable to send their children away to the town to learn to read, write and count would have complained loudly and bitterly.

An optimistic and rational view of the world

The partisans of the contrary view claimed the right to decide the destiny of the ignorant mass of the people.

They, too, knew and loved the people of France, but less perhaps as they were than as they thought they ought to be. On the real, living man with customs and traditions whose value they recognized but which they thought weighed too heavily on the development of the country, they superimposed an idea of man to which they wished all men to conform. The enthusiasm with which they defended the proposals of the compulsory education law can be seen on every page of their speeches, particularly in the conclusion of Jules Ferry's of 20 December 1880:

For us, the book – and by this I mean *any* book, – is
the fundamental, irresistible instrument for the
emancipation of the intelligence . . .

The first thing to be done is to learn to read; it is
the first thing even if it means learning by reading
the *Rosaire de Marie* or the *Bible de Royaumont*. . . .
I say this because I believe in the natural moral
rectitude of the human spirit, in the final triumph of
good over evil, in reason and in democracy.

In these words Jules Ferry reveals the secret of his beliefs –
which were those of many of his contemporaries. He had
confidence in man only because he believed in human reason –
which is the same in every man, and which must therefore be
awakened and cultivated in every man. To achieve this it is
necessary – and it is sufficient – to teach every man to read:
'reading is the irresistible instrument for the emancipation of
the mind': thanks to 'the natural moral rectitude of the human
mind', reason can – must – triumph in every man. Thenceforth,
the people – provided they can read – will be able to free themselves from all prejudices, from all passions, will make sane
judgments on all matters, will make sure of their sovereignty
and with that sovereignty will come 'the final triumph of good
over evil'.

This was the time when the possibilities of science in the
future seemed limitless.

Every child, then, rich or poor, must be able to go to school;
education must be free. Parents who did not appreciate that
their first duty was to see that children learnt to read were
guilty people; they must be punished; education must be
compulsory.[3] Being compulsory, it must be neutral because
there was no State religion. Thursday was reserved for ministers
of the various sects to teach their religion.

Doubtless, Jules Ferry set as much store as his opponents on
the principles of which they had declared themselves the
champion – the family, the Fatherland, even religion which,
in all sincerity, he denied wishing to attack.

The official syllabuses issued in 1887 called upon teachers in
the middle school to give lessons on Duty to the Family, to the
Fatherland and to God. Jules Ferry and most of those who
supported him by their cheers and votes would have been

horrified at the idea of an education which did not extol these sentiments. But, even though they held these sentiments very strongly, they did not form the central point of their doctrine: they believed above all in Man, in Reason, in Progress.

It was not to veneration of the home district, or of the family, or of the Fatherland – even less of God – that they wished the school to be dedicated but to the veneration of Reason.

The first clause of the Law aroused vehement argument, reading as it did:

Primary Education comprises:

(1) Moral and Civic instruction.

The various amendments proposed aimed at abolishing Civics and replacing Moral Instruction by religious instruction.[4] The optimistic and rationalist view of the world was to defeat the pessimistic, traditionalist and religious view at a time when immense material progress was being made and when boundless hopes were arising among the 'sovereign people'. And the votes of the majority faithfully supported Jules Ferry, no matter how brilliant the speeches of the minority might be.

The primary school, therefore, developed after 1882 under the emblem of Reason which alone provided a firm foundation for and ensured the fulfilment of Duty. As for the content of this Duty, the legislators of 1880 and 1882, like Guizot in 1833, thought that what they believed in was rational and, consequently, eternally true.

The school of reason

Reason, by its very nature, is general and universal.

The communal framework, which enclosed the school in so narrow and sometimes so oppressive a manner, now cracked. The teacher was to become a public servant; he was to be paid by the State, on which he was to be completely dependent except as regards his housing and the school buildings which would remain a charge on the communes not only, it must be said, because that was the custom but because Jules Ferry willed it so. There were to be no more communal councils, no local syllabuses or time-tables. Inspection would henceforth be carried out only in the name of the State. All syllabuses and time-tables would be drawn up in Paris; they would be the same for the whole of France.

Education would be the same for all.

From the point of view of the intellect, the aim was to shape the citizen, the whole man; to develop reason in every individual, irrespective of his environment or trade. What mattered, said the regulations of 1887, was that children should take away from the primary school 'firstly, a body of knowledge appropriate to their future requirements; secondly, and particularly, good habits of mind, an open and awakened intelligence; clear ideas, judgment, the power of reflection, order and accuracy in thought and language. The aim of primary education – as has been well said – is not to teach everything it is possible to know in all the subjects it covers but to learn properly that which is essential in each subject and of which no person may be allowed to be ignorant.'

From the point of view of morals, 'one will endeavour to develop in man, the man himself, that is to say a heart, an intelligence, a conscience'. Every pupil on leaving the school should take with him 'together with his little inheritance of elementary knowledge, a treasure still more precious: an upright conscience'. Children would be taught 'to distinguish between the written law and the moral law: the one fixes a minimum of prescriptions which society imposes on all its members under prescribed penalties; the other imposes on every individual, within the depths of his conscience, a duty which no one compels him to obey but which he may not fail to carry out without feeling guilty towards himself and towards God'.

The teacher's mission was quite clearly defined: 'It consists in strengthening, in implanting in the minds of his pupils, by presenting them in the course of the daily routine, these essential ideas of human morality which are common to all doctrines and necessary to every civilized man.'

A school for mankind

These were the regulations appended to the decree of 18 January 1887. Education of the intellect is marked by its universality; moral education is above all the education of the individual conscience and, consequently, of judgment: it is, in essence, based on what is of general application – on mankind as a whole.

The syllabuses, too, put more emphasis on one's duty to

oneself than upon duties to the social group of which one is a member. What is in the foreground is the cult of the individual and, within the individual, the cult of reason.

When Jules Ferry wrote to the teachers asking them to teach their children 'those elementary rules of the moral life which are not less generally accepted than those of language and arithmetic', and when he told them 'to speak out boldly when they were certain of being able to pass on to the children, not their own wisdom but the wisdom of the human race, one of those universal ideas which centuries of civilization have handed down as mankind's heritage',[5] his thoughts went far beyond the French family, beyond France itself to the whole of mankind. And such was, it should be emphasized, the inner meaning – whatever his own personal feelings might have been – of his actions and those of the creators of free, compulsory, secular education. Since their – and Jules Ferry's – principles, so completely secular and so strongly moderate, were based on an unshakeable faith in man's reason, they dedicated the schools of France, across the boundaries of the family and of the nation of which they still wished to preserve the cult, to the service of mankind as a whole.

Traditional France

In so doing they were in the stream of perhaps the most authentic and most universal aspect of a great French tradition. Our greatest writers have always sought to think and to feel in a setting of the world of mankind and not merely in a narrow national sphere.[6]

Moreover, their doctrine had this character of universality only because, in order to assert itself, it was obliged to oppose the Catholic doctrine, also universal in its very essence. The debates in the Chamber of Deputies and in the Senate centred on the idea of secularism. Jules Ferry's letters to teachers, the regulations accompanying the syllabuses in 1887 reveal the obsessions of their authors. They wanted to demonstrate that a morality which was secular, rationalist and (for Jules Ferry at least) spiritual, which was independent of any revealed religion, could exist and be as fine, as noble and as fertile in good works as no matter what religious morality; that it could – indeed, must – be taught in school and that, in addition, it was the only kind that could be taught in a system of compulsory education, entirely managed by the State which was continually striving to become more and more secular.

The rationalist tradition of French thought and the Christian tradition whose influence these men felt, even more particularly when they were in violent conflict, came together, then, to impose on these French patriots of 1880 the idea of a school dedicated, beyond the family and the Fatherland, to the cult of reason and of man.

The morality that they put forward could lead to great advances. It rested on solid foundations which seemed at the time to be indisputable and which would ensure its existence – the Family and the Nation, which bound individuals by precise duties which could go as far even as the final sacrifice. And it was permeated with a higher ideal.

A noble endeavour

What was attempted was fine in conception: the way ahead was clear and certain but it was extremely narrow and skirted dangerous precipices.

These ideas were probably not intended to be put into immediate, general circulation (something which might pre-suppose that they were a new creation) but something to be made explicit and amplified through the school just at a time when the means of communication were developing at unprece-dented speed. It was also a time when changes in the nation's way of life, the emphasis placed by people, even in the most remote parts of the countryside, on material wants in the shape of articles of all kinds manufactured in the cities or imported from abroad inflated the attraction of town life and consequently increased the contagious influence of apparently rational ideas. Again, it was a moment when – judging from the commune where I was born – there was the spontaneous growth among the people of a new religion in which the idea of progress was in the foreground. They wanted to keep their children as far as they could within the natural framework of the environment in which their life was lived and, by so doing, give a body to the soul that they were fashioning in them: but because they placed the centre of their faith elsewhere – in human nature and man's power of reason – and because they were intent on training this power of reason in their children, sharpening their critical faculty, they ran the risk of bringing them up more to discriminate and to criticize than to hold in honour things to which they could devote their life. They thereby risked separating them more swiftly than the general evolution of man made reasonably possible from that corner of the earth which was their birthplace, from the homes where they had grown up and from the Fatherland whose destiny they must both fashion and, at the same time, follow.

Mazières-en-Gâtine school

The central government's policy of providing every commune in France with facilities for free, compulsory and secular education was implemented in Mazières-en-Gâtine with considerable *éclat* immediately after 1880 when new school buildings were erected. This was not surprising in the light of what we know of M. Proust's temperament and how his ideas were in complete accord with those of Jules Ferry – or rather of Paul Bert.

In 1880, 150 were enrolled at the school built by M. Pouzet in 1853 half-way up the slope rising towards Parthenay. This school, which in those days had seemed to be almost extravagantly good, was by now much too small and quite inadequate.

On 29 October 1876 and on 17 November 1878 the town council, under M. de Tusseau, had twice refused to provide separate schools for boys and girls, in spite of the requirement imposed on them to do this by law. They argued that the commune had insufficient funds and that it was not possible to find any suitable site for a new school.

On 6 February 1881, one month after the election of a new council and a few days after his nomination as mayor by the administration, M. Proust had provision made for the expenditure of 20,000 francs for the building of a new boys' school. In so doing he proved the very keen interest he took in 'this most urgent and exciting problem of primary education'.[7]

The site on which his choice fell was a meadow called *Le Pinier* belonging to M. de Tusseau 200 yards along the Niort road. At the same time he requested the appointment of an assistant teacher, the average attendance at the school during the 1880–1 school year having reached 142. The assistant was appointed on 1 October of the following year and, until the new school was ready, held his class in the little room previously used by Mme Popineau.

No difficulties arose over the building of the school, even though the final cost considerably exceeded the estimates. The town council agreed at a meeting on 30 April 1882 to pay 1,660 francs for the site and to allocate 37,800 francs for the building. The teacher was to be magnificently housed: a fine house with four rooms with a kitchen-scullery at the side on the left, a stable-cum-box-room and a hayloft on the right and attic bedrooms for the assistant teachers in the roof. Situated in the midst of the fields, with its slate roof and *jardin anglais* it had all the appearance of a landlord's house. The school playground ran beside the Principal's house and opened on to the road through a high fence. The two classrooms with a very large cloakroom were at the back to the right. They were well lit but the windows were at a good height so that the pupils should not be distracted by what was going on outside. A meadow formed the background to the playground. M. Proust had had big ideas: the school was worthy of a commune which chance had made into the chief town of the *canton*. It was opened in 1882 and the old building became the girls' school. In 1883 a third classroom was added to the boys' school, the number of pupils (140) justifying this action and the appointment of a third teacher.

In 1885 a feeder school was opened at L'Angevinière, a large village about three kilometres from Mazières on the Niort road. Now the school map for the commune was finally drawn.

The feeder school (the hamlet school)

Little need be said about the school at L'Angevinière. In 1886 it contained 36 pupils; in 1887 the enrolment rose to more than 45 and, after 1890, stabilized at around 40 pupils. Masters and mistresses especially followed each other in swift succession from 1886 to 1914. They taught the children of the peasants in the neighbourhood to read, write and count; and that was all that was expected of them. The education that they gave was just as stereotyped and unconnected with the rural environment in which they were living as that of any school in any part of France. They could have given no example of affection for the countryside since twelve teachers followed each other in the space of twelve years: the longest-serving mistress stayed for only five years, most for only one or two years. But the influence of the environment was such that not one pupil from L'Angevinière school sought to continue his education after obtaining the primary school leaving certificate and almost all looked for work within the district. This fact is confirmation of what has been said earlier on the influence of the township which, having become differentiated from the countryside, took the lead in drawing it on toward a more modern way of civilized life. It also illustrates the narrow limits of the influence of the school.

The girls' school

Little, too, will be said of the girls' school. Much could, no doubt, be said of the aims and orientation of the teaching given there but the same general problems will be found when we deal with the boys' school and can be examined with more precision there. The only point to be noted is that several years elapsed before a competent mistress was in charge. Whereas in 1856 the boys' school was already directed by an excellent teacher, the girls' school had to wait until 1886 before it had a good head-mistress. Her assistants were not always of good quality: the town council even asked for one to be removed (council meeting of 3 April 1888).

After 1895 the school had to meet competition from a private Catholic school. This competition, however, was intense only at the time when the mayor and the priest were engaged in their violent quarrels and when minor incidents were blown up into importance by political passion. When emotions cooled down after the death of the curé Proton and the departure of M. Proust, the teachers at the two schools left each other alone without ill-will and even with a certain amount of mutual sympathy. The Sisters of Saint-André were secularized at the time of the law on religious communities and continued to teach without interference in the buildings donated to them by the Jorigné family.

The State school always had more pupils than the private school. It had 80 when it opened and enrolment settled down at around 90 until 1900, after when it decreased first to 80 and later to 70 pupils. The private school never had more than 50 pupils, divided in two classes. These came mainly from isolated farms in the south of the commune or from nearby villages in neighbouring communes. The pupils in the State school came mostly from larger villages in the north of the commune. Probably this is accounted for by the fact that the private school was sited on the southern edge of the village, while the State school was at the opposite end, a fact which may well have influenced parents' choice. It corresponds, all the same, with all that has been said up to now: the scattered peasant population in the south of the commune was generally more closely attached to old ways and paid less attention to education than the more densely settled area in the north of the commune.

I have dealt very briefly with the girls' school, but will now endeavour to examine as closely as possible the development of the boys' school and analyse its influence.

The boys' school: attendance

Primary education was made free in 1882. In point of fact, the number of pupils exempted from fees under the old law had been rising rapidly: 41 in 1879; 72 in 1880; 76 in 1881. Education had become compulsory but attendance during the early years remained very nearly the same as previously. Already by 1880 the great majority of children in the commune were passing through the school.

In 1881 and 1882 there was a sharp increase in enrolment: 240 pupils in 1881 and 278 in 1882 as against 198 in 1880, but this was the moment when work on the construction of the railway line had considerably (and temporarily) increased the school population of the commune. In 1883 enrolment dropped to 164.[8]

The following are the figures for subsequent years:

1884	166 pupils	1888	116 pupils
1885	161 ,,	1889	131 ,,
1886	160 ,,	1890	122 ,,
1887	137 ,, — (feeder school at L'Angevinière opened November 1886)		

Enrolment remained stationary until 1900 (1895, 127; 1900,

135) but after then decreased regularly as the following figures show:

1900	135 pupils	1908	94 pupils
1901	126 ,,	1909	98 ,,
1902	113 ,,	1910	98 ,,
1903	106 ,,	1911	98 ,,
1904	102 ,,	1912	103 ,,
1905	105 ,,	1913	103 ,,
1906	99 ,,	1914	100 ,,
1907	93 ,,		

In this way the decrease in the birth rate was reflected in school enrolment. But, if attendance had not improved in quantity: it had greatly improved in quality. From 1880 almost all children from the township attended regularly: only choir boys were often absent or children from poor families who would go to the 'handouts' which were a feature of every wedding or funeral in the better-off families and who would miss school when they went off to gather firewood.

Country children were even less regular. They stayed at home whenever – and this happened frequently – there was work to be done. In fact, after they had reached the age of eleven or twelve, they hardly attended school except during the four winter months, although it is true to say that this process would continue until they were seventeen or eighteen. Against this were those who left school for good at ten or eleven – those whose parents hired them out to work in the farms herding cattle, leading oxen at ploughing time, helping to feed the cattle in the byre and in the thousand and one tasks the farmer's wife would find for them.

Gradually attendance improved and the average age of the pupils decreased. On 15 November 1883 M. Bouet sent to the Inspector of Primary Schools at Parthenay a list of over-age pupils who wanted to attend the Mazières school. The list contained 18 names. Three were born in 1866 and were now seventeen: two were born in 1867 and were sixteen: six were born in 1868 and were fifteen.

Four years later, on 5 December 1887, he sent in a similar request. This time it contained only 13 names: three born in 1870 were seventeen years old; one born in 1871 was sixteen; two born in 1872 were fifteen. In 1883, then, Mazières school accepted during the winter 11 pupils aged 15 or over. Four years later there were only six in this category. Ten years after that the register shows none. Also the crosses in the register marking absentees were widely spaced.

The following is a table of absentees in 1880–1:

Month	Total enrolment	Pupils absent less than 4 times	Pupils absent more than 4 times
October	106	65	41
November	122	76	46
December	147	66	81
January	158	75	83
February	154	85	69
March	150	53	97
April	139	89	50
May	134	101	33
June	120	77	43
July	121	66	55
August	105	85	20

The same table for 1900–1 shows:

Month	Total enrolment	Pupils absent less than 3 times	Pupils absent more than 3 times
October	110	74	36
November	115	85	30
December	122	90	32
January	135	95	40
February	131	96	35
March	129	92	37
April	118	90	28
May	115	87	28
June	112	75	37
July	108	71	37
August	104	90	14

The improvement is quite clear both in the regularity of daily attendance and the longer period that it covered. The average number of pupils enrolled in June compared with those enrolled in January is in the ratio of 120 : 158 in 1880–1 : it is 112 : 135 in 1900–1. That is to say that 38 pupils only attended during the winter in 1880, a figure which is reduced to 23 in 1900. In 1910 it was down to nine: 88 pupils were on the register in January and 79 remained there in June.

This improvement had been made without resorting to the law on compulsory attendance. In living memory there is no instance of anyone having been brought to court over this matter. But M. Bouet's prestige was growing and one wished to please M. Proust who 'had a long arm'! And one appreciated more and more the value of education. Finally, and above all, the introduction of machines began to bring more leisure time, even to the peasants. When, by 1900, the Brabant plough was used on most farms and machines were used for chopping turnips and swedes for cattle food there was less need for the service of the young workers and the farmers gave up hiring them: so they went to school. Thus economic and social change in the district had more effect than the law on compulsory attendance which was only brought into action – as Jules Ferry had foretold – as a striking demonstration of the moral obligation (which applied to all parents) of sending their children to school.

The school's influence

What kind of teaching did the school provide? What effect did it have on the pupils?

A school's influence depends largely on what is taught there and we have seen the kind of syllabus conceived by Jules Ferry for the primary school and we know the direction towards which it guided the pupils' minds. We have also looked quickly at the 1887 regulations.

A school's influence also depends on the environment which surrounds it and on the adaptation of its syllabus to that environment. We know the conditions of Mazières commune at the time of 1880. M. Proust, a notable anti-clerical, had just defeated the Comte de Tusseau, descendant of the Squires of Petit-Chêne, in the municipal elections. The story of the bells and the cemetery led to conflict with the priest. We know the mental attitudes of the people and how, slowly and surely, a few simple ideas were making their way in under the pressure of new economic and social conditions. Their minds were, in this way, ready to accept an education which aimed above all at awakening and fostering a sense of judgment.

A school's influence depends also and perhaps particularly on the personality of those who teach in it and remain there sufficiently long. Mazières school was fortunate – something which was not uncommon in those days – in having the same headmaster from 1880 to 1916. In his long tenure of office his strong personality influenced the teaching methods of his assistants and left its mark on generations of children who came to him as his pupils. We should know more of him before analysing the influence that he was able to make.

A portrait of the teacher[9]

M. August Bouet was born in 1858 at Vausseroux, a tiny commune in Gâtine, about fifteen kilometres from Mazières. He was the only son of a peasant farmer. He was a brilliant pupil at his village school, so much so that, when he was twelve, his teacher entered him for the scholarship examination for the Lycée. He failed on account of a grammatical error due to his peasant origin (for him at that time the word *vipère* was masculine and not feminine in gender because country folk said: *'un grou (gros) vipère'*). If he had passed he would most certainly have had a brilliant university career. In spite of this disappointment he continued to attend school until he was sixteen when, without ever having left his village, he went to the *Ecole Normale* at Parthenay. In 1878 he passed out top of his class with the full Certificate (*Brevet complet*) which is equivalent to the present Higher Certificate (*Brevet supérieur*) but which was rarely awarded at that time even among students at the *Ecole Normale*. For a few months he taught at Secondigny-en-Gâtine; for a year at Saint-Marc-la-Lande, five kilometres from Mazières. In 1881 he came to Mazières as headmaster. He married a girl from the township and remained there for the rest of his teaching career. In 1925 he became mayor of the commune.

The simplicity of this career, confined to a single appointment, is extremely significant. It indicates, first of all, that throughout his life M. Bouet had more the feeling of being a member of the commune – or, rather, the whole district – in which he exercised his profession than of being a member of a special, outside, body: the teaching force of the *département*. His ambition was to be one of the respected leading citizens among the people with whom he had integrated himself and not one of the most highly regarded public servants in his profession.

This view of life very probably derived from his peasant origins, from a childhood spent in the midst of the countryside with no thought of the possibility of travelling or moving away from it. It would even have allowed him to be content to remain in the rural commune to which fate had sent him, since there he found peasant folk he could understand and love; where he could rediscover the pleasures of his childhood – fishing and gardening. He would even have felt – and with every justification – that he had achieved a good social success. The girl he married was well-off: she was the only daughter of a tradesman in the town who owned several houses. In a sense, this marriage was symbolical of the social transformation which was happening in Mazières, of the increase in wealth and the transference of influence which was taking place. Here was the only son of poor peasants coming, because he was intelligent and industrious, to take up employment as a Government servant and consolidating his situation and movement upward in the social scale by marrying the only daughter of a small shopkeeper in the township who had been able to gain a certain amount of money by reason of the development of trade and an economic revolution in the region.

Because he was known to have money, as much as because he was a good teacher, everyone respected him. He consorted as an equal with the town officials of a higher rank than his own: the justice of peace, the tax inspector, the surveyor. Dressed like them, often superior to them in knowledge and culture, always in his intimate knowledge of country matters, he went shooting with them – a sport in which he excelled.

He was secretary to the mayor. He enjoyed M. Proust's friendly confidence – something of which he was very proud. Among the people of the town he formed strong, if respectful, friendships. And so, throughout his career, he had that feeling of stability and that deep inner contentment which are indispensable to active happiness. The very fact that he showed himself so completely attached to the soil on which he lived and to the customs of the country gives a clear idea of the kind of influence he was to exercise.

As we have said, he was an excellent student at the *Ecole Normale* at Parthenay. He had acquired a broad and solid education much more oriented, it seems to me, towards history and science than to philosophy and literature. In history itself he was much more interested in facts than in ideas; and the curiosity of his mind was directed more to the observation of local things than to more general study. The only writings he has left are a local monograph and a course in agriculture, and a few articles on local history.

At the *Ecole Normale* he had had lessons in the methods and principles of education which are to be found in some notebooks I have been able to consult. The following is an important passage:

> Finally, in the fifth place, we shall consider the
> qualities and, especially, the duties of the teacher.
> These duties are concerned with the following points:
> first, with his private conduct as a man. The teacher
> must be sincerely religious; he must, as much by his
> attitude as by his words, inspire respect for the
> established government, for the law and for the
> magistrates charged with its execution. Also his
> home must be a model of concord and good behaviour:
> he must be prompt in paying his bills and he must
> avoid that sorry mania of wishing to raise himself above
> his station. Besides these general duties, the
> teacher has special duties towards those placed in
> charge of the direction and inspection of primary
> education: to these authorities he owes respect,
> deference and affection.

This was the course given at the Parthenay *Ecole Normale* by M. Brothier, Principal of the college in 1877. M. Bouet was a hard worker and could not understand how anyone could not enjoy work: no one was more severe than he on tramps and idlers. He was thrifty and could not understand how anyone could expect to become well-off other than by hard work and thrift. He would never have that 'sorry mania of wishing to raise himself above his station'. Nevertheless, he was not religious in the sense intended by his Principal, that is, he was not a practising Catholic. He believed, on the contrary, very deeply and very religiously in the existence of a secular morality, independent of any religion. The essential elements of this religion were, moreover, the same as those which were growing spontaneously among the people and which we have noted: faith in progress, belief in the Republic, love of country.

As regards human progress, M. Bouet had *la foi du charbonnier*. This can be seen in the local monograph from which I have quoted several significant examples. After speaking of the farm workers who, from fear of unemployment, tried to put threshing machines out of action by mixing stones with the sheaves of wheat, he compares them with the Weser boatmen breaking up Papin's steamboat. He adds: 'Clearly these happenings cannot last long: but these gross mistakes to which the common people fall prey demonstrate excellently to the government how important it is to educate people, to enlighten them and destroy the prejudices of days gone by.' No shadow of doubt crosses his mind: machines manifest a striking victory of human ingenuity and the power of reason over matter. It would be a sin against reason not to make use of them; they cannot but lighten man's burden and hasten progress: anything that stands against this march forward can be only superstition and prejudice which education will chase from the scene.

He was an ardent republican but in no way a democrat. He would most certainly have been shocked if the mayor of Mazières were a peasant or a tradesman and not a bourgeois like M. Proust. He never envisaged that his best pupils could aspire to a future different from his own, to a career superior to that of a teacher. It was certainly not he who gave Pascal Chaignon, the postman, the idea of sending his son to the secondary school. On the contrary, he supported in good faith and with all his power the conservative views of M. Proust. Later on he was to oppose in the *canton* socialist propaganda whose egalitarian arguments he detested.

He was a true patriot. He belonged to a generation when teachers were not called upon to do military service and so he had never been a soldier. But he gave his daughter in marriage to an officer and, throughout his career, he was continually repeating to himself, to raise in his own eyes his modest but noble profession, 'that in 1870 it was the Prussian teachers who defeated France'. He would never ask himself if the progress in which he believed imposed on him any different duty; he did his utmost to inspire his pupils with a love for their country.

Such, then, was this man who believed in Reason and in Progress, in the nobility of his task but whose thoughts moved only among things that he knew well within a narrow physical field, among men he respected.

When Maurice Barrès addressed the Chamber of Deputies in 1910 on the parlous condition of the village school teacher, 'alone amidst peasants and labourers, isolated in his house by reason of his half-education, unfinished and feeble as it is', he was wrong: many village teachers were like M. Bouet.

When Jaurès, in order to save the teacher from living in an abstract world in the half-knowledge of textbooks, could find the only means of reuniting him with the world of reality was by joining his trade union he, too, was wrong. Many teachers like M. Bouet did live in the real world of the things and the people of the commune where they carried out their duties. And they lived a happy, useful life.

M. Bouet's work, in particular, produced results because he lived and thought according to the moral standards of the life around him, because his teaching went with the grain of the evolution of the people, because in this way he aided that evolution and because he gave his pupils a clearer understanding of the principles governing life around them.

The assistant teachers

He was also helped in this task by some excellent assistants who themselves – and this was typical of the times – sprang from rural origins and were happy to stay in this village which had nothing very attractive about it.

One was to stay there for his whole teaching career. It is true that he was a native of the place, the son of one of the oldest and most respected artisan families in the town: his entry to the *Ecole Normale* has already been mentioned earlier.

As a teacher he was able to return to his village, proud of his family whose prosperity and high standing increased his own power as a public servant. He married a Mazières girl and became headmaster in 1925. He has since retired and is now (1945) Mayor of the commune, enjoying the respect of all.

Another assistant stayed for twelve years at Mazières from

1892 to 1904 and only left to gain further qualifications and return later as a headmaster. Teachers' ambitions in those days were very circumscribed: they were confined to the *canton* and had not spread out to the *département*. He was the only son of a small farmer in the Thouars plain. He was top in the entrance examination to the *Ecole Normale* and passed out first. Through his knowledge of country matters and through his own tastes he remained close to the peasants. He formed close ties of friendship in the town which still bring him back from time to time at the age of seventy, although he lives quite far away. He certainly felt the need to put down roots. But he had married a teacher. Besides this he was too intelligent, was too taken up with general ideas and intellectual work, watched too closely the careers of his fellow-students at the *Ecole Normale* not to swing back and forth between one view of life as sym-bolized by M. Bouet and another in the achievement of success in one's career as measured by the status of the position one holds and the chances for personal advancement that it offers. From 1904 to 1911 he was headmaster at the boys' school of Saint-Marc-la-Lande, five kilometres from Mazières, whose town band he continued to conduct. In 1911, when M. Bouet delayed his retirement, he accepted the post of headmaster of a *cours complémentaire*[10] in the north of the *département* and he finished up as head of a large *cours complémentaire* at Brelous-la-Crèche.

These are the three teachers I had the good fortune to sit under as a pupil from 1900 to 1908.[11]

The infants' class, when I was a pupil there, was taken by the first of these two assistant teachers. He was very young, very patient, very conscious of his profession: and we liked him very much. His chief aim in class was to teach us the three Rs and he got excellent results. After two years of school – three at the most – his pupils could read perfectly well; they knew their multiplication tables and could do long, difficult sums without a mistake. He also gave us an elementary education in the world of ideas and we also had excellent little lessons in history and geography. It is from his teaching and the stories he told that I retain a tender regard for Blanche de Castille and St Louis. It was in his class that, at the age of seven, I learnt that it was the duty of every French citizen to pay his taxes and obey the law. All this was excellent and seemed quite natural to everyone. The windows of the classroom might well look out on to a garden just as those of the most modern nursery school at floor level, but any study of things near at hand had no place whatever in the syllabus. I can remember my sense of wonder as a small boy looking out from my desk on a garden which seemed to me full of mystery and grandeur because it was a place unknown to me and yet was close by the school. I had a quite distinct feeling that everything I saw outside and which so filled me with delight was something foreign to the classroom and a source of dangerous distraction: books, summaries, lessons, problems, dictation – these were the only things worthy of my attention.

The second class was taken by the other assistant. He had the deserved reputation throughout the commune of being a hard and strict task-master. The windows in his classroom were far from being too low: they were high up on the left hand wall. Through them we could only see a bit of the sky and, just occasionally, the end of the branch of a tree waving in the wind. We really did work hard in his class. We learnt the metric system (the metre at that time was understood to be the ten-millionth part of a quarter of the earth's meridian – what glory for the men of the Revolution to have made such a discovery!) and the franc was related to the metre through the medium of the table of measures of weight and capacity. I remember being punished for not knowing the correct measures of weight. We worked out problems; we learnt to read better; we had lessons in history and geography and science and even – at our tender age – in civics. All this was done with an impeccable regularity and from a real desire to get the pupils to understand and to awaken their sense of judgment, just as the regulations recommended should be done. And this was not always achieved without some difficulty. I remember in particular that one day the teacher wanted to explain to us why the republican system of government, based on universal suffrage, was superior to any other. At one point in the lesson he must have thought we did not understand – we were then between eight and ten years old – so he borrowed an example from our daily routine. 'Think,' he said, 'what you do when you go out of the classroom. You stand up. You get out of your desks. The row nearest the door goes out first, the second follows them, then the third and so on. . . .'

He must then have seen that his example was badly chosen and I can still hear him hesitate before going on. But we waited for him and he launched out bravely: 'Suppose I let you vote to decide which row should go out first; this would be an example of universal suffrage.' The idea seemed to us quite astonishing. 'If I don't have you vote,' he added, 'it is because I know you would soon change your minds; it is also because I know better than you what ought to be done; it is not the same thing when it is no longer a question of children but of grown-up men.' This conclusion seemed reasonable to us and our faith in the virtue of a universal suffrage reserved for men – whose judgment was stable and to be relied on – was complete.

This teacher, excellent though he was, had no more interest than his colleague in the first class in relating his teaching to local matters. He, too, put all his energy into giving a firm grounding in fundamentals – reading, writing, arithmetic and basic ideas.

But both of them were integrated in the community. It might be that their teaching did not help to bring us closer to the things around us by rendering us more conscious of them: indeed it might even make us more ready to detach ourselves from them by giving us an idea of the wider world outside and filling our minds with more general concepts; nevertheless, their example of a simple life lived among the events and people of the region kept us close to our milieu, our families and to our village. It was inevitable, too, that the pleasure they felt in living in Mazières showed itself, in one way or another, in sudden glimpses in their teaching. One day it would be a reference in patois to such-and-such a village from where a pupil had arrived late at school because the road was bad. One day it might be an allusion to a game of cards played the evening before: 'You haven't done your homework; you preferred to have a game of "Giles" last night and it is always nice to play "Giles"!' This would be said in a tone of irony but also from a hidden and strong understanding; and the game of 'Giles' would seem to all of us to have all the delights of the forbidden fruit, something of the *summum bonum* of all the pleasures on earth that man can enjoy.

M. Bouet's teaching

In the third – the 'big' – class under the paternal and undisputed authority of M. Bouet we would meet with an atmosphere slightly more different and more closely touched by local matters.

M. Bouet taught the syllabus as prescribed by the 1887 regulations to perfection. On arrival at Mazières he set monthly compositions to be written on single sheets of paper that he took the trouble to bind together. Several series of these compositions have been preserved. From them one can get a very clear idea of the standard of education reached by the pupils. In 1889 the whole of his class (49 of them) at the end of the school year were capable of solving easy problems in arithmetic and of writing short compositions in French without too many mistakes or mis-spellings, even though most of them had not reached the school leaving age.[12]

He did not, however, confine himself to teaching the three Rs. He took great trouble in teaching anything to do with the knowledge of everyday things. He would try to carry out elementary scientific experiments at a time when such a thing was very unusual. Mme. Bouet's tall paraffin lamp was sometimes to be found on his desk surrounded by bottles and flasks. He would heat pieces of iron and show that they could no longer go through the bottle necks. One day he even tried to demonstrate to us the proportion of oxygen and nitrogen in the air: my recollection is that he failed and so we had to trust in his word without the illusion of having it proved to us that the air contains one-third of oxygen to two-thirds of nitrogen.

He neglected none of the subjects in the syllabus he was required to teach and the excellent results he obtained are proved by the constant success gained in the C.E.P.E. examination.[13]

The number of illiterate conscripts decreased. It was in about 1890 that the first pupils who had been through his school were called before the recruiting board. For a period of some ten years there were still a few young men every year who had not received a sufficient education at school for them to be able to write after they had reached the age of twenty-one, but at least they could all read and count. After 1900 there were practically no illiterate conscripts in the commune.[14]

Taken as a whole his teaching was 'universal', that is to say, it was aimed at the training of man to live anywhere and not merely of youths born in Mazières and destined, for the majority, to live their lives there. It is true that a map of the *département* of Deux-Sèvres hung in his classroom; but he rarely used it. He taught the geography of France and the world with great care; the subject for the geography essay on 25 February 1895 was Egypt. In his history teaching he made little use of his great knowledge of local history.

In a region where, in 1900, the only measure of area in common use was the *boisselée*, when firewood was measured by the *corde* and money was counted in *pistoles*, he taught only the metric system. He would certainly have thought that he was failing in his mission if, when setting problems, he had spoken of anything other than *ares*, *stères* or *francs*. In this way he carried out to the letter his task of missionary of the French State, charged with giving his pupils a minimum body of knowledge which would be indispensable to them and which would put them on a level with pupils in the 36,000 other communes of France.

Through this broad, general education he broadened his children's imagination: he gave them confidence to meet, without fear, change of career or locality; he gave them the chance to leave the area if they were forced to or wanted to.[15]

However, he himself was too much of a countryman in all his tastes and was too deeply fixed in Mazières to cut them off from their roots.

A rural education

Because he carried out his duties in a rural commune and because he was also the son of a peasant and was interested in farming matters, he made a place in his teaching for agriculture.

In 1896 he had composed a 'Practical Course in Agriculture' for the Mazières-en-Gâtine district. All his pupils were required to copy it out and keep it by them for their use when need arose. The strong exercise book in which his lessons were bound contains more than a hundred pages written with the great art and extreme care only possible for a teacher of that time; fifty-five pages are devoted to agriculture, twenty to horticulture and twenty to arboriculture.

In the specifically agricultural course there are many lessons, definitions and general precepts which apply to France as a whole. But one occasionally comes across precise, even picturesque, details which show that, while he was writing, M. Bouet had in his mind the little district whose customs, potentiality and needs he knew so well. And the lessons he gave in class were full of anecdotes: a year when there was a drought such-and-such a farmer grew wonderful cabbages while his neighbour's crops failed because he had ploughed deep and the water in the sub-soil had risen. Another had been able to get rid of the *cuscute* in such-and-such a field by using the method that he, M. Bouet, was recommending in his lesson. Yet another had made a good deal of money by culling and improving his stock.

Nevertheless, everything that touched on agriculture proper had but little effect. This was probably because it was a question of theoretical instruction: how could the poor man have found the time to take us out into the fields while he was preparing his pupils for the Certificate? It was also probably due to the fact that a number of the pupils, particularly the brightest, those who were most regular in attendance, lived in the town, knew nothing about agriculture and took no interest in it. M. Bouet committed the error – a very common error – of believing that his school, because it was situated in the country, was essentially a rural school. We know, having followed its development, that, on the contrary, its origin was essentially urban: it was a creation of an initiative from the central government; its success was due to pupils from the town. Finally, it is certain that these lessons in agriculture lacked the effect that he might have expected from them because the farmers' sons felt that they knew more than he about farming.

Very lively discussion often arose between the teacher, confident in what he had read and observed, and this or that young thirteen-year-old peasant already initiated in the practice of farming by his father and despising from the bottom of his heart all this theoretical knowledge he was expected to learn.

This course in agriculture, of which our old teacher was so proud – and justifiably proud – was learnt with complete lack of interest, and only because they had to, by the town pupils:

the country pupils met it with stubborn arguments. In their homes their peasant fathers were amused at the folly of this excellent teacher who wanted to teach people their trade.[16]

Lessons in horticulture and arboriculture were followed with much closer attention and had greater effect for many reasons: we occasionally were taken into the school garden; some lessons were concrete and practical (we loved doing grafts); M. Bouet had a well-deserved reputation as a fine gardener; we all had gardens at home and we could immediately practise there what we had learnt at school – and show results both for our pockets and our self-esteem.

More than one twelve-year-old boy was not a little proud when, for the first time, he pruned the trees in his father's garden. Those youngsters are now men of a ripe old age and many of them owe to their former teacher the fact that they possess fine gardens full of fine trees.

So, anything which smacked of apprenticeship to a definite trade (farming) slid over the pupils' minds, particularly perhaps over those who might have profited most but who shut themselves up in a shell of indifference, if it was not hostility, through which nothing might penetrate concerning something that they wanted to learn only by practical experience. On the other hand, anything in the lessons which might be of general interest, whatever their parents' trade, whatever career the pupils might expect to follow, was listened to attentively and profitably. Thus, this primary school, despite all the efforts of an élite teacher, defined for itself a purpose which was not technical, not specialized but general, consisting not in training producers but in preparing men for life.

Through his teaching of horticulture and arboriculture, even of agriculture, M. Bouet nevertheless managed to a certain extent to keep his pupils close to rural life, to their environment. The very atmosphere created in the class itself by his friendly relations with his children's parents, by his close attachment to Mazières and everything that went on there had the greater effect. He was always anxious to know about everyone's health and the daily events in their life: 'I see that your father has built a fine cattle shed. His cows will have a better home than people used to have in the old days.' The young peasant to whom these words were addressed would stand up, his eyes shining with pride, and his friends would have some feeling of respect for him. In the course of a lesson or conversation M. Bouet would let fall that in such-and-such a meadow you could find excellent mushrooms, that over in that wood there were some fine *cèpes*, that you could catch crayfish in that stream. He was always interested in where hares had their forms, where partridges were nesting. He liked to talk about the state of the crops and then he would reckon in *boisselées* and not in *ares*. 'The other day I walked by your land: tell your father he has got a fine crop of turnips'; or: 'Your father has put the field near the house down to potatoes: how many *boisselées* are there?' etc. Because it was part of what he believed in and was dear to his heart, he never missed the chance of contrasting the free life of the land where everyone worked at his own rhythm with town life, of which he knew little but which he imagined always to be feverish, enmeshed in a thousand and one commitments – and which he detested.

M. Bouet was, therefore, very close to finding, instinctively, what might well have been the true purpose of his teaching in this rural commune in which the people were still relatively unchanged. If only the Ministry regulations, which he put into practice in his own way and according to his temperament but always to the best of his ability, had emphasized the need to train and bring together French youth not by cultivating and developing in them what was common to all but by deepening their knowledge of what was peculiar to each. He would then joyfully and fruitfully have taught local history, local geography: he would have had his pupils observe the trees, plants, birds and insects of the locality; he would have urged them to study local customs if the questions in the C.E.P.E. had not required a wider and more general knowledge. And at the same time as providing his pupils with the means of communicating with other Frenchmen, he would have kept them more closely, more strongly, attached to their own home district. Doubtless he would have prevented very few from leaving: the need to earn their living would have made the same young men leave, and many too would have had that same driving aspiration within them and would have gone. But all of them would have been accustomed to making judgments from facts and the intimate knowledge of the environment in which they had grown up would have given to those who went away, for the rest of their life, a self-assurance and an anchor which in a crisis may have been lacking in some. This might even have made his moral education more effective.

Moral education

Deliberately, at a time when France had a government which was both liberal and centralized, but without religion or even clearly defined and laid-down State articles of faith, he set out to share with his pupils the beliefs by which he ordered his life and to give them a prescription for the journey through life.

His belief in Progress was proclaimed continually in his teaching.

I have found in his monograph on Mazières commune the example of the Weser boatmen smashing the first steamboats, an example dear to his heart which he often quoted in class to condemn hidebound conservatism in every aspect. I can still hear his solemn, rather heavy voice pronouncing the words: *bateliers de la Weser*. He also often used the example of the weavers breaking Jacquard's looms and emphasized the indisputable benefit which the weavers themselves in many factories gained from these looms. He was happy to contrast the lot of peasants in the Middle Ages and even in 1789 with the prosperity and liberty they enjoyed under the Third Republic.

Moreover, it was probably because he believed in Progress, i.e. the possibility of there being a paradise on earth which must be gained and which was not far distant, that his morality was firmly secular. Man's duties towards God appeared in the syllabus. I must confess that I never heard him mention them except when it was a question of reproving a badly brought-up child for having sworn. In every way he endeavoured to remain neutral. He fully acknowledged the charitable rôle of the Church in the Middle Ages. He passed lightly over the Inquisition and one of his best history lessons was on the Wars of Religion. He would quote with great emphasis the example and words of Michel de l'Hôpital and would use the occasion to advocate peace between the political parties which were tearing each other to pieces in Mazières as elsewhere. But, great though the respect is that I bear to his memory, I must admit that I find his reason lacking in depth and that he was too credulous in his own beliefs. Also, the time when teachers were supervised by priests was too recent for him always to be able to render full justice to revealed religion in general and to Catholicism in particular. In the end his religious neutrality came to disappear.[17]

But if he believed in Progress he was, as we know, too closely involved in everyday life and with too strongly rational a mind not to be against all precipitate and violent action. In his teaching he was very severe on the 1848 Revolution and the workers in the National Workshops. I remember making him very angry because I was reading one day a story of the 1870 Commune by Louise Michel. 'Where did you find the book by this old madwoman? I shall tell your father to watch over what you read' and he confiscated the book. He really believed that, in the year 1900 under the Third Republic, all Mazières children had the duty to consider themselves happy with their lot and we were too closely attached to our habits, we lived in too limited a horizon to be able to think he was wrong.

It is hardly necessary to add that he taught us to love the Republic. With obvious enjoyment he gave very clear, lively and dramatic lessons on French history. No shadow of doubt crept into what he taught. France had indeed had a few good kings worthy of unreserved admiration: St Louis, Henry IV. These kings may have had some great ministers (and he picked out for special mention Sully, for whom grazing and arable farming were the twin breasts on which France fed; and Colbert, born among merchants, thrifty and hard-working). But most of the kings had done harm to France: Louis XIV was too fond of war; Louis XV was only fond of pleasure; Louis XVI had deserved his unhappy fate by his total lack of will-power and by his treasonable act. The French Revolution had marked the beginning of a new era in our history. After 1789 good law had begun to win the day: Progress had started its march forward. It had been halted by the Restoration and by the excesses of 1848 which had led to the Empire, but since the coming of the Third Republic there was nothing left to ask for: there was no limit to progress. And so he stopped his teaching of history at 1870.

With great attention and regularity he gave the lessons in morals and civics as prescribed on the time-table. For these he generally used the textbook written by Ernest Lavisse under the pseudonym of Pierre Laloi, published by Colin. This little book was very cleverly written and had been published in editions of several thousand copies. Morals and civic instruction were mingled together in very vivid stories. In this book we learnt all about the organization of magistrates' courts, dealing with the ill fortune which befell careless and unthrifty business men or drunkards and men of violence. We saw, on the other hand, how a man could raise himself up by his own efforts if he used the various resources put at the disposal of the thrifty by a wise and foreseeing State. We saw the value of taxes. We learnt the machinery of elections and the inestimable benefits of universal suffrage. We watched the transformation of a backward commune through the activities of an intelligent and energetic mayor. We looked with admiration on a well-managed farm presented as a model for all farmers. The final story – an extremely moving one – extolled patriotism.

This little book, shining with faith in a democracy in which justice is always seen to be done, in which public officials are always seen to be friendly, intelligent and unbiased, in which taxes are always seen to be fairly shared out and usefully expended, in which, step by step, is formed a picture of a strong and wise Republic guaranteeing order and progress, organized in a rational way on bases which are unshakeable because they are indisputably right – this little book had a tremendous influence. 'Good day, your Majesty,' said the locksmith Jesserand in greeting Frontier the farmer, and we naïvely believed with Frontier that all the electors were their own rulers, men of knowledge and reason. 'Who voted for the taxes? You, me, all of us.' We were impressed with this definition and used it in our play.

The virtues extolled by our teacher, both in his formal lessons and in the trend of all his teaching, were, moreover, the same as those I have referred to earlier. Respect for grandparents and parents, love of one's brothers (a brother, he said, is a friend provided by nature), pity for the weak, neighbourliness – all these were taught in a way we could understand with examples taken from life. As regards one's duty towards oneself, he emphasized temperance and thrift and he even used arithmetic lessons to show how necessary it was to be sober and thrifty. I remember working many problems on how much a workman could save if he did not smoke or drink: by the end of his life, thanks only to his economies, he would be able to buy himself a little house. These lessons were not without effect in an area in the grip of full social mobility where people are thrifty by nature.

In this way he taught us to control our desires and instincts in line with our own well-understood interests. But he also strove to develop in us that part of every individual's personality which must form the base of any moral code worthy of the name: in his teaching he gave cardinal importance to love of one's country.

The French Republic, daughter of the Great Revolution, mother of all progress, was in his eyes worthy of every sacrifice. He read to us and gave us for dictation famous writings which glorified France. Among many others, the passage where Michelet, comparing France with other nations, declares that she had done much more for mankind than any other, seemed to us to be indisputably true and filled us with joy and pride. One day he dictated to us a text on a postage stamp representing France the Sower which moved him to tears: 'In this picture the whole spirit of France can be seen.' Every year he would read to us a passage from an author whose name I forget which described two enemy soldiers, French and Russian, dying on the battlefield. In the morning the survivor awakes surprised to find himself warm: the other, before dying, had covered him with his cloak. 'Little Frenchmen, guess who had died and who it was who had made this sublime gesture. I can see you hope it was the Frenchman. Well then, be happy, it was the Frenchman.' And indeed we were happy.

We learnt to recite poems by Eugène Manuel, Déroulède, and Victor Hugo. We learnt military songs:

> Où t'en vas-tu, soldat de France,
> Tout équipé, prêt au combat,
> Plein de courage et d'espérance,
> Où t'en vas-tu, petit soldat?[18]

Our reading book was entitled *Tour de France*. M. Daniel Halévy in a book recently published[19] made a close, but rather cruel, analysis of this little book. He brings out all the implications of renunciation it contains. We, for our part, could see only one thing: two orphans driven out from their land by Germany who discover France and do their utmost every day to improve themselves and become more worthy of being French. The last sentence of the book uttered by little Julien when he has at last found himself a home, a corner of French soil where he may live, was:

> 'I love France!' 'I love France! . . . France! . . . France!' came the clear echo from the hillside and was taken up again within the ruined farmhouse.
>
> Julien stopped in surprise.
>
> 'All the echoes answer you one after another, Julien,' said André gaily.
>
> 'All the better,' cried the boy, 'I wish the whole world answered me and that every nation on earth said: "I love France".'
>
> 'For that to be,' said Uncle Volden, 'there is only one thing to be done: let every child of the Fatherland strive to do the best he can; then France will be loved as much as she is admired throughout the whole world.'[20]

Such an ending, read to us time after time, could not help moving us and engraving itself on our memory. Even if, as M. Daniel Halévy so rightly remarks, these two children leave Alsace without a backward glance, with no thought of returning, it must also be remembered that, in all the school maps of France, the lost provinces were coloured purple, the colour of mourning.

These moral ideals – work, thrift, progress, republic, country – could have been taught so steadfastly only because they expressed the ideals of France current at the time and reflected in circulars from the Ministry[21] (up to 1900) and in educational journals.

Those books from the school library which, by the hands of the children, found their way into homes also carried with them these ideals. There were some four hundred books in the library, the majority acquired or donated between 1884 and 1895.[22]

The works of classical authors (Bossuet: *Discours sur l'Histoire Universelle*; Voltaire: *Histoire de Charles XII*; Montesquieu: *Grandeur et Décadence des Romains*; Chateaubriand: *Génie du Christianisme*, etc.) were not read. They remain today covered in dust but as new. Biographies of great men, such as *Le Cardinal de Richelieu* by Ornu, *Davoust* by Boudois, *Montcalm* by Bonnechose, *Lazare Hoche* by Bonnechose, *Gambetta* by Bardou, had a few readers. But novels and short stories alone were really popular, among which *Le Roman d'un brave homme* by Edmond About stands first, so similar in the ideals it puts forward to the tales of Pierre Laloi and Ernest Lavisse. This book is the first on the catalogue list. Then came Dickens' novels (*The Cricket on the Hearth, Nicholas Nickleby, A Christmas Carol, Pickwick Papers*), so vivid and moral, so close to the people in their inspiration, the simplicity of the characters and their ideal. Most popular of all, perhaps, were the works of Erckmann-Chatrian, filled with such a complete affection for the corners of the world where his heroes lived, so moving in their republican and patriotic fervour. Then there were others sharing the same patriotic or human theme: Achard's *Récits d'un Soldat*; Harriet Beecher Stowe's *Uncle Tom's Cabin*.[23]

At the little school at Mazières children heard the convinced words of a man of their own town telling them, making available to them and understandable through examples of 'proof', ideas which were current in the wider national sphere and which also – as we have seen – were moving, confusedly, among their own people on all sides. The children were, in their turn, ingenuous agents of propaganda and not without effectiveness. I can, at this moment, see in my mind a little fellow of about nine years old solemnly explaining to an old peasant at the great fireside where they were both warming themselves why the republican régime was superior to the monarchy. His father in the next room was laughing at him, but I can see him, nevertheless, a year or two later explaining to the stoker and the butter-maker at the co-operative dairy why France could not be at war with Germany since she had Russia as ally.

The generous, perhaps over-simple, faith which sprang from the combination of all this propaganda and all these happenings was never more in evidence than at the time of the 1914 elections.

An old senator, once a tannery workman at Parthenay, was campaigning in support of the retiring deputy, the radical candidate, a small landowner in the neighbourhood. The meeting was held in the assembly room at the town hall, a great bare room. It was crowded with people. The senator got round to speaking of the possibility of war with Germany. I can still hear his voice, see his gestures: 'Yes, it is possible that we shall be at war with Germany.' Pause, a shudder goes through the audience. 'You know, Germany does not have the good fortune to be a Republic; she is governed by an Emperor who does just as he pleases.' There were a few laughs: how was it possible to be civilized and not be a Republic! 'What we want, we Republicans, is peace. But if war came, we should tell the Germans, after we have won, to be Republicans like us and the German Republic would be the sister of ours. . . .'

No one clapped; there was not a single movement, not a murmur. But the audience was enthralled; an old man next to me had his eyes filled with tears. Some young men a little further off, young peasants, listened with solemn faces, eyes strained. What a flight of imagination for them!

A few months later war broke out. Fifty-two of the best men of this commune of eleven hundred souls were to die for their country, their republican faith, their belief in progress, their ideal of the brotherhood of man in a war they had not wanted.

It was a fine ideal. The school was by no means the sole agent in building it. Its influence would soon have disappeared, scattered in the mass of the population if it had not interpreted what was best, most certain and most deeply entrenched in French opinion as a whole. It had not been unequal to its task.

1806

A township composed of hardly more than hovels in the midst of fields of heath, broom and gorse. Stunted, puny peasants dressed in coarse canvas garments appear before the recruiting board. Many have legs covered in ulcers and sores: some are epileptic or deaf. Less than a quarter can be declared fit for service, some sham disabilities, all go off against their will. Not one of them knows quite why he has to fight. The Empire, France itself, are for them almost meaningless words.[24]

November 1848

The land is still covered with gorse and bracken, with no roads and no trade. After mass, at one o'clock, smock-clad peasants, cap on head, clogs on feet, ranged behind a few notables, listen to the mayor reading the proclamation of the Republic. But general ideas are incomprehensible to them. They talk only in patois. Three years later when the Republic is overthrown they hardly notice the fact.[25]

January 1881

A country where land clearance has almost been completed and which is covered by a network of excellent roads. A railway line under construction. Trade developing. Many men still wear the smock, but for the most part they wear shoes on their feet and felt hats on their heads. At the municipal elections they have voted against the descendant of their former overlords and for a reforming leading citizen. They dance round a bonfire to celebrate their victory. Ideas are beginning to percolate into the township which has become quite a little centre.[26]

March 1914

All the land is under cultivation. Houses are clean and spacious. Carriages and bicycles throng the vicinity of the town hall. In the Assembly Room men in good solid working clothes or in their Sunday best – jackets, hats or caps, thin shoes or thick boots – listen to one of their own sort, a former workman who has become a legislator. Everyone understands and speaks French. Universal and lofty ideas, spilling over the boundaries of France and embracing the whole world, dazzle the imagination, giving strength to men's resolves.

Around 1880 a revolution had taken place in material things, in the *mores* and in men's way of thought.

The fears expressed by Jules Ferry's opponents had not been realized as far as the commune of Mazières-en-Gâtine was concerned. A new faith had been born, mother of energy and happiness, agent of both progress and stability in society and showing itself capable of inspiring great devotion. We have seen the basic rôle played by economic and social change in its creation, and the need for education, for both economic and ethical reasons, that these changes had brought with them. And we have seen the influence – limited but nevertheless definite – that the school had played in the changes and in the way of life which had resulted.

It should, however, be carefully noted that if this faith

remained living and active it is because the data on which it was founded were real, deeply rooted in every individual and sheltered from any wind of criticism. The sense of judgment of the Mazières school children may well have been awakened (as Jules Ferry had hoped) through their reading and their education: but it had, in fact, been directed and limited by the narrowness of the geographical and social environment in which their thought and imagination had its being. The influence of the teachers could do no more than consolidate this faith because, however accustomed they might be to teach ideas, to awaken and develop judgment in their pupils, however imbued they might be with a rational, and therefore universal, ethic, they remained, in fact, tightly bound to the little district in which they were living. All their tastes, all their habits, their affection for the reality of things within the human environment in which they lived, their perfect contentment with their lot – all these had banished from their minds any doubts of what they were teaching and any wish for any sharp and profound change in society. So much so that these teachers, the champions of an open morality, had helped to give more effectiveness and solidity to the faith that they taught only because they, in fact, lived within the closed morality of the pre-1914 commune which was their home.

three

Conclusion

I have attempted to trace as closely as possible the course of the life of the people of Mazières-en-Gâtine commune over a period of almost a century. In so doing I have tried to discover the needs to which the school responded, how it came into being, how it developed and what was its influence. It is for the reader to draw his own conclusions from this study which I have done my best to keep as objective as possible, despite my personal involvement.

I believe that the salient points regarding the school are as follows:

The establishment of a school in the commune in 1833 was premature. The initiative came from the central government; it was encouraged – or, rather, was not actively discouraged – by the leading inhabitants. But it had little impact. For this to have happened the peasants for whom it was intended would have needed to be other than they were, more ready for contact with the outside world, with a different attitude to life and more open to receive new ideas. Also the school would have needed a teacher who tackled his work with more zest and competence. A few peasant children learnt to count: a few others to read and write their names. For many years that seemed to be quite sufficient.

By 1860 conditions were totally changed. Roads had opened up the country. An exchange economy was beginning to replace the earlier semi-closed peasant economy. Land clearance had begun: people went to market more frequently. They were beginning to think that it was a good – and useful – thing to be educated. The teacher whose enthusiasm had cooled just when it should have risen in response to people's wishes had been transferred at the request of a local authority now alive to the situation. It only needed his replacement by a good teacher for the school to thrive immediately. But the first pupils to attend school regularly and to benefit most came from the township. Mazières-en-Gâtine school, like all primary schools in France, had been given by the creators of French popular education the task of teaching communication through symbols and religious instruction. The first regular attenders, whose example led others to follow, were those who, in their way of life, were the most separated from rural ways. Thus, a school which at first sight would be taken as typically rural demonstrated quite clearly from the outset according with the intention of its creators and with the needs and desires of the people that, on the contrary, its nature was essentially urban. Its design was not to adapt its pupils to the narrow environment in which they lived but to develop their natures and adapt them to a broader society.

By 1882 the school's development had accelerated quite sharply. Land clearance was almost complete. Easier means of communication had raised the standard of living. A railway was under construction. The township had grown and its trade diversified: it had become a miniature administrative and urban centre. The opposition of an anti-clerical and reforming leading citizen to the squire of Petit-Chêne had helped to accustom people to the clash of opinion. A certain number of former pupils from the school had, thanks to the teaching they had received, been able to escape from poverty by earning a better living on the spot or by finding work elsewhere. The education provided by the school was becoming an important factor in economic and social change and in altering the people's attitude.

It was a decisive point in time in the history of the commune.

The school was now called upon to play an economic and social rôle: it fulfilled its task admirably. It may be true that the attempt made by an excellent teacher to direct his teaching towards a vocation, that of agriculture, failed. It was an attempt condemned to failure in advance for, from the outset, it ran counter to the purpose prescribed for the school, originating in an urban setting with mankind as a whole its horizon. On the other hand, enterprises such as the co-operative dairy became practicable. Without these changes in attitude and the general progress of enlightenment they would have been doomed to fail. Thanks to the teaching they received at school many young men were able to adapt themselves to the changed social and economic conditions taking place in France as a whole and in their own village. They could take advantage of the many new openings for employment which were being created by developments in Government service, in industry and in commerce. They found new occupations in their immediate surroundings which enabled them to render useful service and earn a good living with an increased status: or, if they carried on their parents' occupation, to adapt it to the new conditions influencing it. Many of those who, because of poverty, left the commune found themselves better placed than their fellow-pupils who, as independent farmers, were tied to the land and their narrow district by reason of their increased prosperity itself.

The school also had to play an educative rôle from both the intellectual and moral standpoint.

At a time when wider and more general ideas were spreading from all sides into this region formerly so shut in on itself it could have offered an education firmly based on local matters and local people and, in this way, kept its pupils' minds in close touch with concrete reality, giving them a better-informed understanding of their own little district. It could have tried to make France and the whole world more meaningful to all its pupils through the medium of their own commune.

It could, on the other hand, follow the main trend of ideas and look on these little Gâtine peasants as future citizens of France and the world who needed to learn all these things of which it is not permissible for a person to be ignorant. This would mean that the pupils must leave school with a clear idea of Egypt, America, Asia, the history of France and the great nations of Europe – and of much else besides – with the risk of knowing nothing of their own area.

It could, in the final count, bend its efforts towards helping them to gain a deeper and more discerning knowledge of their own personality or try to create in each one of them an abstract ideal of Man.

All the intellectual development and administrative history of France, all the training given to teachers, made it inevitable that the Mazières-en-Gâtine school should receive its syllabus from Paris and offer a prescribed education generally applicable to all France.

It was in 1882, also, that the school was officially withdrawn from the influence of the Church and that the teacher ceased to be the priest's assistant, in the sense intended by Guizot. Doubtless, it was the intention of the creators of the secular school that he should continue to collaborate with the priest through the moral instruction he gave to his pupils: but he did so in full independence; he was no longer the priest's subordinate. This decision had been preceded in Mazières by changes in moral attitudes; circumstances and personalities were such that the teacher could only be an adversary of the priest.

His most important task was to sharpen his pupils' judgment and to awaken their powers of reasoning. But a new religion had arisen under the pressure of profound social, economic and political change. There was belief in Progress; there was faith in the Republic; there was love for France. The physical and social world within which the people of the commune lived remained very restricted; and the very narrowness of the boundaries within which their sense of judgment was confined was a guarantee of the solidity of their faith.

The teachers were too deeply rooted in the countryside. By reason of their personal memories, their tastes and habits they remained too close to the local peasants, artisans and tradesmen who were their neighbours for them not to resist, perhaps unconsciously, by their example and the subjective tone of their classroom lessons what might have been too centralized and 'uprooting' in their teaching. Moreover, they were too deeply and sincerely absorbed in the faith felt perhaps unconsciously but nonetheless profoundly by those who surrounded them not to have become convinced and effective propagandists for the religion of Progress, Republic and Patriotism.

The Mazières school has thus seemed to me always to have been essentially urban and universal in outlook, not rural and localized. At every turn, however, it seems to have depended very closely on the environment in which it existed. The intentions of the central government became practical reality only in so far as the people's minds were prepared for them and when they assumed a form acceptable to them. The diligence of the pupils and the influence the school exerted on them were at all times dependent on the economic and social state of the commune and on the attitude of mind of the people. It did not create the belief that it helped to spread: it was but the mirror which reflected and focused this belief.

Later, when the soldiers returned from the 1914–18 war, having completed the enormous effort demanded of them and innocently expecting the promised results for which they had always looked forward to – perpetual peace, justice for all through the League of Nations – when facts began to show that this hope was vain and life was a perpetual struggle, that the peace had to be won just like the war through sacrifices and efforts which might be less severe but which were harder to find general acceptance, when inflation had shaken the stable basis of life, when buses and cars joined the railway to make travelling a matter of daily occurrence, when newspapers and radio became widespread, when the controls exercised over the power of intellectual logical reason by traditional custom and prejudice gradually weakened, when the trust of those who had cleared the land and seen the roads built had vanished – in short, when all the circumstances which had miraculously come together to ensure the moral equilibrium of the people of the commune in the midst of the rapid changes they were caught up in had disappeared, disorder crept into men's minds. Some listened to the missionaries of new religions who came even into this poor little town to preach Order and Progress. Others remained firm in their faith in the Catholic Church. Most found nothing certain but devotion to one's self-interest.

The school had not created this attitude: it was powerless to remedy it. It could only reflect and accentuate a disordered state of mind. The teachers who followed each other at Mazières instinctively reduced their rôle to that of preparing their pupils for the primary school leaving examination (C.E.P.E.). M. Bouet, now mayor, no longer felt himself in conformity with the sentiments and ideas of his former pupils on many a matter.

Appendix

In response to numerous requests from readers of the original French text, I add a few pages to describe the economic and social conditions in the commune and the attitudes of its people in 1968. They provide a brief analysis of the changes which have taken place since 1914 – changes which have proved vastly greater than those observed between 1850 (when an exchange economy began to replace the subsistence economy) and 1914 and the outbreak of the First World War. These changes over a period of 64 years were themselves enormously greater than any that had taken place between 1650 and 1850, even taking into account the French Revolution. Thus, in the evolution of a little rural commune, is revealed that acceleration of history which is so much a characteristic of the present day in countries of a highly developed technology.

1968: Fifty-four years have elapsed: twenty-one years of an inter-war period when confusion reigned; five years of war and occupation; twenty-three years post-war with the emergence of a new style of life and new attitudes and ways of thought.

Two things are of particular significance: on the one hand, a decrease in the population; on the other, a rising standard of living bringing with it many changes both in the pattern of life and in mental attitudes.

The following table shows the population, first of the commune as a whole, then of the township and villages separately:

	Commune	Township	Villages and farms
1911	1,178	378	800
1936	1,032	349	683
1946	985	280	705
1954	926	368	558
1964	902	410	492

There has been a marked decrease in numbers despite considerable developments in the town and it should be noted that the birth rate is *not* the cause. The average number of births during the last ten years has been of the order of a little more than 16 per annum. Taking into account the fact that the number of young married couples has decreased much more sharply than the population as a whole, this means that most of them, particularly in the country, have three or more children each. In spite of this there were only 492 people in the villages and farms, which is the lowest figure ever recorded. During the nineteenth century the figures varied around the 800 level and all the evidence leads one to believe that they were very similar during the eighteenth century, despite the decade of frightful misery and poverty from 1705 to 1715, when twenty-five households disappeared between 1686 and 1716.

There have been great changes in the pattern of life and work over the past fifty years. A growing number of farmers have bought their farms, being aided in this by the pre-emptive right, sanctioned by law, granted to tenants to purchase the land they are working when it comes up for sale. The *Crédit Agricole* (a State organization) provides financial assistance in these circumstances. At the present time, of 97 farms, 50 are owner-operated. The number of medium-sized farms has greatly increased. Holdings of less than five hectares are practically unknown. Farms of between 10 and 20 hectares have increased in number (13 in 1913; 30 in 1954; 44 in 1967) and those of between 20 and 50 hectares even more (8 in 1913; 19 in 1954; 43 in 1967). There are ten farms of more than 50 hectares.

There has been a general improvement in farming methods: fertilizer is used to a much greater extent and more judiciously; it is the general practice to have soil analysed. Crop yields have improved; 30 quintals of wheat per hectare as against 10 or 12 in 1913 is a current average – which means that as much grain can be harvested from a smaller sown area (194 hectares in 1954 compared with 548 hectares in 1914). This, in turn, allows more attention to be paid to stock farming. Up to 1939 great attention was paid to root crops and sown pasture or grass leys. Since 1945 the shortage of labour has caused the growing of root crops to decrease while the area of permanent pasture has risen to 350 hectares. But these pastures are treated with fertilizer and the cattle are increasingly fed on a carefully balanced and supervised diet of cattle cake. Nothing shows more clearly the change in the attitude of the farmers towards their calling than the measures they have taken to improve their herds and to widen the scope of the activities of their co-operative dairy.

At the beginning of the century the cows on all the farms were of the Parthenay breed, a sturdy local breed whose milk was rich in butterfat. They were used both for transport and ploughing and great efforts were made to improve their milk yield. In the great majority of farms cows are no longer regarded as working animals: they have been replaced by tractors. In 1954 there were 24 tractors in the commune; in 1968 there are 67. Consequently it has been possible to raise herds of Friesian cows which although less sturdy and smaller have a much greater milk yield (5,500 to 6,500 litres per lactation of 300 days as against 3,000 to 4,000 for the same period). Such a change would have been unthinkable 60 years ago: the peasants of that time did not know – and did not wish to know of – any breed other than the Parthenay, their own home breed.

From this development the co-operative dairy received more than 10 million litres of cows' milk in 1967 and was able to distribute almost $5\frac{1}{2}$ million francs to its members. In addition, it added to its activities the collection of goats' milk (756,000 litres in 1967) which was processed in association with a neighbouring co-operative. And, what is of particular importance, in order to make industrial use of the skim milk which before 1914 was returned to the suppliers to be fed to their pigs, a union of 16 co-operatives in the region was established in 1961 to manufacture powdered milk and cattle food etc., and now forms an important enterprise.

All this is a striking demonstration in a rural commune of the law of concentration operating in the French industrial world – and indeed throughout the whole world.

There is nothing surprising in the peasants now having the

outlook of managers of undertakings alert to any opportunity for profit. Through the press and radio they are keep abreast of prices ruling in Paris and the region. Many of them subscribe to agricultural journals. They are quick to work out their costs of production and to improve their methods of farming and animal husbandry. In this they are helped by the *Direction des Services Agricoles*, but more and more are now capable of taking individual initiative. No doubt, everything is not perfect: there are still farms which are too small and too many hidebound conservative farmers. There are still too many fields enclosed by hedges. The cattle byres, the pig sties and poultry yards need, if not modernizing, at least to be improved, but over the whole industry there have been great changes which have produced considerable progress in productivity, in material welfare and the pattern of life.

Not all the houses have been brought up to date, but almost everywhere are to be found radio receivers, electric pumps for raising water, Butagaz cookers, more and more washing machines and, besides the tractors and agricultural machines, a car. Before 1914 there was only a single motor car in the commune; in 1954 there were 150 and 219 in 1968. Some of the farmers and shopkeepers in the town own vans for transporting their goods as well as a car for pleasure journeys.

These changes in the peasants' way of life have obviously been of benefit to the township and are linked there with other factors which will now be examined.

Several new houses have been built along the Niort road. In the middle of the township dilapidated houses have been pulled down and rebuilt. One of those mushroom-shaped water towers which are dotted all over the French countryside is a sign that running water has been installed there. The two butchers are doing a very good trade. The two bakers sell less bread these days (an average of 300 grammes a day per person instead of the 600 grammes in 1914). They no longer bake enormous five kilogramme round loaves and sell even less and less of the two kilogramme variety but mostly 750 gramme loaves (formerly a very unusual size) and, increasingly, even *baguettes* of 250 grammes which were never seen in the old days. In particular, they make and sell cakes and confectionery on an increasing scale. Five grocers, who for a long time now have given up selling material and clothes, have prosperous businesses. A chemist has opened and has many customers. Three garages are physical evidence of the importance of motor vehicles in the region. A quarry two kilometres from the town produces 150 cubic metres of stone daily, using the most modern plant and employing 20 workers. Electricity, installed in the town in 1929 and now extended to the whole of the countryside, has warranted the establishment of an electrician who has two assistants and sells radio sets and domestic appliances. So we see the township as a busy little place with a good deal of motor traffic, including coaches which stop there for connexions to Parthenay and Niort.

Only artisans are losing ground. Around 1850 we saw the clog-maker doing well; then, towards 1885 the cobbler appeared and also prospered. For over 10 years now there has been no clog-maker in Mazières: there is only one cobbler and he is doing poorly. There is no wheelwright. There is now only one harness-maker and, to make a living, he has turned to making mattresses which have taken the place of the old feather bed. On the other hand, the building and alteration of houses had led to an increase in the number of carpenters (three) and masons (three). A house decorator employs a workman – and has plenty of commissions. Four dressmakers are able to make a living, working at their homes.

But two social categories in particular have been the basis of the township's development. First, that which is classified on the register as *rentier*, of whom there were only three in 1911. The people involved were local notables living on the rents of their farms. Today the register lists 65 such people in the township and 56 in the villages. Some of them have savings – certainly quite modest – on which they live, others a little land, but all are safeguarded from poverty by the State old people's allowances. It would be true to say that, before 1914, they would have been registered as 'day labourers' (*journaliers*) and this change in classification – and of fortune – is a sure sign of an increase in material well-being and social justice.

The other social category is that of the public servant. The number of postmen in Mazières had decreased in 1911 because post offices had been established throughout the surrounding countryside. Postal delivery for the whole canton is now organized from Mazières and is undertaken by motor van – a further example of the centralizing effect of technical development. Because of this the number of postal employees has risen to five.

Teachers have increased still more. We saw the uncertain start of the school at Mazières, followed by its development and the central rôle that it played in the economic, social and moral evolution of the commune. But today the elementary primary education of children from the age of 6 to 14 years is no longer considered sufficient, even by parents. A law recently passed lengthens the period of compulsory education to the age of 16. But, even before this law came into force, a secondary school (*Collegè d'enseignement général* – C.E.G.) open to all pupils in the canton had been established. It prepares them for an examination known as the *Brevet d'enseignement du Premier Cycle* taken at the age of 15 or 16–17, a good pass in which permits the holder to continue his education at the lycée. In October 1968 the C.E.G. received an entry of 55 new pupils from all the communes in the canton. Its total enrolment is 188. Pupils are transported by coach and have their midday meal at the school canteen. Impressive buildings have been erected near the old school built in 1882.

If one considers that, when I left to go to my secondary school (*collège*), I was the only pupil from the boys' school to continue my education and that, in the *collège* hostel, I found only one other pupil who came from our canton, one can measure the extent of the change that has taken place.

A widespread increase in material comfort, a higher standard of living, more time for leisure, and greater ease in travel, thanks to trains, coaches and private cars – such are the main characteristics of changes brought about during the past half-century. Through them the whole state of mind of the people has been transformed.

The closed world of 1850 has vanished; the limited pre-1914 world has widened its horizon: the roots by which the people were attached to the soil on which they lived and to their old habits of life have withered. No longer is the world seen and judged purely from the standpoint of Mazières: now Mazières is judged from without, even by those whose home it is. And people are ready to leave it if there is a better life to be found elsewhere. This is true for the artisans and shopkeepers of the township, where one finds newcomers who have been attracted from a considerable distance to set up in business through the most unexpected channels – an advertisement in a newspaper, the advice of a business agent. It is true, also, in the villages where, however, old habits retain their hold to a greater extent.

Not only the physical but also the social world has broadened. Most of the peasants have rid themselves of their inferiority complex. They know that their calling demands intelligence and know-how, and they no longer have their fathers' and grandfathers' uncritical respect for the local officials – and particularly for teachers. There is no local notability to whom one would shrink from comparing oneself. The château of the seigneurs at Petit-Chêne is now occupied by a poultry farmer: La Minardière is now an Old Men's Home. The doctor who is now the mayor is respected and even loved, but he does not have the fear and reverence owed to his distant predecessor, M. Proust.

The wider views and understanding of the world in general, the tentative beginnings of which we noticed at the turn of the century, have now found their way into every household through the press (practically everyone reads a newspaper these days), through the radio and television. Czechoslovakia, Vietnam, Israel and the Middle East form the subject of daily conversation. By contrast the war in Indo-China which cost France so dear in human life is almost forgotten and the Algerian war, of such recent history, is mentioned less and less frequently. All attention is now directed towards the future. Whereas former generations were almost obsessed with their memories and the old folk of before 1914 were perhaps too willing to talk about the past, today the most important happenings slide over the surface of people's minds, leaving no trace behind them. In the school where previously there was a general interest taken in history and geography, there is a tendency to emphasize more the breakthroughs in industry and the victories of science and technology. This people, formerly so stable, now exhibits all the traits of a people on the move.

They would have recovered their equilibrium without great difficulty had not one important factor intervened to destroy the virtues peculiar to their stable way of life. The constant fall in the value of money which ruined the wealthy and enriched the debtor and which has undermined all confidence in the State has been of fundamental influence in a change in attitude. Before 1914 everyone had complete confidence in the value of the franc and in Government funds; the rural notables who, for generations, had lived on their dividends were living symbols of the stability of the currency throughout all the vicissitudes of history. To get into debt was a shameful thing; one made every possible effort to save money; from childhood one learnt to temper and control one's wants within the bounds of the possible and, with a sense of complete security, one shaped for oneself a future which, if it lacked grandeur, had a comfortable stability.

Today everyone knows that the future is uncertain and that one must constantly reshape it for oneself. The old people have gone who, in 1914 and 1915, offered their gold to the State and who had never believed that that same State, victory once won, would buy back their gold at twenty times the price from those who, when the country was in its hour of danger, had refused to make any sacrifice. Their pleas had few to hearken to them: in any case all this belonged to the past and only the future mattered. The new generations have become accustomed to finding their equilibrium in this disequilibrium and certain precautions have found their way into their *mores*.

Rents are fixed in relation to the price of wheat or meat; even wealthy farmers will not retire without keeping some of their land; shopkeepers and artisans go on working as long as it is possible. Everyone plans his life bearing in mind his experience of a never-ending inflation. As soon as one has any money one makes haste to invest in things which will bring in a good return or which are useful or pleasant. This state of affairs is much to the liking of the children and young people: they get their bicycles when they are seven or eight and their mopeds or scooters at 15 or 16. The spirit of the community which, in 1914, united society on the basis of a few well-understood principles – Progress, the Republic, Patriotism – was unable to resist this perpetual drift, these continual readjustments and the shock of new events and ideas.

Above all, all confidence in the State was lost. The image of a strong, wise Republic in which justice was always seen to be done, whose officials were valuable and efficient servants, where taxes were put to useful purposes and order and progress equally guaranteed has vanished. The Ministers and politicians of the Fourth Republic were continually the objects of the most improbable and unjust accusations and this attitude among the people certainly aided, if it did not make inevitable, General de

241

Gaulle's seizure of power in 1958. The institutional changes that he introduced were considered necessary by many and the candidates who supported him regularly received the majority of votes at elections. The elections held while the fears engendered by the events of May-June were vivid in people's minds resulted in an increased Gaullist majority. It all seems as though the electorate, weary of politics, disturbed in its mind by a world it has given up trying to understand, placed itself for all important decisions in the hands of a man whose past record inspired confidence. In this attitude immediate self-interest played a greater rôle than principles: the contrary was the case before 1914 (see pp. 182-3).

All this can very probably be traced to the disappearance of the uncomplicated faith in Progress which permeated the whole of life, nourishing the most solid virtues. The miracles of science and modern technology, reflected in the radio and television, give rise as much to anxiety as to wonder, making clear to the more awakened minds the fact that France must from now on learn to live in a world that has outstripped her.

The ethic of Progress has been replaced by a more personal ethic which is constantly straining to adapt itself to a new economic world, to a crumbling currency and to new techniques. The family itself has been affected. At the turn of the century good parents obeyed an unwritten law which required them to see that their children were educated in order that they should be able to carry the family name as high as humanly possible. Faith in Progress involved self-denial and individual sacrifice. Today every individual has his eyes set on the future; fathers no longer feel that they are prolonging their own lives or those of their ancestors in the shape of their children or that these are in their turn the main stem from which branches will spring. They are still anxious that their children shall be happy but know full well that they are going to have to live their own lives in their own fashion and according to their own desires. They are, therefore, less willing to make sacrifices on their behalf and their affection tends to turn to indifference. The strength and sometimes cruel tightness of the links binding the family together have been loosened by social conventions which now allow young couples, thanks to children's allowances, to buy a television set as soon as they start a family and which, through 'old age pensions', release them from the obligation to care for their parents when they are old. The family circle is no longer bound by those economic chains which forged its unity in previous days!

Patriotic sentiment has itself undergone change. It no longer consists of that intense love of the soil, of being deeply rooted in ancient customs, the fruits of an enclosed, stable life from which the soldier of 1914 drew part of his courage. Love of one's country springs more and more from individual self interest. France is loved because one has a feeling of belonging to a country where life is relatively easy and whose prosperity is likely to increase. Pride in her greatness, perhaps because this is no longer seen to be a possibility, has been renounced. One feels she should be strong only in so far as this strength is seen to be essential for her dignity, her precarious security and her prosperity. No doubt noble and generous ideals still find their way into men's minds. During the time of the Occupation the commune behaved in exemplary fashion. Everyone listened secretly to the English radio, admired England's struggle and awaited confidently the intervention of the Americans. All the young men rose up spontaneously as soon as circumstances permitted to help in throwing out the invader, but many today smile at their enthusiasm of those days. What holds most attraction for them now is individual success and the new techniques at man's command.

Over the years France has always followed the path traced for her by her geography, her history and the genius of her people, relying on the strength of a peasantry great in numbers, firmly rooted in its soil, submissive and courageous. This peasantry was the pendulum which balanced the wildest oscillations at the summit, a reservoir of men who ensured success for the most daring of projects undertaken within its compass.

If the facts which have been disclosed during the course of this study are valid (as I believe them to be) for many rural communes, then the social and economic situation and the mentality of the French countryside have greatly changed. Not only has the peasantry decreased in numbers, not only will it decrease still further, but it is well on the way to being overwhelmed in all its customs and attitudes by an industrial civilization. The whole of society is becoming sensitive to oscillations at the summit: the effect of the pendulum is seen only in the clash of opposing opinions which are reflected throughout the whole of the land. These opinions, in their turn, are the source of the gravest of problems. The reserves of idealism and energy which were inherent in a closed society are disappearing and a rootless people has not yet discovered a common faith which will ensure its equilibrium.

ROGER THABAULT

notes

Part One

Notes to chapter two

1 Dauzat, A., *Les noms des lieux*, Delagrave, p. 34.
2 In the country dialect 'Les Gâts' meant, 30 years ago, uncultivated fields full of reeds and heath still existing at that time.
3 'Les Naides' are marshy areas unsuitable for cultivation.
4 *Mémoires de la Société de Statistiques des Deux Sèvres*, 1886.
5 The whole estate of Pressigny was in the possession of the de
Breuillac family from 1672 (Ledain, B., *La Gâtine historique et
monumentale*, Parthenay 1897.)
6 The commune of Verruyes in 1790 had a population of 1,450; in
1936 this had become 1,625 when all land had been cleared and
many people were engaged in local trade.

Notes to chapter three

1 Today the sixteenth of Frimaire, year three of the French
Republic one and indivisible, before me Jean Robin, Mayor of
the Commune, deputizing as official registrar of births, deaths
and marriages of citizens appeared in the Town Hall, François
Veillon, cultivator/farmer, aged sixty-five; René Guichard,
farrier and national agent of the commune, aged fifty-three; and
Jean Vivier, joiner and secretary of the commune, aged sixty-
one, all of this commune.

The aforesaid reported to me that Citizen Cavoroc, formerly
curé of the said commune of Mazières, had died in his house at
the hour of 8.30 in the morning, having been murdered in his bed
by a band of brigands who thereupon ransacked his house as well
as several others in the said town. Upon this statement I
immediately proceeded to the domicile and confirmed the death
of the said Bertrand Cavoroc, the pillage and damage committed by the fire set by the brigands to the buildings of the

said house of which two rooms and a roof of a chapel of the church were burnt. In accordance whereof I have drawn up this present statement, the witnesses having signed with me hereunder

Jean Vivier   Robin, Mayor
Guichard, national agent.

2 Today 16 vendemaire, year IV of the French Republic one and indivisible, in the presence of us Jean Robin, Mayor and acting as registrar of deaths in this commune, upon a declaration made to me by Citizen Louis Vivier, municipal officer, aged about 49 years, by citizenesses Prudence Morel, aged 23 and Anne Marie Morel, her sister, aged 22, all of the said commune, who have stated to us that Pierre Morel, health officer residing in this commune aged 46 years and father of the two informants and husband while living of Henriette Françoise Rousseau had been killed between the communes of Allonne and La Boissière. In view of the difficulty of proving this death by a police officer in accordance with article 2, section 3 of the Criminal Police Law since the country is in insurrection and occupied by the enemy, we have thought it well to proceed to report the fact of death of the said Pierre Morel, surnamed Delisle who was killed on 13th inst. at four o'clock in the evening and, having been unable to proceed myself to the spot to confirm the said death because of the danger I should have encountered, I now abide by the report of the informants and give certificate of death, they signing with me with the exception of the two women.

. . . .

Robin, Mayor.

3 These are probably oral traditions collected by M. Bouet in his childhood. I have received confirmation of the facts from M. Georges Picard who, from an indictment from the Public Prosecutor which relates all the events of the Chouannerie in Gâtine in 1832, is preparing an important study for the Société des Antiquaires de l'Ouest.

4 The history of the de Breuillac property will be examined later.

5 In addition to the de Breuillac properties of which part, as will be seen later, were sold as assets of émigrés, there were seven sales of church property: on 11 March 1791, Borderie de la Gagnerie, belonging to the priory of Ternant, to François Gaillard, farmer, for 8,075 livres; 29 March 1792, Borderie de la Folie of the priory of Saint-Marc to Jacques Bonnet of Mazières for 4,600 livres; 12 May 1791, the farm of Les Tailles belonging to the Hospitalières de Niort to Charlot, a merchant of La Chapelle-Bâton for 16,100 livres; 20 May 1791, lands and pasture of the curé of Mazières to Gallard, merchant-farmer at Verruyes;

20 September 1792, Borderie de la Chapelle at Ternand to Louis Bernard of Parthenay for 2,300 livres; 7 February 1793 the farm of La Dronière to Tilleux, manufacturer at Parthenay for 25,200 livres; 16 Floreal, Year III, Borderie de Monbail belonging to the Commanderie de la Lande to Fleau of Verruyes for 21,000 livres.

6 Archives of Saint-Georges.

7 Extract from a report on the state of agriculture in Parthenay district submitted to the committee for the Exposition Universelle of 1855, published by the Statistical Society of Deux-Sèvres in 1855.

8 Open letter on the improvement of morals, cultivation and domestic animals in Deux-Sèvres and Poitou, pp. 358–9. Published in the works of J. Bujault by Guillemot, Niort: Favre. Appears to have been written in 1832.

9 Works of J. Bujault, p. 68. His almanac, much read in the region, had great influence, especially in the plain towards Niort and Melle.

10 The memorandum of Prefect Dupin depicts the state of the houses in Year IX thus: 'The lack of skilled building workers is more noticeable in the countryside where it has more dismal effect. Almost everywhere the houses are very small, sunk more than a foot below ground level, often windowless and receiving light only through a low door almost always closed. Furniture is piled on top of itself in the one room, with four or five beds. Tubs, on which is placed food for the fowls and pigs and which are never washed, contribute to the pollution of the atmosphere and a drain dug in front of the door in which to rot the manure completes the foulness of the dwelling.'

11 The first statistics enumerating the population by inhabited places date from 1851. In 1851 the town of Mazières had 210 people: the commune 976. There were 40 houses, 53 families in the town: 149 houses in the rest of the commune, 154 families comprising 760 persons.

12 This date is carved on the facade of the house – that of the notary Gaillard, tenant farmer of M. de Breuillac.

13 This does not tally with Balzac's summary judgment. 'In France, as far as 20 million people are concerned, the law is nothing more than a notice in black and white fixed to the door of the church or the town hall. . . . Many cantonal mayors make bags for currants and seeds from copies of the *Bulletin des Lois*. As for the mere mayors of communes, it is frightening to learn how many can neither read nor write, and to see the way in which records were kept.'

¹⁴ Reply from the mayor of Mazières to a letter from the sub-prefect of Parthenay, dated 23 October 1849:

> In reply to your letter of 23 October 1849 in which you ask me to inform you of the royal ordinances and ministerial orders authorizing the establishment of cattle fairs and markets held in the commune of Mazières, I have the honour to state that the fairs have long since ceased to operate. At one time (before 1789) they flourished and stock dealers from Berry would come to purchase the horses which they now find at Saint-Maixent. But to tell you, Sir, how and by whom they were established is quite impossible: there is no reference in the records to these fairs.
>
> As for the market, it was established by a Ministry order of 22 April 1837. Last year and at the beginning of 1849 it had little importance: the only goods sold were fowls, butter, cheese and a little fruit. For several months now it has completely failed.

¹⁵ I can only explain this predominance of feathers over wool in an area where there were poultry, but also sheep, by the poor quality of the wool from the sheep, the necessity and difficulty of treating it before use and, no doubt, by the survival of old customs dating to the time when poultry abounded but there were few sheep.

¹⁶ A letter from the mayor of Mazières dated 4 September 1856 speaks of the complaints of the baker about the high cost of flour.

¹⁷ Quoted by Dion, *Le Val de Loire* (p. 469), Arrault et Cie, Tours 1934.

¹⁸ Mazières town council often had to defend its roads against this kind of encroachment (Council Meeting, 23 November 1845).

¹⁹ Memorandum quoted, p. 88.

²⁰ *Galipotes* were men changed into dogs or sheep; *loups-garous* were men changed into wolves.

²¹ No explanation of this term can be found.

²² Op. cit., p. 367. Prefect Dupin writes thus: 'The Gâtine peasant is more religious, industrious and a harder worker: his coarsest manners have something patriarchal about them. Isolated in the midst of his farm holding, leaving it only to go to market or mass, he rules over his family: his wife is less a companion than a senior servant; before she dares to sit at table she must await his command. His faith in agreements is unshakeable; he respects his landlord and makes every effort to pay his dues on time. He has little desire to acquire land; his cattle are his only wealth and, before the war, he hoarded. He is inclined to inde-

pendence but will yield without a murmur to authority whenever he sees it to be just. By nature he is serious and melancholic. If he has become distrustful, it is because he has been deceived/cheated (p. 194 – Second memorandum on statistics in Deux-Sèvres by Citizen Dupin, prefect, Year X).

23 *Dominus*, disait le prêtre
Vobiscum dit l'ageasson
La pibole
Vobiscum dit l'ageasson
Pibolon.

24 In these times a journey of 39 km. there and back frightened no one. I have heard of the case of a teacher of these parts who every three days would walk 10 km. to go and fetch bread where he could find it at one sou the kilo cheaper than at home. The beadle at Mazières continued to walk to Parthenay (15 km. there, 15 km. back) even though he was wealthy and even though a public service was available for him to go by carriage.

25 In 1850 the Registrar's Office thought of establishing a bureau at Reffanes to serve the cantons of Mazières-en-Gâtine and Reffanes. This was the Mayor's answer: 'The proposal to establish a Registry Office at Reffanes for Mazières canton to which you refer in your letter of the 11th inst. can have neither my assent nor that of the people of my commune for it is an absolutely absurd idea: more than three-quarters of the population of Mazières have less contact with Reffanes than they have with Paris.'

26 The Mayor added to his letter: 'If it were possible for the new service to be discharged by M. Moreau who is now acting, this would be most useful for this man is of exemplary punctuality.'

Notes to chapter four

1 Op. cit., p. 119.
2 2nd memo, published in Year X, pp. 211–17 *passim*.
3 Return of schools in Parthenay district in 1835 and 1836.
4 Prefect Dupin wrote in Year IX (op. cit., p. 125): 'In twenty years' time the rural communes will not provide one man who can read and write: then, no more local government.'
5 *Mémoires de Guizot*, Michel Levy, 1860., Vol. III, chaps. XV and XVI.
6 Quoted by Léard and Glay, 'L'école primaire en France', *La cité française*, p. 274.
7 Prefect Dupin, in the Year X, was moved by very similar feelings when he regretted the absence of schools: 'If one understands

that the unhappy Vendeé war was fostered only by the ignorance of the peasants and that nevertheless ten years earlier there existed colleges at Parthenay, Thouars, Bressuire, Saint-Maixent, Niort and Melle and small schools in every village, can one not be anxious over what the future holds?'

8 When Guizot was writing his memoirs (in 1860) his work had suffered contact with reality. More than one sentence gives the impression that he had wondered if, as had been stated after the 1848 revolution, mass education had not been a danger for society. His conclusion was quite clear. He declared that popular education was a necessity; it would have been useless to oppose its development. He added: 'Primary education is not a panacea which cures all moral ills in a people and suffices for its intellectual health. It is a powerful influence – for good or ill according to how it is directed and contained within its limits or pushed beyond them' (p. 81).

9 In writing his memoirs in 1860, Guizot saw clearly that this excessive centralization constituted a weakness. After analysing very lucidly the reasons that had led the English not to abandon their empirical system of education which had regard for 'the variety and separateness of existing establishments', he added: 'I can understand how the English reached this conclusion, and I commend them for so doing. In France we do not even have to ask ourselves the question which led them to make this decision. Here all the leaders and various establishments of public education have disappeared, the teachers and assets, the corporations and financial foundations . . . In the matter of public education as in the whole of the organization of our society, an overall system based on and maintained by the State is for us a necessity: it is a condition our history and national genius force on us. We desire unity, the State only can provide it. We have destroyed everything and must recreate' (*Memoirs*, Vol. III, p. 24). It is possible to say that Guizot could still have recreated while still respecting diversity. In reality he had a systematic mind; he loved unity and in that followed the rationalist and centralizing tradition of France.

10 Niort, Imprimerie Th. Martin 1904.
'Elementary Certificate' = *Certificat d'études primaires élémentaires (C.E.P.E.)*

11 The following note from Dauthuile's book shows, moreover, that this was not an isolated instance. In the same report (discovered in the departmental archives concerning the books used in schools of the Melle district in 1832) we find this strange remark: 'The reading primers have, up to now, been completely misunderstood by teachers, and so they make no use of them.

The inspectors generally find them relegated to a corner of the classroom as relics too respectable to be touched. As teachers become more enlightened and intelligent, a larger supply of primers will be distributed.'

[12] Simon de Nantua is a travelling merchant who teaches people by means of useful and amusing talks. The talk on the necessity for vaccination against smallpox was particularly impressive.

[13] This is a popular version of the well-known chivalry novel of the same title. The exploits of Renaud and the aid which their miraculous horse Bayard never failed to bring to the four knights in distress formed the subject of more than one fireside story.

[14] It should be noted in passing that in 1852 there was no long holiday at Mazières school. The regulations of the committee of Parthenay district specified that, in the towns, the holiday should be from 15 September to 15 October. In the rural communes the dates were fixed by the local committee and could not exceed one month. The Mazières committee cannot have paid much attention to its school.

[15] *v.* Sub-Prefect's letter quoted above, p. 119.

[16] A *coche* is a piece of wood – a slender branch of a tree – a little thicker than the thumb, about 30–40 cms. long and split in two. The buyer and the seller each have their own half. At the time of a transaction the seller joins the two parts together and cuts a nick (*coche*) in the presence of the buyer. For the baker, so many nicks means so many loaves: for the miller, so many sacks supplied.

Part Two

Notes to chapter one

[1] The distance from Secondigny to Mazières was 13 km.

[2] The text of the decree of 30 October 1848 concerning agricultural education reads as follows:

The National Assembly has adopted
And the Head of the executive authority promulgates the decree in the following terms:

Preliminary Clauses

Article 1: Agricultural vocational education is divided into three classes. It comprises:

Class 1: *Farm Schools* where elementary practical instruction is given;

Class 2: *Regional Schools* where instruction is both theoretical and practical;

Class 3: *National Agronomic Institute.*

Article 2: The cost of vocational agricultural education at all levels is provided by the state.

Section One

Farm Schools

Article 3: The Farm School is a rural farm operated with skill and at a profit in which apprentices, selected from among land workers and admitted without fee, perform all the tasks receiving as well as remuneration for their work instruction which is essentially practical.

Article 4: In each *département* of the Republic there will be established one farm school as a first step. This organization will be progressively extended to each sub-prefecture (*arrondissement*).

Article 5: The salaries and wages of the teaching staff are met by the State. The State also bears the cost of boarding which, together with the pay of the pupils, is allocated to the Principal to meet the cost of food and other expenses occasioned by the admission of apprentices.

[3] Note on the organization of farm schools issued by the Echo Republicain No. 74 on 12 August 1849 (*Journal des Deux-Sèvres*).

[4] The Petit-Chêne estate is barely 5 km. from the plain.

[5] I was fortunate enough to find among the papers of M. Bouet, head teacher at Mazières school from 1881 to 1916, a manuscript giving full information on the agricultural course taught at the Petit-Chêne farm school in 1850 and 1851.

[6] This was an error, as the facts show.

[7] Op. cit.

[8] In a letter of 10 October 1850 the mayor of Mazières wrote: 'Potatoes are becoming more and more diseased: they yield at least ten for one . . . but the farmers will be obliged to give up growing them as has already happened on several farms where they are replaced by swedes.'

[9] *v.* the chapter on the school on this point.

[10] I had occasion while undertaking my research in the area in July 1939 to refer to this practice in the presence of an old farmer, now retired, and of his 50-year-old son who had taken over the farm. The old man exclaimed loudly. He remembered perfectly well having had in 1895 or 1896 a splendid crop in a field he named – because he had mixed lime and manure. Nothing like it had been seen before. The son listened to him calmly,

a little amused by all the excitement. A careful man, he expressed no opinion of his own but answered me with an evasive gesture when I questioned him directly: 'That's what they say: mustn't mix lime and manure.' In that gesture and in the way a man I knew to be intelligent and hard-working there was a totally new trust – both touching and judicious – in those men of science who teach methods of farming contrary to the proved but narrow experience of his father.

Notes to chapter two

1 This marked increase in the number of 'non-residents' deserves a closer look. It is particularly noticeable in properties of less than 5 hectares (54 as against 35), i.e. those comprising often not more than a house and a garden, or perhaps a field. By examining the cadastral register I was able to discover that six of these small owners were sons and heirs of families formerly resident in the commune, chiefly in the town, who had left to earn a living elsewhere. It is the first sign – to be confirmed later in more detail – of movement in a population previously firmly rooted in its homes.

2 Note that between 1835 and 1850 only 25 houses were built.

3 I have often heard my maternal grandmother tell the story of a peasant who was offered asparagus for the first time and began to eat it at the thick end. She did not like it at all and her gaffe was the subject of much mirth in the countryside.

4 The first important saw-mill to be established at Parthenay dates from 1884. Its production hardly began to exceed local demand before 1895 and it is only then that it began to compete in Mazières with the local pit-sawyers and the saw-mills at Niort.

5 It would be foolish to imagine that the Government's effort was always successful. Jacques Bujault, in a letter published in his book (pp. 298–321), reports a curious act of the central administration in setting up stud farms at Saint-Maixent, thereby compromising – without creating anything of value – the whole mule industry of the district. These studs were not closed down until 1863.

6 It is most regrettable that the P.T.T. administration does not keep records which would enable one to follow the development of each post office: I should have been able to find most useful information for this study. I am, however, most grateful for the kindness of the Directeur des P.T.T. at Niort in enabling me to glean these few details from the Mazières office file.

Notes to chapter three

[1] M. Guillemot, professor of agriculture at Niort, wrote a footnote in his edition of the Almanach of Jacques Bigault (p. 103) published in 1867: 'we could have wished to have heard the strong voice of the reformer thunder out against the inferiority, the state of slavery in which woman is kept in the country. She is not the companion, the equal of the master of the house, but his chief maidservant, never – or almost never – taking part in the conduct of business affairs. If, occasionally, when striking a bargain, he takes advantage of asking his wife's advice, this is not his true motive: he simply wants to gain time. It is to be hoped that education will cause this dreadful disparity between husband and wife in the countryside to disappear.'

[2] No bourgeois had more than two children, as noted above.

[3] Note that the farmer whose account book was examined above (p. 67) was also a Republican under the Empire: He was one of the few farmers who could read.

[4] 249 of the electorate of 350 had voted. M. de Tusseau obtained 201 votes: the opposition candidate with the most votes was M. Frère who obtained only 97 votes.

[5] Electorate of 307; 257 electors voted; M. de Tusseau obtained 190 votes.

Notes to chapter four

[1] In actual fact the woodshed was not built until 1861 (Resolution of 21 July). M. Popineau was then teacher and secretary at the town hall.

[2] The school was attended by children from nearby villages situated outside the commune.

[3] Even the daughters (aged 13, 12 and 9) of the gendarmes quartered in the town did not go to school.

[4] From the records of the *Ecole Normale*.

[5] Details taken from a study made of the *Ecole Normale* by M. Sejourné, Principal of the college from 1896 to 1924 published by M. Duthuile, Inspecteur d'Académie des Deux-Sèvres (op. cit.).

[6] See his remarks when recommending him for the post of telegraph agent.

[7] See p. 121.

[8] Mme. Popineau was paid as sewing teacher even though she possessed her *brevet élémentaire*: she received 100 francs a year.

[9] The introduction of the *'volontariat'* in the army recruiting law

of 1872 and the possibility of doing only one year of military service, if one could pass a relatively easy examination, may have had considerable influence in these decisions.

Part Three

Notes to chapter one

1 Council resolution of 24 June 1866.
2 There were 50 Italians, 3 Spaniards and 1 Swiss among 280 workers (return of non-resident inhabitants in the commune in 1881).
3 Council resolution of 9 December 1879.
4 Resolutions of 9 June 1882 and 23 February 1883.
5 Resolution of 18 May 1889.
6 I have to thank the statistical service of the S.N.C.F. for the figures of incoming and outgoing traffic at Mazières–Verruyes station from 1885 to 1914.
7 Letter dated 26 December 1854.
8 By 1900, when the factory had developed, it was necessary to pipe water from a spring one kilometre distant.
9 We shall see, when we come to examine the township, how the shoemakers took over from the clog-makers.
10 It was told that only one of the milkmen could not read, but he kept in his head all the necessary figures which he would repeat on arrival at the dairy: he had added up the total in his head. Later on he learned to write down the figures against names that he could not read by knowing where they came on the form.
11 His duties were to inspect the quality of the milk and take samples for analysis.
12 The money was distributed by the elected delegates, some of whom could neither read nor write, which was something of a disadvantage, but no one doubted their honesty.
13 It would be false, however, to conclude that this success meant that the peasants' distrust and anarchical individualism was conquered. In 1897 a mutual insurance society against stock mortality was founded under M. Proust's patronage. Despite all his efforts it had a difficult start. In 1900 it had only 130 members with a capital of 145,000 francs. The number of members and the relatively small capital insured show that the society had a measure of success only among the small farmers for whom the loss of a beast was a disaster. Later, the society gained more members but it was never really successful.
14 Treading out the grain by oxen on the threshing floor.

15 It must be remembered that this station serves several communes.

16 From answers to a questionnaire given by the Mayor of Mazières, 28 October 1865.

17 We shall have occasion to remark on the departure from the commune of a considerable number of young men who were expected to stay on as farm workers.

18 This drop in population in 1896 can probably be ascribed to the agricultural crisis in 1893.

19 In 1885 Mazières station received by slow train 189 tons 900 of building material; 333 tons 700 in 1890; 680 tons in 1900; 396 tons in 1910, excluding 120 tons of 'various metal goods' and 89 tons of timber for building of furniture.

20 The first iron Venetian shutters in the region were put up in 1906.

21 Not without some hesitation and resistance: every time cap was changed to hat there was quite a drama.

22 The use of wine in every house and at every meal was an event of great importance which has remained for all the old folk the symbol of the coming of prosperity. The following are the figures for receipts of wine and vinegar at Mazières station: 1885, 252 tons 200; 1890, 385 tons 100; 1900, 792 tons; 1910, 1,240 tons (the last figure including all kinds of drink).

23 As already mentioned, a cobbler had set up in Mazières a depôt for fertilizer under the Deux-Sèvres Farmers' Union.

24 Which did not prevent the building still being known for many years as 'les Halles'.

25 To them should be added the departure of a few clever young men who left the commune to continue their studies and enter the priesthood. Only three were involved and one left the seminary to take his *baccalauréat* but died before he found employment.

26 For 1910 only the figures for passengers leaving Mazières–Verruyes are known.

27 Before the 1914 War there were only two motor-cars in Mazières: one bought by the doctor, the other by the estate agent.

28 Even in 1880 veritable set battles took place from which the combatants came away with black eyes, broken noses and torn clothes. Twenty years later all this had stopped.

29 Note – and this is significant – that this band owed its existence only to the personal authority of M. Proust and, a little later, of the schoolmaster who conducted it, to the attraction it had for the youths who saw in it a chance of doing their military service in the regimental band – and to their pride in knowing how to play music. And so we find in this special kind of school

the same elements which led to the success of the primary school: the personal authority of the teacher – and this time of the leading citizen, practical use and the feeling of dignity gained. Note, too, that this special school had an egalitarian tendency among the young, independently of their social class or of where they lived. It contained, in particular, an almost equal number of youths from the town and the country.

30 Melchior de Vogüe remarks in *Les Morts qui Parlent* that the Gascon peasants were responsive only to the tone of political speeches, to the gestures and all the external signs of the speaker's convictions – not to the meaning of the words he spoke. This would seem to me to be equally true of the Gâtine peasants of that time.

31 It was in 1892 that Brieux produced *Blanchette*. In 1900 the play was several times put on by local amateur theatrical societies.

32 Pascal Chaignon's son did go to the *collège* at Saint-Maixent. He passed his *bac.* and joined the P.T.T. but died when he was twenty-five. Pascal became postmaster in a village in the south of the *département*. His wife was heartbroken at her son's death and did not long survive him. Pascal ended his life sadly even though he had brought his elder brother to a nearby farm where he lived happily in easy circumstances amid his numerous family of children.

33 As we have seen, this progress was due much less to any particular form of government than to a general change in the conditions of life in France and the world as a whole. It had been started by the Empire, and before the Empire under the Second Republic, with the building of roads provided for by a law – the *Loi Montalivet* – passed by Louis Philippe's government. The continuity of French life under different régimes is clearly evident from this, but people will always judge only from what they can see and they will always ascribe their well-being to the government which happens to be in power at the moment when they become conscious of their well-being.

34 It was enough for any politician to be connected, closely or at a distance, in one way or another, with any doubtful concern for him to be for ever discredited. A Deputy who criticized the conduct of the Panama administration on the floor of the Chamber of Deputies was marked by his action for the rest of his life. It was not a question whether or not he was one of the politicians who had been bribed: he shared in the general censure levelled at all involved in such a complicated affair of which only one thing was clearly understood and that was that in some mysterious way the small savers had lost their money. It was reasoning by

contiguity or by participation, not by causality; or, rather, it was a reflex action of emotion and not reasoning at all.

35 M. Proust occupied the office of Mayor from 1881 to 1905 and M. de Litardière from 1905 to 1925.

36 V. G. Picard, op. cit., p. 322.

37 V. G. Picard, op. cit., p. 323.

38 One can be for or against war, for or against soldiers: Hugo, like the people, a man of the people, is at one and the same time for and against war, for and against soldiers: and he turns this to three accounts, a maximum exploitation.

This is exactly what the people do and in this, as in so many other respects, Hugo is the people's chief representative. Like Hugo, man of the people, the man in the street uses war and the soldiers for at least three purposes, all contradictory: he demands from the soldiers the military parades which they alone can provide, the July 14 reviews and all other shows; he expects from war and the soldiers an exercise in malediction, of moral disapproval which is sentimental, public, oratorical, official, philanthropic, scientific, eloquent, learned, socialist and revolutionary; and thirdly he wants from war and the soldiers inspiration and an exercise in imagination when – now going back in to the past, now interpreting the present, now anticipating the future – he wants to convince himself that he has not lost the taste for adventure; when, in fact, he is tired and bored with his picture of peace. (Charles Péguy, *Notre Patrie*, pp. 79–80, N.R.F. edit.)

There were never any military parades at Mazières but they would have been loved.

Before 1914 'exercises in malediction' against the Army would have evoked no response. People were very responsive to the 'exercises in imagination' that Péguy speaks of.

39 These figures refer only to children who were at home at the time in 1901. In fact, among the families with only one child (36) and the 12 couples with none, there were some whose children had left home. There were also young married couples who would later have a family. This remark is not valid where the town is concerned where the figures have been corrected through further enquiries with each family. Thus the difference between the corrected figures for the town and the uncorrected figures for the country, striking as it is, is not adequately represented.

40 It should also be noted that the disappearance of very large families among the poor was generally thought to be a good thing and this was so because the State made no provision for them and abandoned them to their fate. Young peasant women

who got married around 1900 had a real terror of having many children.

Notes to chapter two

1 I consider, moreover, that any move to make the school anything other than this vehicle of general education would be in vain and would be dangerous for any State which tried to make it. I would refer the reader to the discussion held on this matter at the headquarters of the *Union pour la Vérité (Bulletin de l'Union pour la vérité* June/July 1936) and to a letter I wrote to M. Guy Grand *(Bulletin,* Jan. 1937). Certain arguments in that letter and discussion remain valid today.

2 Just as today (1945), the people of Morocco prefer the army officers or civil administrators who do not interfere with their customs – even if to our eyes these appear somewhat cruel – to those who try to make them follow new ways in search of a new kind of happiness of which they have no conception.

3 In fact, Jules Ferry was precise on this point: in his mind it was less a question of judicial sanction than of a moral sanction created by a law. 'These compulsory laws,' he said, 'have above all a moral value: everywhere where compulsion has operated over a number of years, it has had the effect of imbuing the public conscience with a new duty' (Speech to the Chamber of Deputies, 27 November 1880).

4 e.g. the text of the amendment proposed by Jules Simon on 12 March 1882: Article 1 – Teachers shall teach their pupils their duties towards God and towards the Fatherland.

5 See his letter dated 17 November 1882.

6 Our great writers who were responsible for guiding French thought lived at a time when the quarrels of the King were of little interest to those of his subjects who were not making or suffering from war, a time when France was incontestably the greatest power on the continent of Europe and when, even in defeat, she could consider herself stronger than her conqueror. This explains their attitude. In 1880, barely ten years earlier France had for the first time seen the true measure of her weakness. She had been overwhelmed, invaded and, from her defeat, there had arisen across the Rhine a powerful empire of redoubtable dynamism. In the Prussia of 1807, crushed, invaded, humiliated, a philosopher of liberal views and accustomed to abstract thought had drawn up the plan for a national system of education: his conception of education was very different from that of the patriot from the Vosges – J. Ferry – later in France. The latter was to die 'with his eyes fixed on the blue line of the

Vosges mountains', but he had launched the school on the wider sea of humanity beyond the frontiers of France and thought of it as a means and not an end. In his speeches to the German nation, Fichte may have formed the Prussian teacher who is said to have conquered us in 1870 and, beyond the teacher, have fashioned German thinking in which idealism and nationalism are so closely mingled. 'Mankind can only realize itself through Germany. Germany is the only possible country for the development of the mind. . . . She has the right and the duty to impose her ideas on the world.' Nothing shows more clearly the essential difference between French patriotism, which seeks to place France at the service of mankind, and German patriotism, which puts Germany over all others and believes it has the right to impose German ideas on the rest of the world.

[7] Extract from the council resolution of 6 February 1881.

[8] The State school for girls was now open. 96 pupils were enrolled, which was many fewer than at the boys' school. Much less attention was paid in the district to the education of girls than to boys.

[9] I have attached all the more importance and care to this portrait in that it seems to me to be typical of a whole generation of teachers. Practically all teachers who came to work in the Mazières-en-Gâtine *canton* between 1870 and 1900 resembled M. Bouet in many respects.

[10] *Cours complémentaire* may be described as a secondary school less academic than the lycée, with a practical bias.

[11] The pages which follow have been written, in large measure, from my own recollections checked from enquiries made among several ex-pupils of varied ages and social background, from studying numbers of exercise books and text books in use at the time. The very personal note that they convey may seem surprising in a work which is intended to be objective, but any other approach to making a correct analysis of the influence of Mazières school and of its rôle in the development of sentiments and ideas in the commune would have been impossible.

[12] Here, for example, are the results from the compositions of 25 January 1895. M. Bouet had 60 pupils in his class (30 in the top division, 30 in the lower). The top division had been given a fairly difficult spelling exercise, consisting of some 17 or 18 lines from Michelet's essay on the lark. The results were as follows: 0 mistake, 3; $\frac{1}{4}$ mistake, 2; 1 mistake, 2; $1\frac{1}{4}$ mistakes, 2; 2 mistakes, 1; $2\frac{3}{4}$ mistakes, 1; 3 mistakes, 1; $3\frac{1}{4}$ mistakes, 1; 4 mistakes, 1; 8 mistakes, 2; 9 mistakes, 1; 10 mistakes, 2; 11 mistakes, 2; 12 mistakes, 2; 17 mistakes, 1; 18 mistakes, 1. More than half had fewer than 5 mistakes.

In arithmetic the results were still more remarkable. The first seven pupils who presumably were those entered for the C.E.P.E. were set special problems, rather more difficult than the rest. All got more than half marks. These are two problems set to the remaining 23 pupils: 'I have paid two-fifths plus three-sevenths of the cost of a house I have bought and I still owe 1,200 francs: what is the total cost of my house?' 'A circle has a diameter of 80 metres. What will be the perimeter of a rectangle of the same area with one side 25 metres long?' All the pupils, except one, got more than half marks.

The results in French were not so good. The pupils were required to describe how they had spent a Thursday holiday with their friend Jean. Except for the first ten or twelve essays, which were fair, and even good, efforts, all the others were poor in ideas and style. Their authors were clearly unaccustomed to think up imaginary but realistic adventures or to analyse what they had actually done. Most of their sentences were joined together by conjunctions like 'and' and 'then'. Some compositions contained spelling mistakes and errors of grammar. But the miracle is that all were perfectly legible and comprehensible. The same is true of the work of the lower division pupils who were asked to describe 'A Good Scholar'.

13 The Mazières school records show the following results in the examination:

1885,1; 1886, 0; 1887, 2; 1888, 3; 1889, 2; 1890, 6; 1891, 6; 1892, 2; 1893, 4; 1894, 3; 1895, 2; 1896, 8; 1897, 1; 1898, 7; 1899, 8; 1900, 7; 1901, 5; 1902, 5; 1903, 5; 1904, 9; 1905, 7; 1906, 2; 1907, 5; 1908, 7; 1909, 5; 1910, 2; 1911, 2; 1912, 6; 1913, 6; 1914; 5.

14 The recruiting registers give the following figures:

	Conscripts	Illiterate		Conscripts	Illiterate
1881	13	9	1885	10	7
1882	10	6	1886	10	6
1883	9	5	1887	6	3
1884	8	1	1888	9	4
(Only one completely illiterate from 1885 to 1888)					
1889	9	5	1897	14	1
1890	12	3	1898	13	0
1891	10	2	1899	9	2
1892	11	2	1900	16	0
1893	9	5	1901	12	2
1894	13	1	1902	13	0
1895	14	3	1903	9	0
1896	11	2	1904	9	0

	Conscripts	Illiterate		Conscripts	Illiterate
1905	15	1	1909	7	0
		(born at	1910	18	0
		Allone)	1911	15	0
1906	13	0	1912	10	0
1907	15	0	1913	8	0
1908	17	0	1914	13	0

[15] See p. 159 and the emigration of the young men.

[16] I asked thoughtful old farmers if they had gained anything useful from these lessons in agriculture. One of them remembered that M. Bouet advised them not to mix lime with manure: another recalled that he recommended covering the manure heap with a layer of earth. The others remembered nothing.

[17] I can still remember precise incidents and I must say that, in most cases, M. Bouet was only replying in class to attacks made by the priest, who, in his sermons and elsewhere, spoke too often about the secular school. This is a matter of too important a schism in the moral history of France for it not to be mentioned: it is also too painful to be examined at length.

[18] Where art thou going, soldier of France
All fully armed, ready for battle,
Full of courage, full of hope,
Where art thou going, my little soldier?

[19] *La République des Ducs*, pub. Grasset.

[20] *Le Tour de France* by Bruno, pub. Belin.

[21] Particularly in the fine circular of 23 April 1884 concerning the keeping of the monthly Logbook and printed on the cover of all these logbooks.

[22] After an important purchase of 60 volumes in 1904 the Mazières library ceased to expand. (Records of the popular library at the Mazières public school, compiled in 1917.)

[23] At the end of the 1888 school year the top division of M. Bouet's class were required to write an essay on the following subject: 'Write to your friend François telling him the pleasure you have in reading the books in the school library. Encourage him to read a great deal and tell him about a story you have recently read.' These are the titles of the books they had read: *Le Conscrit de 1813* by Erckmann-Chatriau (read by two pupils); *Le Vaisseau 'Le Vengeur'*; *L'Auberge* by Spessart (2 pupils); *La Vie de Duguay-Trouin*; *L'Arbre de Noël* by X. Marmier; *Les Exilés de la Forêt* by Mayne Reid; *Naufrages Célèbres, Histoire de Marius Lelong* (the story of a young man who gave his life for

France), *Jeanne d'Arc, L'Ecole buissonière* by G. Marcel; *Le Tueur de Lions* by Gérard (2 pupils); *Histoire de célèbre Pierrot* by Assolant, *Vie de Lazare Hoche* by Bonnechose.

[24] See Prefect Dupin's report on p. 16.
[25] See p. 48.
[26] See p. 113.

Index

265